THE BEST OF

THE

WORD FOR YOU TODAY

365 DAYS OF STRENGTH AND GUIDANCE | VOLUME 5

BY BOB GASS

The Best of The Word for You Today, Volume 5

International Standard Book Number: 978-1-61584-852-2

Copyright© 2009 by Celebration Enterprises
Roswell, GA 30075

DEDICATED

TO: ....

FROM: ....

DATE: ....

HOW TO
GET THE MOST OUT OF THIS DEVOTIONAL

SET ASIDE A DEFINITE TIME
EACH DAY TO READ IT.

Ask God, "What are You saying to me?"

IS SOMEONE YOU KNOW HURTING?

Give them a copy. It could change their lives.

ARE YOU IN BUSINESS?

Give it to your clients and customers.

DO YOU WORK IN A HOSPITAL...A PRISON...
A REHAB CENTER...OR A RETIREMENT HOME?

This devotional is the perfect tool
for reaching people with God's love.

WHY USE SO MANY TRANSLATIONS?

For two important reasons. First, the Bible was originally written using 11,280 Hebrew, Aramaic, and Greek words, but the typical English translation uses only around 6,000 words. Obviously, nuances and shades of meaning can be missed, so it is always helpful to compare translations.

Second, we often miss the full impact of familiar Bible verses, not because of poor translating, but simply because they have become so familiar! We think we know what a verse says because we have read it or heard it so many times. Then when we find it quoted in a book, we skim over it and miss the full meaning. Therefore we have deliberately used paraphrases in order to help you see God's truth in new, fresh ways.

INDEX OF ABBREVIATIONS

*All scripture references are from the
King James Version, unless otherwise noted.*

AMP	Amplified Bible
CEV	Contemporary English Version
GWT	God's Word Translation
NAS	New American Standard
NCV	New Century Version
NIV	New International Version
NKJV	New King James Version
NLT	New Living Translation
NRS	New Revised Standard Version
PHPS	The New Testament in Modern English
TEV	Today's English Version
TLB	The Living Bible
TM	The Message

OLD TESTAMENT

ABBREVIATIONS

Genesis	Ge	Ecclesiastes	Ecc
Exodus	Ex	Song of Solomon	SS
Leviticus	Lev	Isaiah	Isa
Numbers	Nu	Jeremiah	Jer
Deuteronomy	Dt	Lamentations	La
Joshua	Jos	Ezekiel	Eze
Judges	Jdg	Daniel	Da
Ruth	Ru	Hosea	Hos
1 Samuel	1Sa	Joel	Joel
2 Samuel	2Sa	Amos	Am
1 Kings	1Ki	Obadiah	Ob
2 Kings	2Ki	Jonah	Jnh
1 Chronicles	1Ch	Micah	Mic
2 Chronicles	2Ch	Nahum	Na
Ezra	Ezr	Habakkuk	Hab
Nehemiah	Ne	Zephaniah	Zep
Esther	Est	Haggai	Hag
Job	Job	Zechariah	Zec
Psalms	Ps	Malachi	Mal
Proverbs	Pr		

NEW TESTAMENT

Matthew	Mt	1 Timothy	1Ti
Mark	Mk	2 Timothy	2Ti
Luke	Lk	Titus	Tit
John	Jn	Philemon	Phm
Acts	Ac	Hebrews	Heb
Romans	Ro	James	Jas
1 Corinthians	1Co	1 Peter	1Pe
2 Corinthians	2Co	2 Peter	2Pe
Galatians	Gal	1 John	1Jn
Ephesians	Eph	2 John	2Jn
Philippians	Php	3 John	3Jn
Colossians	Col	Jude	Jude
1 Thessalonians	1Th	Revelation	Rev
2 Thessalonians	2Th		

THIS YEAR—PERSEVERE (1)

We will reap a harvest if we do not give up.

GALATIANS 6:9 NIV

Perseverance means: *(1) Succeeding because you're determined to, not because you're entitled to.* Achievers don't sit back and wait for success because they think the world "owes them." No, if you're wise you'll ask God for direction, stand firm on the Word He has given you, go forward and refuse to quit. You must adopt the attitude of the man who said, "We are determined to win. We'll fight them until hell freezes over, and if we have to, we'll fight them on ice." Recalling the trials he'd faced, Paul said: "I started, and I'm going to finish. I've worked much harder, been jailed more often, beaten up more times than I can count, and at death's door…And that's not the half of it" (2Co 11:23-28 TM). One word describes Paul—relentless. *(2) Recognizing that life is not one long race, but many short ones in succession.* Each task has its own challenges and each day its own events. You have to get out of bed the next morning and run again, but it's never exactly the same race. To be successful you must keep plugging away. It's said that Columbus faced incredible difficulties while sailing west in search of a passage to Asia. He encountered storms, experienced hunger, deprivation and extreme discouragement. The crews of his three ships were near mutiny. But his account of the journey says the same thing over and over: "Today, we sailed on." And his perseverance paid off. He didn't discover a fast route to the spice-rich Indies; instead he found a new continent. The scriptural key to success is—running the race each day (See Heb 12:1-2). So, this year—persevere.

THIS YEAR—PERSEVERE (2)

We will reap a harvest if we do not give up.

GALATIANS 6:9 NIV

It's said that Walt Disney's request for a loan was rejected by 301 banks before he finally got a "yes." Yet he built the world's most famous theme park. So, this year remember: *(1) Perseverance is needed to win the prize.* At a sales convention the manager said to 2,000 of his firm's sales force, "Did the Wright brothers quit?" "No!" they responded. "Did Charles Lindbergh quit?" "No!" they shouted. "Did Lance Armstrong quit?" "No!" they bellowed. "Did Thorndike McKester quit?" There was a long, confused silence. Then a salesperson shouted, "Who in the world is Thorndike McKester? Nobody's ever heard of him." The sales manager snapped back, "Of course you haven't—that's because he quit!" Quitters never win, and winners never quit. *(2) Perseverance turns adversity into advancement.* Paul writes, "Everything that has happened to me here has helped to spread the Good News" (Php 1:12 NLT). Paul didn't give up—he rose up! How did he do it? He found the benefit to him personally that comes from every trial. One Christian author writes: "Today we're obsessed with speed, but God is more interested in strength and stability. We want the quick fix, the shortcut, the on-the-spot solution. We want a sermon, a seminar or an experience that will instantly resolve all problems, remove all temptation and release us from all growing pains. But real maturity is never the result of a single experience, no matter how powerful or moving." Growth is gradual. The Bible says, "Our lives gradually becoming brighter and more beautiful as God enters...and we become like him" (2Co 3:18 TM).

THIS YEAR—PERSEVERE (3)

We will reap a harvest if we do not give up.

GALATIANS 6:9 NIV

Observe two more things about perseverance: *(a) Perseverance means stopping not because you're tired, but because the task is done.* Diplomat Robert Strauss quipped, "Success is like wrestling a 1,000-pound gorilla. You don't quit when *you* are tired—you quit when the *gorilla* is tired." When you're fresh, excited and energetic you work at a task with vigor. Only when you become weary do you need perseverance. The Apostle Paul recognized this: "Let us not become weary in doing good, for at the proper time we will reap a harvest if we do not give up." Fatigue and discouragement are not reasons to quit, they're reasons to draw closer to God, rely on our character and keep going. We underestimate what it takes to succeed. When we haven't counted the cost we approach challenges with mere interest; what's required is total commitment! *(2) Perseverance doesn't demand more than we have, but all that we have.* Author Frank Tyger observed, "In every triumph, there is a lot of try." But perseverance means more than just trying or working hard. Perseverance is an investment. It's a willingness to bind yourself emotionally, intellectually, physically and spiritually to an idea, purpose or task until it has been completed. Perseverance demands a lot, but here's the good news: everything you give is an investment in yourself. Each time you do the right thing—seek God, work hard, treat others with respect, learn and grow—you invest in yourself. To do these things every day takes perseverance, but if you do them your success is guaranteed.

THIS YEAR—PERSEVERE (4)

We will reap a harvest if we do not give up.

GALATIANS 6:9 NIV

Perseverance is a trait that can be cultivated, and the initial step to cultivating it is to eliminate two of its greatest enemies. These are: *(1) A lifestyle of giving up.* A little boy was promised an ice cream cone if he was good while accompanying his grandfather on some errands. The longer they were gone the more difficult the boy was finding it to be good. "How much longer will it be?" he asked. "Not too long," replied the grandfather, "we've just got one more stop." "I don't know if I can make it, Grandpa," the little boy said. "I can be good. I just can't be good enough long enough." As children we can get away with that, but not as mature people, and certainly not if we expect to succeed in what God's called us to do. *(2) A wrong belief that life should be easy.* Paul told Timothy he must "endure hardness, as a good soldier" (2Ti 2:3). Having the right expectations is half the battle. Clinical psychologist John C. Norcross found the great characteristic that distinguishes those who reach their goals from those who don't—expectation! Both types of people experience the same amount of failure during the first month they strive for their goals. But members of the successful group don't expect to succeed right away; they view their failures as a reason to recommit and refocus on their goals with more determination. Norcross says, "Those who were unsuccessful say a relapse is evidence they can't do it. They are the ones who have a wrong belief that life should be easy." Bottom line: "We count them blessed who endure" (Jas 5:11 NKJV).

THIS YEAR—PERSEVERE (5)

We will reap a harvest if we do not give up.

GALATIANS 6:9 NIV

Here are three more enemies of perseverance you'll have to defeat each day of this year: *(1) Lack of resiliency.* Harvard professor George Vaillant identifies resiliency as a significant characteristic of people who navigate the different seasons of life from birth to old age. In his book *Aging Well* he writes, "Resilient people are like a twig with a fresh, green, living core. When twisted out of shape the twig bends but it doesn't break; instead it springs back and continues growing." That's an excellent description of perseverance. We must not become dry, brittle and inflexible. We must draw on God's grace and endeavor to bounce back no matter how we feel. *(2) Lack of vision.* Everything that's created is actually created twice. First it's created mentally, then it's created physically. And where does our creativity come from? God, our Creator, who made us in His likeness (See Ge 1:27). A God-given vision will keep you moving forward when nothing else will. The lack of one will stop you dead in your tracks. *(3) Lack of purpose.* Rich Demoss remarked, "Persistence is stubbornness with a purpose." It's very difficult to develop persistence when you lack a sense of purpose. Conversely, when you have a passionate sense of purpose, energy rises, obstacles become incidental and perseverance wins out. A world champion boxer put it this way: "Champions aren't made in the gyms, they are made from something they have deep inside them—a desire, a dream, a vision. They have last-minute stamina. They have to be a little faster, and they have to have the skill and the will. But the *will* must be stronger than the *skill.*"

THE IMPORTANCE OF SMALL THINGS

*Whoever sows generously will
also reap generously.*

2 CORINTHIANS 9:6 NIV

Have you ever gone to a restaurant with somebody whose meal cost $8.00, and watched them struggle over the tip? They have $2.00 in change, and they know that leaving just $1.00 might be thought of as stingy. Yet do they leave $2.00? Not on your life! That would be too much. Instead they'll waste ten minutes getting change for that second dollar so they can leave $1.50 tip and save themselves fifty cents, rather than "sow generously" and leave a little extra. What would have happened if they'd left the full $2.00? They would have made the waiter or waitress's day. Fifty cents may not seem like much, but the message that goes along with it can mean the world to someone. It says, "Thanks, you did a good job, I appreciate you, you're valuable." Maybe this message gets lost—your server just sweeps up the tip without counting—but you, the one who "sows generously" will still "reap generously." What an opportunity. We can increase the happiness of *others,* and bless *ourselves,* with just pocket change. This is just one tiny example of the many ways in which the small things we do have surprisingly big repercussions. Small acts of kindness set the tone for our day. Going the extra mile—whether it's a slightly larger tip, an unexpected compliment or gift, or just holding a door open for someone—costs very little and gets you a lot. And here's one more thought: we can have mountain-moving faith, understand and explain all the deep doctrines of the Bible and get top marks for personal holiness, yet God's Word says that without love "I am nothing" (See 1Co 13:2).

KEEP YOUR PEACE

The wisdom that is from above is…peaceable.

JAMES 3:17 NKJV

Have you ever gotten into an argument before church and felt like a hypocrite during the entire service? Understand this: the Devil knows that God's Word can only be "sown in peace" (Jas 3:18), so he will do everything he can to keep you from receiving it and being blessed by it. That's why you must do whatever it takes to keep your peace. There's power in peace! If the Devil can't get you upset he has no power over you. He only gains control when you "lose it." He plans to get you upset in order to steal your peace, confuse you and make you run in circles. Don't let him.

James writes, "The wisdom that is from above is…peaceable." In *The Message* Eugene Peterson paraphrases this Scripture: "Real wisdom, God's wisdom, begins with a holy life and is characterized by getting along with others. It is gentle and reasonable, overflowing with mercy and blessings, not hot one day and cold the next, not two-faced. You can develop a healthy, robust community that lives right with God and enjoys its results *only* if you do the hard work of getting along with each other, treating each other with dignity and honor" (vv. 17-18 TM). Notice, getting along with others can be "hard work."

So next time you get worked up about some issue, ask yourself, "What's the enemy trying to do here? If I give in to these emotions what will the result be?" When you're stressed out you lose your joy, and when you lose your joy you lose your strength because "the joy of the Lord *is* your strength" (Ne 8:10). So today, pray, exercise self-control, and keep your peace.

START YOUR DAY WITH GOD

*In the morning I lay my requests before you
and wait in expectation.*

PSALM 5:3 NIV

We think everything rests on our shoulders, but it doesn't! It's God's world, not ours. At the beginning of each day God reminds us that He has His way, that He controls outcomes, and that He cares about every detail of our lives.

The way we get up in the morning sets the tone for our entire day, so try this: first thing tomorrow, get alone with God for a few minutes. Don't try to make it last an hour, just start with five minutes. Go over your plans for the day. If you have a calendar, look over it with Jesus. As you're going through it you'll have some concerns. Just hand them over to Him. Maybe you'll notice a meeting or a particular problem you're worried about. Ask Him for wisdom. If He doesn't give you an immediate answer, realize that it's because He wants you to trust Him. He has something better in mind, something that you haven't thought of yet. So many of us start our day anxious, hurried, fearful, or rushed. But we don't have to. We're going to start our day anyway; why not start it with Jesus? Do we have any better offers? We're going to have a first thought anyhow, a first word, so why not let it belong to God, before Whom all our anxieties flee? We can do this. We really can. We can start our day with God.

Take a moment and meditate on this Scripture: "Satisfy us in the morning with your unfailing love, that we may sing for joy and be glad all our days" (Ps 90:14 NIV).

YOUR RECORD IS CANCELED!

He canceled the record...against us...
by nailing it to [Christ's] cross.

COLOSSIANS 2:14 NLT

How would you like to have a list of all your sins and short-comings made public? Not a pleasant thought, eh? Does such a list even exist? It does, and it's a lengthy one. It details all the bad decisions you've made, the hateful acts, the unforgiving attitudes, the prejudices, the greed, the lust, the lies; the Bible says God has recorded them all. But you've never seen the list, have you? No, and neither has anybody else. That's because: "He forgave all our sins. He canceled the record of the charges against us and took it away by nailing it to [Christ's] cross" (vv. 13-14). Knowing full well that the price for our sins was death, "Christ died...once for all, the righteous for the unrighteous, to bring you to God" (1Pe 3:18 NIV). Note the words "forgave" and "canceled the record of the charges against us." If those words don't thrill your soul, nothing will!

Jesus set aside His divine robes and put on our sin-stained garments of *shame*: the shame of hanging naked before His friends and family; the shame of failure where it seemed for a while that Satan was the winner and Jesus the loser; the shame of our transgressions as "He...bore our sins in his body...so ...we might...live for righteousness" (1Pe 2:24 NIV).

Is there a limit to His love? If there is, David the adulterer never found it. Nor Paul the persecutor. Nor Peter the liar. Nor the thief on the cross. And you won't find it either. When Jesus cried from the cross, "It is finished," God wrote "Paid in full" over every sin you'd commit—from the womb to the tomb!

HOW'S YOUR GIVING?

Give, and it will be given to you.

LUKE 6:38 NIV

When it comes to giving, the Bible clearly teaches us two things: *(1) We should give, expecting to receive!* You say, "If I get more, I'll give more." No, you've got it back to front. Jesus said, "Give and it will be given to you...the measure you use...will be measured to you" (Lk 6:38 NIV). The level of your giving determines the level of your receiving. So break through your barriers of fear and put God to the test, He won't disappoint you. *(2) We get back more than we give.* Paul writes, "Now he who supplies seed to the sower and bread for food will...increase your store of seed and will enlarge the harvest of your righteousness" (2Co 9:10 NIV). Notice, some of the seed [money] God gives us is for food (our own needs), and some is for "a harvest of righteousness." What does that mean? Paul explains: "He has scattered abroad his gifts to the poor; his righteousness endures for ever" (2Co 9:9 NIV). To be truly righteous we must show compassion toward the hurting and give generously to those who are unable to provide for themselves. The Bible says that when we give to the poor, we lend to the Lord and He will repay us (See Pr 19:17). Imagine the interest God pays! Jesus describes it as: "Good measure, pressed down, shaken together and running over." There's no lack of money in this world; God just wants to get it into the right hands!

And by the way, giving is not just how the church raises its budget, it's how God raises His children so that His work gets accomplished and they get blessed in the process. So, how's your giving?

HOW TO RECEIVE GOD'S WORD (1)

Open your ears to the words of his mouth.

JEREMIAH 9:20 NIV

What attitude brings the greatest benefit when hearing or reading God's Word? *Receive it as God's Word—not man's!* It's propagated by us, but originated by Him. "When you received the word of God...from us, you welcomed it not as the word of men, but as it is...the word of God" (1Th 2:13 NKJV).

Here are four things you must always remember about your Bible: *(a) It's authoritative.* "They were astonished at His teaching, for His word was with authority...they were all amazed...saying, 'What a word this is! For with authority and power He commands the unclean spirits, and they come out'" (Lk 4:32-36 NKJV). The forces of darkness around us must recognize and submit to God's authoritative Word. So stand on it! *(b) It's creative.* "By God's word the heavens existed and the earth was formed" (2Pe 3:5 NIV). His Word alone was enough to create all that exists. He doesn't have to strive or sweat, He just has to say it and it's done. So speak God's Word! *(c) It's effective.* "My word...will not return to me empty, but will accomplish what I desire and achieve the purpose for which I sent it" (Isa 55:11 NIV). Every Word God speaks is on a mission and is guaranteed to accomplish it in accordance with His will, His strategy and His timing. So put God's Word to work! *(d) It's dynamic.* "The words I have spoken to you are spirit and they are life" (Jn 6:63 NIV). When you receive it as the Word of God, it produces life-changing results. It can't just sit there and do nothing, it must generate, for it is "the word of God, which also effectively works in you who believe" (1Th 2:13 NKJV)!

HOW TO RECEIVE GOD'S WORD (2)

My words will by no means pass away.

MARK 13:31 NKJV

How can you get the maximum benefit out of God's Word? *Receive it as a permanent Word, not a temporary Word.* Given our culture's "disposable" mentality we don't expect to hold onto things too long. We're constantly replacing them with more up-to-date technologies. But not God's Word! "Heaven and earth will pass away, but My words will by no means pass away." It never needs updating; it's perfect and can't be improved upon. That's why Jesus instructs us to let "my words remain in you" (Jn 15:7 NIV). In twenty-first century vernacular: "Program your mind with the Scriptures." How do you do that?

(1) "Let the word of Christ dwell in you richly" (Col 3:16). Give it permanent residence, not just visitor status. Take it in richly, meaning copiously, abundantly. Call it "operation saturation!" To help us, this passage in The Living Bible adds: "Teach them to each other and sing them out in psalms and hymns and spiritual songs." What a great way to reinforce your grasp on the Scriptures. (2) "Do not let this Book of the Law depart from your mouth; meditate on it day and night...do everything written in it. Then you will be prosperous and successful" (Jos 1:8 NIV). To retain it permanently, talk it out, think it out, walk it out! You say, "But my memory doesn't retain things too well." No problem. "The Counselor, the Holy Spirit, whom the Father will send in my name...will remind you of everything I have said to you" (Jn 14:26 NIV). If you'll read, teach, sing, talk, think and walk in God's Word, His Spirit will supernaturally refresh your less-than-perfect memory of it.

HOW TO RECEIVE GOD'S WORD (3)

All that the Lord has said will we do.

EXODUS 24:7 NKJV

How can you make God's Word more personal and effective in your life? *By receiving it as a practical, not a theoretical Word.* The Bible is not God's attempt to offer illuminating insights, interesting theories or good advice for our consideration. No, it's an authoritative, indisputable statement of eternal truth for us to live by. It's intended for real-world application. "Therefore whoever hears these sayings of Mine, and does them, I will liken him to a wise man who built his house upon the rock" (Mt 7:24 NKJV). The obedient builder's rock-solid foundation withstood the storm's violence. Conversely, "Everyone who hears these sayings of Mine, and does not do them," Jesus says, is a fool, and the storms will erode his foundation (vv. 26-27). Now, Jesus didn't condemn this man for building an inadequate structure, or failing to hear, understand and believe His words, but for failing to act on them. "Do not merely listen to the word, and so deceive yourselves. Do what it says…the man who looks intently into the perfect law …not forgetting what he has heard, but doing it—he will be blessed in what he does" (Jas 1:22-25 NIV). If we think reading, knowing, and even believing God's Word fulfills our obligation to it, we're self-deceived. Because it's God's Word, His intention for it must be fulfilled. That requires not just *believing,* but *behaving* the Word. James didn't say, "he will be blessed in what he believes," but "he will be blessed in what he does!" When Moses read God's Word to the Israelites, they said, "*All that the Lord has said we will do, and be obedient.*" Amen.

AMAZING GRACE

To me...grace was given, to preach...
the unfathomable riches of Christ.

EPHESIANS 3:8 NAS

When John was eleven his father, a master seaman, groomed him for the British Navy. But John lacked discipline. Arrested for desertion, demoted and flogged, he scoffed at authority and mocked Christian crew members. One night he awoke and found his cabin filling with water; the ship's side had collapsed. Normally that kind of damage sinks a vessel within minutes, but a buoyant cargo bought them extra time. John heard another sailor shout, "We're all goners!" and his life flashed before him. In that moment he repented and gave his heart to Christ, a prayer he might easily have forgotten, given the ship *didn't* sink that night. Instead he remembered it long after he retired from the sea to—become a minister and writer of verse. Paul says, "We have...forgiveness...according to the riches of His grace" (Eph 1:7 NKJV). John Newton could join Paul in saying, "To me, the very least...grace was given, to preach...the unfathomable riches of Christ."

Little stories tell big stories, and the big story here is the hymn Newton wrote symbolizing his conversion to Christ. You've probably sung it once or twice. *Amazing grace! How sweet the sound that saved a wretch like me! I once was lost but now am found, was blind but now I see. Through many dangers, toils and snares I have already come; 'tis grace hath brought me safe thus far and grace will lead me home.* The grace that saves us is "unfathomable." We'll never understand it. That's why the last verse of the hymn says, *"When we've been there ten thousand years, bright shining as the sun; We've no less days to sing God's praise, than when we first begun."*

FREE TO BE QUIET

He opened not his mouth.

ISAIAH 53:7 NKJV

Sometimes it's wise to wait, to say, "I don't have the answer right now but I'll think about it, pray, and get back to you." Your need to rescue someone, or impress them and make points, will come back to bite you. The Bible says, "A prudent man keeps his knowledge to himself, but the heart of fools blurts out folly" (Pr 12:23 NIV). Allow wisdom to determine your response, not ego!

When people are anxious for answers they'll pressure you into speaking before you have all the facts or have taken time to pray and consider the situation. If you ask Him, God will tell you *what* to say and *when* to say it. His promise is: "I have put my words in your mouth and covered you with the shadow of my hand" (Isa 51:16 NIV). Ego says, "Don't just stand there, say something." Wisdom says, "Don't just say something, stand there!" Quietly ask God for insight. One insight from Him can settle things in a hurry. Someone else's need to *know* shouldn't determine your need to *speak*.

When Jesus stood before Pilate in judgment He said, "Do you think I cannot call on my Father, and he will at once put at my disposal more than twelve legions of angels?" (Mt 26:53 NIV). Yet the Bible says, "He opened not his mouth." When He was brought before Pilate, Jesus just stood there and said nothing. That's because *He* was not on trial, Pilate was. Jesus knew His destiny, and most importantly, He knew His Father intimately. And when you know God, you can face anything with confidence—and be free to be quiet. What a wonderful place to be!

THE ROMAN ROAD TO SALVATION

The gift of God is eternal life.

ROMANS 6:23

Does your life feel empty? Do you long for peace, the knowledge that your sins are forgiven and the assurance of a home in heaven? Today place your trust in Christ and make Him Lord of your life. "How?" you ask. Take the Roman road to salvation. (Found in the Book of Romans.)

Step 1: "We've compiled this long and sorry record as sinners...and proved that we are utterly incapable of living the glorious lives God wills for us" (Ro 3:23 TM). Face it, we're all sinners to the core, desperately in need of a Savior. *Step 2:* "Work hard for sin your whole life and your pension is death. But God's gift is real life, eternal life, delivered by Jesus" (Ro 6:23 TM). The gospel means "good news" and here's the good news: your sins (all of them) have been paid for at the cross. *Step 3:* "God put his love on the line for us by offering his Son in sacrificial death while we were of no use whatever to him" (Ro 5:8 TM). You can't earn salvation by good works or deserve it by having good character. God offers it to you freely. All you have to do is receive it by faith. *Step 4:* "You're not 'doing' anything; you're simply calling out to God, trusting him to do it for you. That's salvation...say it, right out loud: 'God has set everything right between him and me!'" (Ro 10:9-12 TM).

Now pray these words: "Lord, I surrender my life to You. Come into my heart. By faith I receive the gift of eternal life. Thank You for setting everything right between You and me, in Jesus' name, amen."

THE GRACE TO DO IT!

Pray for those who mistreat you.

LUKE 6:28 NIV

There's no way to go through life without being hurt. But if you think what the person who hurt you did was bad—wait till you see what bitterness will do. It will extend your pain, infect your attitude, control your moods and cause you to lose friends. Few things are worse than a person who only wants to talk about "what *they* did to *me*." Get rid of the score cards. Burn them! If you know where they're hidden you haven't let them go yet. Jesus said, "There is a connection between what God does and what you do. You can't get forgiveness from God, for instance, without also forgiving others" (Mt 6:14-15 TM).

"But you don't know what I've been through." No, but in reading the Scriptures you'll discover what *Jesus* went through. Would you like to compare notes? His family thought He was mad. Some of those He healed called for His death. Even His disciples bailed out when the going got tough. Then add to that the weight of carrying the sins of the whole world, and you've more than reason to harbor bitterness. But instead He preached forgiveness—from a cross! And His Word to you today is: "Bless those who curse you, and pray for those who spitefully use you. To him who strikes you on the one cheek, offer the other also. And from him who takes away your cloak, do not withhold your tunic either. Give to everyone who asks of you. And from him who takes away your goods do not ask them back" (Lk 6:28-30 NKJV). You say, "That's hard to do." Yes, but God will give you the grace to do it!

HOW TO BUILD A STRONG TEAM (1)

Love cares more for others than for self.

1 CORINTHIANS 13:7 TM

Many of us would rather settle for achieving less, than put up with "people-problems." But fulfilling a great dream usually means having a great team. And great teams are made up of people with strengths—and weaknesses. God seldom calls us to do the job alone; He calls others to stand with us. So, do you know who belongs in your life?

Jesus chose twelve disciples to help Him fulfill His mission on earth. One of them doubted Him, one denied Him and one betrayed Him. Yet He called them, knowing what they were—and could become. After listing hardships that would make your worst day look like "a walk in the park," Paul writes, "Besides everything else, I face daily the pressure of…all the churches" (2Co 11:28 NIV). How did Paul evangelize Asia, guide the church and write half the New Testament? Through a team; he introduces them in Romans 16. Let's look at one of his team-building secrets. It's called:

Love. If you don't genuinely care about people they'll sense it and they won't stay with you. If you've a high turnover in your relationships, that could be your problem. Even your best team members will go through times that affect their performance. Jeremiah got so stressed out that he wanted to quit the ministry and go into the motel business (See Jer 9:2). Paul advised his right-hand man Timothy to "use a little wine because of your stomach and your frequent illnesses" (1Ti 5:23 NIV). Here's a helpful prescription for the stress that goes with people-problems. Write it down on a 3x5 card and read it regularly. "Love cares more for others than for self."

HOW TO BUILD A STRONG TEAM (2)

*They committed themselves to the teaching
of the apostles, [and]...life together.*

ACTS 2:42 TM

The success of the New Testament church was driven by two things: (1) A sound scriptural foundation. (2) A sense of belonging. On good teams, players extend trust to one another. Initially it's a risk because your trust can be violated and you can get hurt. At the same time they are giving trust, each team member must conduct themselves in such a way as to earn the trust of others by holding themselves to a high standard. When everyone gives freely and bonds of trust develop and are tested over time, they begin to have faith in one another. They believe that the people next to them will act with consistency, keep commitments, maintain confidences and support each other. The stronger their sense of belonging becomes, the greater their potential to work together.

All teams have disagreements. The leader of one mega-church writes, "Let's not pretend we never disagree. We're dealing with 16,000 people and the stakes are high. Let's not have people hiding their concerns to protect a false notion of unity. Let's face the disagreement and deal with it in a good way. The mark of community is not the absence of conflict, it's the presence of a reconciling spirit. I can have a rough-and-tumble meeting with someone, but because we're committed to each other we can leave, slapping each other on the back, saying, 'I'm glad we're still on the same team.'" Those who built the New Testament church overcame moral and financial problems, doctrinal differences and prejudice. How? Through "a reconciling spirit." As a result, they are credited with "turning the world upside down" (See Ac 17:6).

HOW TO BUILD A STRONG TEAM (3)

Happy is the man who…
gains understanding.

PROVERBS 3:13 NKJV

An important key to building a strong team is being open to new and different ideas. One of your greatest dangers as you become older (or more successful) is that your thinking can become institutionalized—which is just another word for "fossilized." To remain successful you must create an environment in which the free exchange of information and ideas takes place. If people had not been permitted to try things we'd still be traveling by horse and carriage, dining by candlelight, and dying a lot earlier from preventable diseases. It's said that knowledge is doubling every five to ten years. That lets us know how much we didn't know—when we thought we knew it all.

"Happy is the man who finds wisdom, and the man who gains understanding." We must honor what we've learned by building on it, but we never stop asking, "Is there a better way?" Champions don't ease up because they're ahead of the competition; they're still accelerating as they cross the finish line. The competition keeps you sharp. You need them.

Irish singer Bono said something worth noting: "I would be terrified to be on my own as a solo singer…I surround myself with…a band, a family of very spunky kids, and a wife who's smarter than anyone…you're only as good as the arguments you get. So maybe the reason why the band hasn't split up is that people might get this: even though I'm only one quarter of U2, I'm more than I could be if I was one whole of something else." Solomon put it this way: "As iron sharpens iron, so a man sharpens…his friend" (Pr 27:17 NKJV).

GO BACK TO WHERE YOU MET HIM

Simon Peter said to them,
"I am going fishing."

JOHN 21:3 NKJV

When Peter decided to go fishing that night, he may have been making a decision to get away from everything and go back to where he first met the Lord. That's a good move! When you get discouraged you'll either go back to the One who can save, keep and satisfy, or you'll go back to whatever was going on in your life before you met Him. That's *not* a good move! Peter fished all that night and caught nothing. There's a lesson there for you.

God said to the church in Revelation: "You have persevered …and have labored for My name's sake and…not become weary. Nevertheless I have this against you, that you have left your first love. Remember therefore from where you have fallen; repent and do the first works" (Rev 2:3-5 NKJV). Has your love for God grown cold? If so, you need to go back to where you first met Him, to seek Him again like you did before you'd heard so much and seen so much, before the pressures of life had worn you down. "But I'm busy doing the work of the Lord," you say. Busyness and barrenness go hand in hand together. It's possible to look like a saint in the courts of Babylon, yet be a backslider in the courts of Zion. Three times Jesus asked Peter, "Do you love Me?" Finally Peter said, "Lord, You know all things; You know [the extent to which] I love You" (Jn 21:17 NKJV). Oswald Chambers said, "Beware of anything that competes with your loyalty to Jesus Christ. The greatest competitor of devotion to Jesus, is service to Him." Think about it.

CUTTING OFF EARS

Keep your tongue from evil.

PSALM 34:13 NIV

When Jesus was betrayed by Judas, He just stood there, even though He could have called twelve legions of angels to His defense. Then the mob came, laid hands on Him and arrested Him. Peter, ready to defend Jesus, drew his sword and cut off the High Priest's servant's ear. Impulsive, quick-on-the-draw Peter was thinking, "We don't have to take this!" But Jesus said, "No, that's not how you handle things!" Then, "he touched the man's ear and healed him" (Lk 22:51 NIV). Peter was talking when he needed to be listening, and doing things when he didn't need to be doing them. He needed to learn how to wait on God, to exercise humility and discernment. God had great plans for Peter, but if he wanted to reach people for Christ he couldn't do it by taking out his sword and chopping off ears when he felt angry. There's a lesson here.

Our abrasive words can cut off people's ability to hear. We can't just fly off the handle whenever we feel like it. We must be sensitive to God: If He tells us, "Say nothing," we must stand there quietly, even if it means letting someone think they're right even when we know they're not. We must say, "Yes, Lord," and accept that He doesn't owe us an explanation. How many times do we prevent somebody's spiritual growth, or God's blessings from coming into our own lives, because we don't control what we say? Perhaps you think that compared to adultery or stealing this is no big deal? Think again: "He who guards his lips guards his life, but he who speaks rashly will come to ruin" (Pr 13:3 NIV).

GOD'S GOT YOU COVERED!

I will give it into your hand.

JOSHUA 8:18 NKJV

Before going into battle God said to Joshua: "Stretch out the spear that is in your hand toward Ai, for I will give it into your hand." It's amazing how courageous you become when you know God's got you covered. When you know He's behind you, you can say, "No weapon formed against me will prevail" (See Isa 54:17). Remember as a child how secure you felt in a fight, knowing your big brother or sister was behind you? Well, God is backing you up!

The problem is, we say all sorts of things without first checking to find out if God's behind us. When Satan says, "Jesus I know, and Paul I know; but who are you?" (Ac 19:15 NKJV), you must know two things: (a) That you are in right standing with God. (b) That it's His fight as well as yours. Jesus said, "Whatever you bind on earth will be bound in heaven, and whatever you loose on earth will be loosed in heaven" (Mt 18:18 NIV). There must be agreement in both realms. Jesus taught us to pray, "Your will be done on earth as it is in heaven" (Mt 6:10 NIV), because if it's not approved where He is, it's not approved where you are either. Your confidence comes from knowing you're operating according to God's will.

The Bible calls us "laborers together with God" (1Co 3:9), so don't go off and do your own thing. Don't try moving anything the Lord doesn't want moved, or raising anybody from the dead except the Lazarus He calls forth. We do on earth, *only* what we know He's declared to be His will in heaven. That way we *know* we're covered.

WHAT WILL YOUR LEGACY BE?

He did what was right.

2 KINGS 22:2 NIV

Josiah's grandfather, Manasseh, was a violent king who filled "Jerusalem from one end to the other with [the people's] blood" (2Ki 21:16 NLT). His father, King Amon, died at the hands of his own officers. "He did what God said was wrong," reads his epitaph. Josiah was only eight when he ascended the throne. Immediately he chose righteousness, and didn't stop doing what was right all his life (See 2Ki 22:2). What's the point? We can't pick our parents, but we can pick our role-models.

When Josiah was rebuilding the temple he discovered a scroll containing God's law. As he read it he wept, realizing his people had drifted far from God. So he sent word to a prophetess and asked, "What will become of our people?" She told Josiah that since he had repented when he heard God's Word, his nation would be spared (See 2Ch 34:14-27). Wow! An entire generation received grace because of the integrity of one man.

So, you can rise above your past and make a difference. Your parents may have given you your DNA, but God can give you a new birth and a new beginning. "You are God's children whom he loves, so try to be like him" (Eph 5:1 NIV). Just like Josiah, you cannot control the way your forefathers responded to God, but you can control the way *you* respond to Him. Your past does not have to be your prison; you have a say in your life, you have a voice in your destiny, you have a choice in the path you take. Choose well and some day—generations from now—others will thank God for the legacy you left.

"CLING-FREE" RELATIONSHIPS

Therefore shall a man
leave his father and his mother.

GENESIS 2:24

God said, "Therefore shall a man leave his father and his mother, and shall cleave unto his wife: and they shall be one flesh." God said that to Adam and Eve, the first two people on earth, who had neither father nor mother to leave, nor children, yet, to leave them.

Have your children left home? If so, you've discovered that you don't adjust overnight to your sense of loss. After all, you've invested yourself, your time, your labor, your love, your faith and your hopes in them. They're your most precious possessions, your pride and joy; now they're leaving and taking a big chunk of you with them. The empty nest can be both shocking and depressing. But it's been Life 101, ever since Eden. That's why God laid it out for Adam and Eve so early in the parenting game. Knowing that one of the hardest parts of parenting is letting go, God was saying, "Letting go takes time. Start preparing yourself now, *before* you have children."

Our kids are born leaving! From their first steps, they're on an outbound orbit, returning periodically to tank up on reassurance (or funds) and leaving again to become their "own person," couple or family as God intended. So begin early, "letting out the line," gradually increasing their freedom as they can handle responsibility. God gives us two principles for a healthy marriage in Genesis 2:24: *leaving and cleaving.* Your child must leave you in order to cleave to the partner God is giving them. So invest in their happiness by having your *own* life and letting them have *theirs*. Making it easier for them— makes it easier on you!

HAPPINESS KEYS (1)

If you know these things.

JOHN 13:17 AMP

If you want God's best, don't just think about how to invest your money, think about how to invest your life. Jesus said, "If you know these things...happy...are you if you...[do them]." Living this way means:

(1) Making time for friends and loved ones. "Let no one seek his own, but each...the other's well-being" (1Co 10:24 NKJV). George Eliot wrote: "Oh, the inexpressible comfort of feeling safe with a person; having neither to weigh thoughts nor measure words, but to pour them all out, just as they are, chaff and grain together, knowing that a faithful hand will take and sift them, keep what is worth keeping, and then, with the breath of kindness, blow the rest away."

(2) Giving thanks. If you can't be grateful for what God has given you, look around you and be grateful for what He's protected you from. The enemy doesn't have to steal anything from you, just make you take it for granted. "From the fullness of his grace we have all received one blessing after another" (Jn 1:16 NIV). The excitement of a new car or a salary increase soon passes, but anytime you stop to count your blessings you start feeling better.

(3) Practicing contentment. A gardener who'd tried everything to get rid of dandelions wrote to the Department of Agriculture for help. "What can I try next?" he asked. "Try getting used to them!" came the reply. In life, you get what you focus on! That's why Paul writes, "Fix your thoughts on what is true, and honorable, and right, and pure, and lovely, and admirable. Think about things that are excellent and worthy of praise" (Php 4:8 NLT).

HAPPINESS KEYS (2)

*Blessed...are those
who hear the word...and obey.*

LUKE 11:28 NIV

Jesus said, "[Real] life is not measured by how much you own" (Lk 12:15 NLT) but by how you live. That's why it's always wise to:

Challenge yourself. Examine how you spend your leisure time. After a long day it's easy to "vege out" in front of the TV, but you'll be happier if you are physically and mentally active. Go for a walk, play with your kids, take time to read God's Word and pray, even when you don't feel like it. Jesus said that in order to follow Him, we "must give up the things [we] want" (See Lk 9:23 NCV).

Reach out to others. The smallest good deed is worth more than the most grandiose intention, so if you want to help yourself, help others. Not only will it make you feel better, being around other people who are giving of themselves keeps you connected to a larger cause. The enemy doesn't mind you talking about your faith as long as you don't practice it, whereas God never teaches us anything without giving us an opportunity to put it to work. That's why Jesus said, "Blessed...are those who hear the word...and obey."

Be more patient. A man who rode the ferry to work prided himself on his punctuality. But one day he overslept. Fearing he'd be in trouble with his boss, he raced to the dock only to see the boat six feet out from the terminal. Taking a leap, he landed on the deck. Smiling, the captain said, "Great jump! But if you'd waited another minute we'd have docked and you could've walked on." Don't be in such a hurry; give it a little time. "Patience...can...overcome any problem" (Pr 25:15 CEV).

NEED MORE STRENGTH? WAIT ON GOD!

They that wait upon the Lord
shall renew their strength.

ISAIAH 40:31

God usually doesn't tell us *how* He will answer our prayers, or even *when*. But He does promise those who wait on Him one thing—strength. The word "wait" in this Scripture pictures a Hebrew word used in the making of rope. Every rope starts out as a thread, and every strand added just increases its strength. So each time you wait on the Lord you add another thread to the rope; you get a little stronger, a little more able to cope. Do you feel like you're just hanging on by a thread today? Spend more time in God's presence and God's Word, and watch your thread turn into a rope. But waiting is not always passive, sometimes it's active, like waiting on a customer, seeing that his or her needs are met. In this case, waiting is not so much a *position* as it is a *focus*.

The Bible says, "Thou wilt keep him in perfect peace, whose mind is stayed on thee" (Isa 26:3). Whether it's sitting prayerfully in His presence or actively carrying out His will, you have God's assurance that your strength will be renewed.

If you're at the end of your rope today, grab hold of these three promises: (1) "Wait on the Lord; be of good courage, and He shall strengthen your heart; wait, I say, on the Lord" (Ps 27:14 NKJV). (2) "Wait silently for God alone, for my expectation is from Him" (Ps 62:5 NKJV). (3) "As the eyes of servants look to the hand of their masters...so our eyes look to the Lord our God" (Ps 123:2 NKJV). *Do you need more strength? Wait on God!*

HOW LONG WILL THIS ATTACK LAST?

Having done all...stand.

EPHESIANS 6:13 NKJV

The size of the prize determines the severity of the fight. The enemy knows your vulnerabilities and he'll push you to your limits. When he does, remember: "Blessed is the man who endures...when he has been approved, he will receive the crown" (Jas 1:12 NKJV). "Approved" means victory qualifies you for greater things. "Endures" means your staying power is being tested. So, "having done all...stand." You say, "How long will this attack last?" The Prince of Darkness hindered Daniel's prayers for twenty-one days (See Da 10:13). Goliath defied the armies of Israel forty days and nights (See 1Sa 17). Your enemy is relentless; you must be, too. When it comes to prayer, *your* persistence overcomes *his* resistance. "You have need of endurance, so that after you have done the will of God, you may receive the promise" (Heb 10:36 NKJV).

David didn't get into trouble with Bathsheba until he left the battlefield. It's the safest place to be. So stay there, keep fighting and God will come to your aid. When Joshua needed extra time to defeat his enemies, the sun stood still. God was saying, "As long as the sun doesn't go down you won't go down either, for the same power that's holding it up is holding you up." Isn't that great?

Jesus healed people in different ways. Some He spoke to, others He touched. One day He told ten lepers to go and show themselves to the priest. And the Bible says: "As they went, they were cleansed" (Lk 17:14). They were probably wondering, "*When* will it happen? *How* will it happen?" Faith doesn't demand details, it just keeps moving obediently forward, believing God for the right result!

DON'T BE A HYPOCRITE

Do not be like the hypocrites.

MATTHEW 6:5 NIV

Jesus is the only person in the New Testament who used the word "hypocrite." And there may be a reason why. Archeologists have discovered a city named Sepphoris, built by Herod the Great when Jesus was a boy. You could see it from a hillside on which His hometown of Nazareth was located. It housed a giant amphitheatre. The actors who put on plays there were called *hypokrites*. They wore masks so that the audience could identify the different characters each was intended to portray. At the end of the performance they would take off their masks and the audience would cheer and clap for them. So, practicing hypocrisy means wearing a mask designed to impress or deceive others. Ouch!

Then Jesus talks about three specific areas in which we tend to practice hypocrisy: *(1) Giving.* "When you give...do not announce it with trumpets, as the hypocrites do in the synagogues and on the streets, to be honored by men" (Mt 6:2 NIV). *(2) Praying.* "When you pray, go into your room, close the door and pray to your Father, who is unseen. Then your Father, who sees what is done in secret, will reward you" (Mt 6:6 NIV). *(3) Judging.* "In the same way you judge others, you will be judged, and with the measure you use, it will be measured to you...How can you say to your brother, 'Let me take the speck out of your eye,' when all the time there is a plank in your own eye? You hypocrite, first take the plank out of your own eye, and then you will see clearly to remove the speck from your brother's eye" (Mt 7:2-5 NIV). So, the Word for you today is—don't be a hypocrite!

GO OVERBOARD FOR THE LORD!

*Peter heard him say, "It is the Lord"
...and jumped into the water.*

JOHN 21:7 NIV

After the disciples had fished all night, catching nothing, Jesus said to them, "Throw your net on the right side of the boat" and they caught 153 fish. That's how it works; one word from Him, and suddenly everything changes for the better.

Then we read, "The disciple whom Jesus loved said to Peter, 'It is the Lord!' As soon as Simon Peter heard him say, 'It is the Lord,' he...jumped into the water" and went straight to Jesus (Jn 21:7 NIV). Notice, Peter had to decide whether to leave his fish and go to Jesus, or stay behind and enjoy what he'd worked hard for. It's a test we all face when we've accomplished our life's objectives, our nets are full, and we've finally "made it." The challenge is—do we stay and guard our blessings, or go overboard for the Lord and commit ourselves fully to Him?

Paul briefly refers to his career success: "You know my pedigree...from the elite tribe of Benjamin...defender of...my religion...meticulous observer of...God's law" (Php 3:3-6 TM). Career-wise, Paul was a "Who's Who." But listen to him now: "Things I...thought were so important are gone...dumped...in the trash so that I could embrace Christ" (Php 3:8 TM). Paul realized that his true identity lay not in his *accomplishments,* but in his *relationship* with Jesus. Do *you* feel that way? That night it probably felt like Peter was forfeiting everything, yet when he reached the shore he found Jesus busy—cooking fish! Whatever you need, God has it. Whatever you give up, He will repay many times over. Whatever you're willing to walk away from, ultimately determines what He can trust you with.

THE RIGHT PLACE; THE RIGHT PEOPLE

For such a time as this.

ESTHER 4:14 NIV

Esther won a beauty contest, married a king, lived in a palace, uncovered a plot to exterminate the Jewish people and saved them. Her story shows us the importance of being in the right place, and being influenced by the right people. So:

(1) Where you are today is no accident. Mordecai, Esther's mentor, challenged her and changed her life by saying, "Who knows but that you have come to your royal position for such a time as this?" Esther didn't set out to be queen, but once she was, she had to decide between her comfort and her calling. It's a choice we all make. "What's my calling?" you ask. It could involve your job, your marriage, your tasks as a parent, your friendships. It could involve the neighborhood where you live or volunteering at your church. One thing is certain: when God calls, it's "your time." We're tempted to think we're "treading water" right now, waiting for some other time or more important opportunity. No, you don't get to choose your time; God does that! The Psalmist said, "My times are in thy hand" (Ps 31:15).

(2) God sends special people to guide us. Without Mordecai in her life Esther might never have understood her calling. And without his help she might never have embraced it. So, who's your Mordecai? Who knows you well enough to help clarify your calling? Who loves you enough to challenge you when you get off track, or strengthen you when you want to quit and turn back? Not one of us is a composite of all of life's virtues; we all have blind spots and weaknesses. That's why God sends others—and why we need them!

DEAL WITH YOUR UNHEALED WOUNDS!

Physician, heal yourself!

LUKE 4:23 NKJV

Did you know that in the Old Testament a priest could not serve in God's house if he had a scab, which is an unhealed wound or a bleeding sore (See Lev 21:20)? Why? Because when you've a scab you're not up to par. You can't get close to others in case they bump into you and knock the protective cover off it. You're not at your best because the pain-drain is sapping your strength. You're afraid to talk about your scab in case people reject you, so you wear a mask, live on two levels and become insecure and controlling. Worst of all, you're so busy working for God and taking care of others that you don't think you've time to stop and take care of yourself. The Bible says: "Physician, heal yourself!"

Does this mean people with "issues" can't work for God? No, quite the opposite. It's the broken, who become masters at mending. But first *you* must take time to be healed. Jesus said that when the blind lead the blind they both fall into a ditch (See Mt 15:14). It's hard to talk about victory to others when you yourself are living in defeat. It's hard to bring emotional healing to others when you're still battling the unresolved issues of your past. When you are still bleeding, you can't treat people's problems with the same kind of aggressive faith you'd have if you'd already worked through the problem. Is it wrong to have a wounded heart? No, but it's wrong not to deal with it. So, spend time with God and let Him make you whole so that He can use you to minister more effectively to others.

IT'S TIME TO GET AWAY

Come aside…and rest a while.

MARK 6:31 NKJV

Luke records: "He departed and went into a deserted place. And the crowd sought Him and came to Him, and tried to keep Him from leaving them; but He said to them, 'I must preach the kingdom of God to the other cities also, because for this purpose I have been sent'" (Lk 4:42-43 NKJV). Examine the life of Christ: the *control* He exercised, the *criticism* He evoked, the *communion* He enjoyed with God, then follow His example!

Jesus said no to good things so that he could say yes to the right things. That's not easy. God may want you to leave where you are, but you're staying. Or He may want you to stay, but you're leaving. How can you know? Get away from the crowd and meet with Jesus in a deserted place. This word "deserted" doesn't mean desolate, just quiet—a place to think, to pray, to hear from God, to refuel and re-chart your course. Hell hates to see you stop!

Richard Foster points out that in contemporary society the Devil majors in three things: noise, hurry, and crowds. If he can keep us engaged in "muchness" and "manyness," he will be satisfied. He implants taxi meters in our brains. We hear the relentless tick, tick, tick telling us to hurry, hurry, hurry, time is money, resulting in this roaring blur called the human race. But Jesus stands against the tide saying, "Come to Me, all you who labor and are heavy laden, and I will give you rest" (Mt 11:28 NKJV). Will you come? Will you follow the One who often "withdrew…into the wilderness, and prayed" (Lk 5:16). A thousand voices will tell you not to. Ignore them!

SPIRIT SIGNALS

The man without the Spirit does not accept
the things that come from the Spirit.

1 CORINTHIANS 2:14 NIV

Paul says: "The man without the Spirit does not accept the things that come from the Spirit...they are foolishness to him...because they are spiritually discerned." Pastor Jon Walker writes: "*Spirit warnings* alert you to impending danger. A friend of mine was driving towards a green light when he was strongly prompted to hit his brakes. As he did so a semi-truck ran a red light. Had it not been for my friend's instant obedience he'd probably have been killed. *Spirit stop signs* red-flag you not to go somewhere. A dog I owned...was used to being on a leash and when I took him to a neighbor's field to run, I'd simply say 'No' when he approached a place he shouldn't go. He'd done nothing wrong, and my warning wasn't a rebuke—it was a caution for his own protection. *Spirit timing* is God telling you the time is not right. In grad school I planned to buy a computer through a discount program. When I turned in my paperwork, however, they told me it had been discontinued. I was very angry at God. Two months later the university re-opened the program [offering] upgraded models bundled with software that cost extra two months ago—the whole package was cheaper than the previous one...Turns out God knows what he's doing!"

Be sensitive to Spirit signals. Trust God's Spirit to guide you in the decisions and details of your life. Keep a list of the times He has prompted you; it'll sensitize you and strengthen your resolve to obey. Remember, God's promptings always line up with His Word—even when they don't line up with *your* ideas.

LEARN TO BE CONTENT (1)

I have learned the secret of being content.

PHILIPPIANS 4:12 NIV

Sometimes contentment means:
(1) *Learning to be happy with less.* A hard-charging executive decided to spend a few days in a monastery. "I hope your stay is a blessed one," said the monk who showed him to his cell. "If you need anything let us know. We'll teach you how to live without it." Happiness isn't getting what you want, it's enjoying what God's given you. Paul said he had learned to be content, "Whether well fed or hungry, whether living in plenty or want. I can do everything through him who gives me strength" (vv. 12-13). *(2) Reminding yourself things could be worse.* Snoopy was lying in his doghouse one Thanksgiving Day, mumbling about being stuck with dog food while all those humans got to be inside with the turkey and gravy and pumpkin pie. "Of course, it could have been worse," he finally reflected, "I could have been born a turkey." Reminding yourself, "It could be worse" can be a powerful developer of contentment. *(3) Understanding that what you seek is spiritual, not material.* Paul says to beware of "greed, which is idolatry" (Col 3:5 NIV). Our problem isn't just that we want more, it's that the condition which underlies all our wanting is that we really want God. As Augustine said, "Our souls will never rest, until they rest in Thee." Why would God let us feel at home, when this world is not our home? Our dissatisfaction, if we let it, can sharpen our spiritual hunger and cause us to pray, "Your kingdom come, your will be done on earth as it is in heaven" (Mt 6:10 NIV).

LEARN TO BE CONTENT (2)

I have learned the secret of being content.

PHILIPPIANS 4:12 NIV

Michael Drosnin wrote a book about a man who wanted more wealth, so he built one of the biggest financial empires of his day. He wanted more pleasure, so he paid for the most glamorous women money could buy. He wanted more adventure, so he set air-speed records, built and piloted the world's most unique aircraft. He wanted more power, so he acquired political clout that was the envy of senators. He wanted more glamour, so he owned film studios and courted stars. Drosnin tells how this man's life ended: "He was a figure of gothic power, ready for the grave. Emaciated, only 120 pounds stretched over his six-foot-four-inch frame...thin scraggly beard that reached its way onto his sunken chest, hideously long fingernails in grotesque yellow corkscrews...Many of his teeth were black, rotting stumps. A tumor was beginning to emerge from the side of his head...innumerable needle marks ...Howard Hughes was an addict. A billionaire junkie."

So here's the question: If Hughes had pulled off one more deal, made one more million and tasted one more thrill, would it have been enough? The illusion of gratitude is that we will experience it more, if we get more! No, making sure a child gets everything they want destroys their initiative and dulls their sense of gratitude and contentment. Don't you find it interesting that the man who wrote, "I have learned the secret of being content" also wrote, "In every thing give thanks: for this is the will of God in Christ Jesus concerning you" (1Th 5:18)? You cannot *make* yourself a more grateful or contented person, but you can *pray* for it and *open* your heart to it.

THE TRUTH ABOUT DAVID'S BROTHERS

Then he consecrated Jesse and his sons.

1 SAMUEL 16:5 NKJV

David's seven brothers were each circumcised: a mark of divine ownership. Yet not one of them would fight Goliath. Why? Because:

(1) They allowed the fears of those around them to erode their faith. Fear is contagious; if you listen to it long enough you'll get infected. Now, you shouldn't be isolated from the world, but you must be insulated against its negative influences. Listening to Goliath wore David's brothers down, so who are you listening to? Get God's opinion and build your life around it. Allow His Word to settle every issue. *(2) They had no personal track record with God to fall back on.* There are no insignificant battles in life. The little battles equip us for the big battles which shape our destiny. The lion he killed as a boy was big, the bear was bigger, and Goliath was bigger yet. But David wasn't intimidated. "The Lord, who delivered me from the paw of the lion and…the bear…will deliver me from the hand of this Philistine" (1Sa 17:37 NKJV). Stand on your "God moments." What you believe in a crisis will be determined by the experiences you've had with God in the past. *(3) They had looks that impressed but not hearts that sought God.* So He disqualified them, saying, "The Lord does not see as man sees; for man looks at the outward appearance, but the Lord looks at the heart" (1Sa 16:7 NKJV). David's spiritual core was formed while observing creation and having fellowship with his Creator. "As the deer pants for the water brooks, so pants my soul for You, O God. My soul thirsts for God, for the living God" (Ps 42:1-2 NKJV). Can you say that?

TODAY, GOD'S LOOKING OUT FOR YOU!

The Lord turn his face toward you
and give you peace.

NUMBERS 6:26 NIV

When Dallas Willard was a child he lost his mother. He writes about a little boy whose mom also died. Every night he toddled into his dad's room to ask if he could sleep with him. Only when his father promised to sleep with his face turned towards him, did the little guy feel safe enough to doze off. Willard writes: "We can get by with a God who doesn't speak. Many of us at least *think* we do. But it's not much of a life, and it's certainly not the life God intends or the abundant life Jesus came to make available."

Moses prayed, "The Lord turn his face toward you and give you peace." Isn't it wonderful to know God watches over us, guides and protects us 24/7? In fact, the most common promise in Scripture isn't about salvation or heaven. No, the most frequent promise in the Bible is, "I will be with you" (Jos 1:5 NKJV). It's the one God made to Enoch, Noah, Abraham, Sarah, Jacob, Joseph, Moses, Mary and Paul. And it's the one that kept them going! David said, "Even when I walk through the darkest valley, I will not be afraid, for you are close beside me" (Ps 23:4 NLT). God was constantly reminding His people that He was with them through the Tabernacle, the Ark of the Covenant, the manna in the wilderness, and the pillar of cloud and fire that went before them. Just like He's reminding you today, "Do not be afraid or discouraged...the Lord...is with you" (Jos 1:9 NLT). Be at peace today, God is looking out for you!

THE WAY THAT'S BEST FOR YOUR CHILD (1)

Through wisdom a house is built,
and by understanding it is established.

PROVERBS 24:3 NKJV

You say, "I raised all my children the same way, how come this one is a problem?" *(1)* Congratulations on succeeding with your other kids! You're ahead of the curve. A good family rule is: Pray about your shortcomings; focus on your successes. Don't obsess over one particular child, shortchanging the others of your time and attention. Though it doesn't feel natural, reduce your intense concentration on your problem child. Stop "fixing" them, enjoy all your children, and watch things improve. *(2)* Children develop at different rates and in different ways. Many problem children are just late arrivers; give them the time they need. *(3)* Most families have a "black sheep." They make us uncomfortable by not doing life like the rest of us. Accept what you don't like about them till God either changes them or teaches the family mature, unconditional, non-controlling love through them. *(4)* You do your best as an imperfect but loving parent, then your children, not you, make their own choices. The prophet Samuel's sons "did not walk in his ways. They turned aside after dishonest gain and accepted bribes and perverted justice" (1Sa 8:3 NIV). Embarrassing and disappointing, yes! But no charge of spiritual or parental failure is laid on Samuel's doorstep. As godly a man as ever lived, he "walked the talk." But when push came to shove, his sons had their options and chose not to do likewise. *(5)* However dysfunctional your child may be, under God their greatest asset is a parent who responds by faith not by fixing, by praying not prying, and who gets out of God's way and lets Him work.

THE WAY THAT'S BEST FOR YOUR CHILD (2)

Train up a child in the way he should go.

PROVERBS 22:6

You say, "She's such an obedient child, but her brother breaks every rule!" Or, "Our first child's so organized; our second's a disaster area!" Children are created unique. Dealing with that reality is a parent's great challenge. Look at God's directives in Proverbs 22:6. *(1) "Train up a child."* Thoughtful, loving, productive, happy children don't just evolve—they're trained. Our latchkey generation has proved "A child left to himself disgraces his [parents]" (Pr 29:15 NIV). Wise parents choose their child's direction, then maintain it by positive reinforcement and consistent discipline. They mold their child's attitude and behavior in line with God's Word. Solomon's reference to a child in this Scripture indicates a pre-teen who can still be molded. If you miss those early training years your job's tough, but with God's help, not impossible. *(2) "In the way he should go."* Ever hear of "cross-grain parenting"? It's trying to make your child something they're not meant to be. Forcing square pegs into round holes invites rebellion in spirited kids and creativity-destroying conformity in compliant ones. This Scripture in The Amplified Bible advocates training a child, "In the way…[in keeping with his individual gift or bent]." Study your child's gifts, then direct them accordingly. Putting square pegs into square holes reduces resistance, invites cooperation and recognizes your child's God-ordained destiny. When it's their path, not yours, they'll commit to it. *(3) "When he is old he will not depart from it."* When they're in the place God designed them for, nobody needs to manipulate, control or threaten them. They're invested, creative, challenged, fulfilled and happy to grow up in the square hole God shaped for them!

LEARN TO LIVE LIKE JESUS

Learn from me...
and you will find rest for your souls.

MATTHEW 11:29 NIV

You'll notice that unlike us, Jesus didn't suffer from the fear of failure. That's because He never entertained the thought that He *couldn't* do something His Father had already assured Him He *could*. And He didn't suffer from a fear of lack either. Even though He lived a simple life He was responsible for supporting Himself and a team of others. How did He do it? He prayed a lot, and stayed in sync with His heavenly Father. Consequently He knew how to catch fish when they weren't biting, or find tax money in a fish's mouth when He needed it. (Yes, Jesus paid His taxes!) Now God may not provide for you in similar fashion, but He's promised to take care of you (See 1Pe 5:7). Today Jesus is saying to you, "Come to me...learn from me...and you will find rest for your souls [emotions and mind]."

Stress is brought on by our need to know everything ahead of time—to be in control. Even after we pray and supposedly turn the situation over to God, we develop a "backup plan" in case He doesn't handle things the way we think He should. Do you do that? You don't put your money into a bank then stay awake all night worrying about it, do you? Have at *least* that much confidence in God. Each time you begin the downward spiral of "How? What? When? Where?" stop and give it back to God. Not the little God of your understanding, but the big God whose track record speaks for itself, whose faithfulness never fails, and who has earned the right to ask you, "Is any thing too hard for [me]?" (Ge 18:14). In other words—learn how to live like Jesus.

YOU'LL BE REWARDED

*Your Father who sees in secret
will...reward you openly.*

MATTHEW 6:4 NKJV

Dr. Tony Campolo writes: "I know a man who loves to use his money to help people who will never know it was him. When I told him about a student who was hoping to become a minister but was going to have to drop out of school for financial reasons, he contacted the college and arranged to have the student's bills paid. That student became one of the best preachers in my denomination. Hundreds have become Christians under his leadership. Thousands have been influenced by his sermons—and he never did find out who put up the money! Behind it all was a person with resources, and the desire to do something that would live on. It surprises me more people don't do this. Many keep their money tucked away, and when they die they leave it to people who don't really need it. What a waste, when they could make a difference in so many lives."

A lost opportunity to give is a lost opportunity to receive, because "Your Father who sees in secret will Himself reward you openly." Imagine what it will be like on Judgment Day when God tells somebody you helped anonymously that it was you. There will be rewards handed out to people who don't even remember doing the things they're being honored for, like making a phone call that landed somebody a job, paying their light bill, encouraging them when they're down, or leaving a bag of groceries on their doorstep. Even when those who've benefited from your kindness forget, *God remembers, records and rewards.* Jesus said if all you can do is give somebody "a cup of cold water...you will...be rewarded" (Mt 10:42 NLT).

BE WISE WITH YOUR MONEY

Then Isaac sowed in that land,
and reaped in the same year a hundredfold.

GENESIS 26:12 NKJV

Where money is concerned, the Bible teaches us that we are to:

(1) Save for a rainy day. "There is…treasure…in the dwelling of the wise. But a foolish man squanders it" (Pr 21:20 NKJV). Learn to live within your means and teach your children to do the same. Instead of maxing out your credit cards remind yourself that you can live happily without most of the stuff advertisers are peddling. Before you make another purchase, pray. Just because your banker approves the loan doesn't mean it's wise, or that God approves the expenditure. All boats rise with the tide; they also go down with it. Joseph instructed Pharaoh to "gather all the food of those good years…Then that food shall be as a reserve for…seven years of famine" (Ge 41:35-36 NKJV). Live by "the Joseph principle," and save.

(2) Sow in the time of famine. The Bible says, "Whoever sows generously will also reap generously" (2Co 9:6 NIV). You say, "But things are tight for me right now." Don't withhold because you are afraid of not having enough. Give God a seed to work with and He'll make sure you have a harvest when you need it. God's ability to provide is not limited by the world's economy. Do what Isaac did: "There was a famine in the land… Then Isaac sowed…and reaped in the same year a hundredfold; and the Lord blessed him" (Ge 26:1, 12-13 NKJV). Who blessed Isaac? The Lord! When God tells you to give, give in faith, confident that at the right time, in the right way, and in exactly the right places, you'll receive!

WHAT'S THE "TAKE AWAY?"

*I must leave everything I gain to people
who haven't worked to earn it.*

ECCLESIASTES 2:21 NLT

In business we talk about the "take away." It's your net profit, your bottom line reward.

Here's a truth you need to know before they tag your toe, arrange your funeral service and lay flowers on your grave: when you live for yourself and fail to fulfill God's purpose for your life, the "take away" is not worth the investment. Solomon writes, "So I turned in despair from hard work. It was not the answer to my search for satisfaction in this life. For though I do my work with wisdom, knowledge, and skill, I must leave everything I gain to people who haven't worked to earn it. This is not only foolish, but highly unfair" (Ecc 2:18-21 NIV). Or as author John Capozzi puts it, "The executive who works from 7 a.m. till 7 p.m. every day will be very successful. He will also be fondly remembered by his wife's next husband."

The day is coming when all the stuff you've striven, strained and stressed out to acquire will make no difference. Your résumé and job title will no longer impress anyone. No one will care what clothes you wore or what cars you drove, except your relatives who plan to wear them, drive them or sell them. If you're wise you'll plan to exit this life with a "take away" that involves these three things: *(a) Satisfaction,* that comes from having fulfilled your God-given assignment here on earth. *(b) Success,* that's measured in terms of eternal rewards, not temporal ones. *(c) Security,* that comes from knowing Jesus Christ as your Lord and Savior. These are the only "take away" worth living for!

SUCCEEDING ON THE JOB (1)

He who is slothful in his work,
is a brother to...a great destroyer.

PROVERBS 18:9 NKJV

God's interested in *what* you do for work; He's also interested in *how* you do it. The truth is, your prospects for the future are determined by your work ethic. For the next few days let's look at some work habits from the book of Proverbs to avoid or acquire if you want God's blessing.

Laziness. "I went past the field of the sluggard...the ground was covered with weeds, and the stone wall was in ruins ...I...learned a lesson...A little sleep...folding of the hands... and poverty will come on you like a bandit" (Pr 24:30-34 NIV). Laziness produces lack just as surely as a thief will rob you. The Bible says lazy people are: *(a) Procrastinators.* "A little sleep... folding of the hands." They say, "I'll do it tomorrow," but tomorrow never comes. *(b) Expensive to maintain.* "He who is slothful in his work is a brother to...a great destroyer." They complain, cut corners, cripple businesses and cause hardship. *(c) Quitters.* They quit before the job's finished. "The lazy man does not roast his game" (Pr 12:27 NIV). He hunts the deer but he won't clean it. Unfinished projects fill his life: Half-built cupboards, half-painted rooms, half-tidied garages. Sound familiar? *(d) Masters of excuses.* "The sluggard says, 'There is a lion outside!' or, 'I will be murdered in the streets!'" (Pr 22:13 NIV). When he runs out of credible excuses he goes for ridiculous ones. He "will not plow by reason of the cold" (Pr 20:4). "You want me to get sick, going to work in this weather?" Or if it's warm, "It's way too nice for work!" Whatever your work, do it conscientiously. Don't let laziness rob you of success.

SUCCEEDING ON THE JOB (2)

Go to the ant...consider its ways and be wise.

PROVERBS 6:6 NIV

When it comes to having a work ethic, "Go to the ant, consider its ways and be wise." These tiny giants of industry teach us valuable principles for living. Observe three things about them:

(1) The ant "has no commander, no overseer or ruler" (Pr 6:7 NIV). Nobody has to get it out of bed in the morning or coax it to get moving. Nobody supervises its work or enforces quality standards on it. Nobody needs to micromanage its time on the job or make sure it starts punctually, puts in a full day, pulls its weight and doesn't quit early. It's self-motivated and driven by its own high standards, not by rules, regulations or the fear of being fired. (2) It "stores its provisions in summer and gathers its food at harvest" (Pr 6:8 NIV). While everybody else is complaining about the heat (the weather, the economy, politics, etc.), the hard-working ant just keeps preparing for the future. Later, in the more moderate temperatures of harvest time, it continues gathering. Disregarding the conditions, it works. Then while others are struggling to survive it feasts on the fruit of its labor. "Watch and learn," is God's counsel. (3) The ant is no haphazard, disorganized drifter wandering around aimlessly, looking for something to do. He knows exactly what he's there for and where and how to do it. He's goal-directed, focused, determined and unstoppable. You can't keep a good ant down! "Consider...and be wise."

"But my job's a dead end," you say. As long as you're in this job do it "heartily, as to the Lord" (Col 3:23). Prove yourself where you are and God will promote you to better things.

SUCCEEDING ON THE JOB (3)

The wicked...earns deceptive wages.

PROVERBS 11:18 NIV

If you want to succeed in life practice *honesty!* One poll cited by Paul Harvey stated that 40 percent of American workers admitted stealing on the job, and 20 percent felt justified! Their rationalizing includes: "Everybody's doing it, why shouldn't I?" "The boss can afford it, he won't miss it." "It's only small stuff, it won't make any difference." "The company owes me, I'm just taking what's mine." "I deserve it, I've worked hard and never been acknowledged." What does God's Word say about this? "The wicked...earns deceptive wages." God says deceiving your employer by stealing time and materials, or delivering an inferior product and service, is "wicked." That's strong language! Of all people, employers and customers should be able to trust followers of Christ to be honest, work for their wages and provide the highest quality service.

And for the record, it's *not* smart to steal, even if you don't get caught. "Ill-gotten gains do not profit" (Pr 10:2 NAS). You may take it but you won't benefit by it. "Wealth obtained by fraud dwindles" (Pr 13:11 NAS). You can't do the wrong thing and get the right result. Not only will you have trouble, you'll bring trouble on those who love and need you most. "He who profits illicitly troubles his own house" (Pr 15:27 NAS). The job loss, damaged reputation, humiliation, legal costs and consequences are a "bill" the whole family pays for, often ending in shame and divorce and affecting several generations. Your spouse deserves an honest partner. Your children deserve a role model they can emulate, confident the path you walk is safe for them to follow.

SUCCEEDING ON THE JOB (4)

The hand of the diligent makes rich.

PROVERBS 10:4 NRS

If you want to succeed on the job here's a character quality you need to develop: *diligence.* When asked, "What's your biggest challenge?" employers usually say, "Finding and keeping good people." It makes or breaks any business. "A slack hand causes poverty, but the hand of the diligent makes rich." Diligence calls for being self-disciplined, motivated, alert, dependable, and entails following through. The Bible says, "Diligence is...precious" (Pr 12:27 NKJV) because it's so hard to find.

Diligent workers are worth their wages: "The plans of the diligent lead to profit" (Pr 21:5 NIV). In God's system the boss should profit by you and you should profit by him. Indeed, diligent people *plan* to be profitable employees. Do you want to prosper? See that your employer prospers! Diligent workers rejoice in this, lazy workers resent it. Diligence, not politics and manipulation, will get you promoted. "Diligent hands will rule, but laziness ends in slave labor" (Pr 12:24 NIV). In God's economy you determine whether you become "ruler" or "slave" by how hard you're willing to work. Lazy employees complain about the unfair boss, the stacked system, the "company men" who look out for the boss and the boss who looks out for them. They want the privileges others get but they're not willing to work for them. "The sluggard craves and gets nothing" (Pr 13:4 NIV) because "his hands refuse to work" (Pr 21:25 NIV). "But the desires of the diligent are fully satisfied" (Pr 13:4 NIV). They get it all: the satisfaction of a job well done, a reputation for integrity, the trust of others, job security, profit, promotion, and most importantly, the Master's "Well done."

SUCCEEDING ON THE JOB (5)

He who looks after his master will be honored.

PROVERBS 27:18 NIV

Another Bible characteristic to acquire for job success is *thoughtfulness*. That's so, whether you're a general in the army or a "GI Joe," the company president or the nightshift janitor. Character is not class-conscious. You don't demand respect, you earn it every day. If you're in a leadership role, the Bible says: "Know well the condition of your flocks, and pay attention to your herds" (Pr 27:23 NAS). Good employers and supervisors make it their business to know the needs, strengths, weaknesses, potential and motivational levels of their workers. As a result employee sick time is reduced, morale improved and quality and production soars. A pay increase isn't always the best motivator. Sometimes your thoughtfulness, understanding and interest in your employees are a more powerful motivator. The old "kick them in the pants" philosophy is a sure-fire way to generate resentment and undermining. Respect and caring invites cooperation, makes allies, not adversaries of employees and employers, and brings out the best in everybody.

If you're an employee God promises, "He who looks after his master will be honored." It's not cool to bad-mouth the boss, even if your peers egg you on. Ultimately those around you will distrust you because they know that at some point you'll do the same to them. Speak well of your boss, honor him or her and submit to their authority (See Ro 13:1-7). If you can't, say nothing and look for another job; otherwise you'll be judged for undermining them. In the parable of the talents Jesus said that the workers who took care of their boss's interests were rewarded richly. Yes, God will honor you for respecting even a difficult boss!

SUCCEEDING ON THE JOB (6)

Do you see a man skilled in his work?
He will serve before kings.

PROVERBS 22:29 NIV

Nothing contributes more to job success than *skillfulness.* Skilled workers excel by study, practice and hard work. Second best is unacceptable. Such people are "always in demand ...they don't take a back seat to anyone" (Pr 22:29 TM). Skillfulness isn't genetic; you don't inherit it, you work for it. You burn the midnight oil, stretch to your limits and refuse to "settle." Watch a skilled craftsman; your esteem rises at their attention to detail, refusal to cut corners, patience, dedication and pride of product. They inspire confidence, respect and trust. There's no more practical demonstration of genuine Christianity than being a skilled worker. When they speak people listen. If you doubt that try sharing your faith with those who see you being dishonest, shoddy and careless. Better to be silent till you earn the right to be heard!

Whatever your work, "Do it...in the name of the Lord Jesus, giving thanks to God the Father through him" (Col 3:17 NIV). We should be "raising the bar" because we're Christ's representatives. We should set the industry standard for excellence. Knowing we follow Christ should give employers and customers confidence they'll get nothing but the best.

The skillful worker can't lose, because God promises that their work will inevitably attract the attention of people who'll promote them and reward them. "Do you see a man skilled in his work? He will serve before kings" (Pr 22:29 NIV). They may start at the bottom of the ladder, but their destination is a rung higher up.

GRATITUDE

Give thanks in all circumstances.

1 THESSALONIANS 5:18 NIV

In order to have a grateful heart you must learn to be grateful for flawed people and imperfect gifts. Be grateful when your child attempts to make the bed, even though they make it imperfectly. Be grateful when your spouse expresses affection, even if they do it awkwardly. Be grateful that your body still moves around, even if it's more wrinkled and lumpy. Don't wait to *feel* thankful. The thinking and the doing—leads to the feeling. "Give thanks in all circumstances" calls for a decision and an act of your will, not an emotional response. It's why Americans call their annual holiday Thanksgiving—not thanks feeling.

James Dodson wrote a moving book called *Final Rounds*, in which he talks about the last months of his father's life. They were both avid golfers, and when his father had been diagnosed with a terminal illness James took him to Scotland so they could play golf together at some of the world's most celebrated courses. At one point James's dad asked him about his marriage and family. James's answer was evasive; he was so consumed by his work that there was little time left over. These were the words of a dying father to his son: "I wish I could slow you both down…The danger of great ambition is that you work so hard, you may some day wake up and find that the things you really wanted, were the things you had all along." Paul writes, "Wake up, O sleeper, rise from the dead, and Christ will shine on you" (Eph 5:14 NIV). Every once in a while we do wake up. And when we do, what we wake up to is *gratitude* for the things we take for granted.

WIN YOUR CHILDREN FOR CHRIST

All your sons [and daughters]
will be taught by the Lord.

ISAIAH 54:13 NIV

In the early 1800's, the Swiss educator Johann Pestalozzi wrote, "The best way for a child to learn about God, is to know a real Christian. The best way for them to discover the power of prayer, is to live with parents who pray." Did you know that statistically, 85 percent of all children raised this way develop a strong personal faith in Christ before they're thirteen?

At this point some questions arise, like: *(1) "Am I responsible for my child's choices?"* Ultimately, no; potentially, yes! If you want to determine the spiritual health of your family, first check your own heart, vision, hearing and appetites. *(2) But my kids are already grown; isn't it too late?* No, God's name is "Redeemer." He can give you another chance. Repent and commit your life to Christ, that's how generational cycles of failure are broken and God is brought back into the picture. *(3) But what if I'm afraid to bring a child into this evil world?* That's the whole point; it's children of the light who push back the darkness. Instead of reacting out of fear or selfishness, win your family to Christ and use them to impact the world. "By faith Noah, when warned about things not yet seen, in holy fear built an ark to save his family. By his faith he condemned the world and became heir of the righteousness that comes by faith" (Heb 11:7 NIV). *(4) But how can I compete with the negative influences around me?* Every study confirms that you, the parent, have the greatest influence—greater than friends, school or media—in determining the character and direction of your child.

LEARN TO TAKE TIME OFF

On the seventh day he rested from all his work.

GENESIS 2:2 NIV

Are you tired all the time? Even after sleeping? Do you keep going to the doctor but he can't find anything wrong with you? You may be experiencing the symptoms of burnout. Long periods of overexertion can cause fatigue, sleeplessness and stress. Some other signals of burnout are crying for no reason, being easily angered, insecurity, negativity, irritability, depression, cynicism and resentment toward the blessings of others. Recognize any of these in yourself?

One reason God established the Sabbath was to keep us from burning out. The law of the Sabbath simply says we can work six days, but on the seventh we need to rest; also to spend time worshipping God and having fellowship with His people. Even God rested after six days' work. Now since God doesn't get tired, clearly He's giving us an example we should follow. In Old Testament times the land had to rest after six years. No sowing and reaping were permitted in the seventh year (See Ex 23:10-12). During this time everything recovered and prepared for future production.

We argue that we cannot afford to take time off. The truth is, we can't afford not to! You say, "But I would never get anything done if I did that." Then you're *too* busy and something needs to change in your life. When you're too busy to obey God's commandments, and even follow His example, you'll pay the price. What you sow, you reap. If you sow continual stress with no rest to offset it, you'll reap the results in your body, your mind, your emotions, your health and your relationships. So, rearrange your priorities and learn to take time off!

THE PRAYER GOD ANSWERS

Their cry for help...went up to God.

EXODUS 2:23 NIV

Just when the Israelites thought life couldn't get worse, it did! Pharaoh withheld their straw and ordered them to produce the same daily quota of bricks. At that point three things happened: *(1) "The Israelites groaned in their slavery"* (v. 23). It's what we do when we feel so bad that words can't express it. We groan, first within ourselves, then to whoever will listen, finding relief in venting our frustrations. But lasting help requires more than just talking to yourself and others. So, they raised the decibel level and: *(2) "Cried out...for help."* God had seen them grit their teeth and white-knuckle it through another day. But since they were talking to everybody but Him, nothing changed. However, as soon as "their cry...went up to God...[He] heard their groaning" (v. 24). He just wanted a prayer to answer. David declared, "He hears My voice and...has inclined His ear to me...I shall call upon Him as long as I live" (Ps 116:1-2 NAS). Instead of complaining, pray! Give God a prayer to answer and He'll answer it. "Why would God listen to someone like me?" you say. Because: *(3) "God remembered His covenant with Abraham...and...took notice of them"* (Ex 2:24-25 NAS). God answered their prayers because of a covenant He made with their father. He took notice of them because they were Abraham's children. They got it "on credit." So do you! "God for Christ's sake hath forgiven you" (Eph 4:32). God's mercy and favor is yours today because you belong to Christ. "My Father will give you whatever you ask in my name... Ask and you will receive, and your joy will be complete" (Jn 16:23-24 NIV). How good is that?

GOOD WILL COME OUT OF IT!

God planned good to come out of it.

GENESIS 50:20 GWT

Before World War II Josefina Guerrero was the toast of Manila, young, vivacious and married to a wealthy medical student. Then in 1941 she discovered she had leprosy. Immediately she began treatment, but when Japan invaded the Philippines all the leprosariums were abandoned. Despite her disease Joey joined the underground, smuggling food, clothes, medicine and messages to POW's. She mapped out fortifications along the waterfront and the location of anti-aircraft batteries. When guerillas discovered a newly-sown minefield where the 37th Division was scheduled to land in Manila, they asked her to get the message through. With little thought for her own life she trudged through miles of enemy encampments with the map taped to her back and delivered it safely. Because of her courage many dangerous missions were completed and the U.S. War Department awarded her the Medal of Freedom with silver palm for saving untold American lives. Amazingly, Joey was never caught. In fact, Japanese soldiers had a horror of the ragged little woman who shuffled through the streets of Manila. And even when she *was* stopped they didn't detain her long, once they recognized the swathed bandages and lesions of advancing leprosy.

George Mueller said, "In a thousand trials it's not just five hundred that work for our good, but nine hundred and ninety-nine—plus one!" The Scripture, "God planned good to come out of it," means that no disaster, disease or delay can keep Him from turning it into something worthwhile. Understanding that God forgives your past, knows your present and has planned your future, lets you walk in the confidence that—nothing can ever happen to you that's beyond the scope of His grace and redemption!

ARE YOU TRUTHFUL?

The Lord detests lying lips.

PROVERBS 12:22 NIV

The most famous story about lying in American history is the one about George Washington chopping down a cherry tree. When his father asked him who did it, George supposedly said, "I cannot tell a lie; I did it with my little hatchet." That was in a biography written by Parson Weems in the nineteenth century—he made the whole story up. Incredibly, the most famous story about not lying in America, was a lie. And truthfulness is still in short supply. Politicians spin promises, telemarketers scam the elderly, job seekers pad their résumés, repair shops inflate their bills, students steal essays from the internet to pass tests and spouses lie to each other about money and infidelity.

Financial expert Larry Burkett estimated that fully 50 percent of people who claim to be Christians cheat on their income tax returns. The IRS maintains what is informally called a "cheaters account," to which people with guilty consciences can send money they know they owe. There's a story that the IRS received one letter that read, "My conscience is bothering me because of cheating on my taxes, so I'm sending $10,000. If my conscience doesn't clear up, I'll send in the rest of what I owe." We want to follow the rules, but we're prepared to break them if we can get away with it or think that's what it takes to win. Now since everybody seems to do it maybe you think it's no big deal. Wrong! God's Word says: "The Lord detests lying lips, but he delights in men who are truthful."

BE A "BUILDER-UPPER!" (1)

Do good to people who need help.

PROVERBS 3:27 NCV

During the 1920's, the Chisholms were the epitome of American high society. Everlina, their housekeeper, had been with them for forty-five years, and when her niece came over to play they took the little girl under their wing. She sang beautifully and Mrs. Chisholm, a trained musician, asked if she'd like to become a professional singer. She was thrilled! Her most prized possessions were recordings of famous opera singers, and when the Metropolitan was on the radio she was spellbound. That day she took the first step towards realizing her dream, and guests of the Chisholms were amazed by the girl who sang the classics with a talent and sensitivity far beyond her years. Elizabeth Chisholm continued to sponsor her education by sending her to study at Juilliard. And as a result, the world was introduced to the phenomenal talent of *Leontyne Price, the darling of the Metropolitan Opera.*

The Bible says, "Do not withhold good...when it is in the power of your hand to do so" (NKJV). Bible expositor William Barclay said, "One of the highest human duties, is the duty of encouragement." As a follower of Christ you are commanded to build others up by highlighting what's good instead of magnifying what's bad, by seeing them as unique individuals instead of stereotypes, by respecting instead of ridiculing, by forgiving instead of shaming, by modeling unconditional love instead of love with strings attached, by applauding each step of growth instead of saying, "You'll never change," by seeing their God-given potential instead of seeing them as problems to be handled. Come on, get your theology off the drawing board and put it into practice! Today, be a "builder-upper."

BE A "BUILDER-UPPER!" (2)

Encourage and strengthen him.

DEUTERONOMY 3:28 NIV

God knew that Joshua would need all the help he could get in leading the Israelites into the Promised Land. So He told his mentor, Moses, "Encourage and strengthen him, for he will lead this people across and will cause them to inherit the land" (vv. 27-28). God recognized that Moses was the best man to strengthen and encourage Joshua because he'd dealt with pressures and "people problems" at the Red Sea, and again in the desert when Israel grumbled against God—and him. Everybody needs encouragement, including you! You need others to cheer you on when you've been battered by setbacks and circumstances. German poet Johann Wolfgang von Goethe said, "Correction does much, but encouragement does much more." It rekindles your spirit and gives you the oomph to keep going. One well-known pastor wrote, "Nothing can uplift more than the encouragement of a friend or loved one. It's the oxygen of the soul. Having run two miles, a person may need to pause and catch his or her breath before running another two. Before facing a formidable task, or even the wearying routines of life, a person needs to pause for encouragement before tackling the work ahead. So become oxygen to the souls of those around you. Strengthen them to persevere for the Kingdom. Encourage them with God's promise to work good in all things."

Stop and think about somebody who could use a little encouragement, and before today is over, make it a point to get in touch with them. "Let us pursue the things…by which one may edify [build up] another" (Ro 14:19 NKJV).

HOW TO RESOLVE THE OLD ISSUE

The Lord has taken away your sin.

2 SAMUEL 12:13 NIV

There's no point asking God for other things when you haven't made things right with those you need to forgive, or ask forgiveness from. Jesus said, "If you are offering your gift at the altar and there remember that your brother has something against you, leave your gift there in front of the altar. First go and be reconciled to your brother; then come and offer your gift. Settle matters quickly with your adversary" (Mt 5:23-25 NIV). Don't be led by your wounded ego, be led by God's Word.

You say, "But the person I had the issue with is no longer around. I can't get a hearing, yet in my heart I'm still troubled about it." In this case the Bible says, "Confess your faults one to another, and pray one for another, that ye may be healed. The effectual fervent prayer of a righteous man availeth much" (Jas 5:16). Share your feelings with someone worthy of your trust. Pray with them, openly confessing your wrongs and the guilt you feel. You'll be surprised how prayer and the presence of an affirming friend can provide you with the peace of mind you seek.

After David murdered Uriah, his lover's husband, his guilt was overwhelming. It just about wiped him out. When he could take it no more, he broke his silence and sought God's forgiveness. But Uriah wasn't around to hear his confession; he'd been dead almost a year. So he turned to Nathan the prophet and poured out his heart saying, "I have sinned." Nathan listened patiently, then said, "The Lord has taken away your sin." Follow David's example, and then move forward with confidence.

SEEING YOURSELF THE RIGHT WAY

*Am I now trying to win the approval of men,
or of God?*

GALATIANS 1:10 NIV

Too many of us have made it our life's work to change somebody else's opinion of us. We're determined to prove to them that we're valuable. Now, you can't be like the guy who quipped, "I like talking to myself, because I like dealing with a better class of people." But neither can you base your worth on the opinions of those who put you down. When Harry Truman was thrust into the presidency by the death of Franklin Roosevelt, Sam Rayburn, Speaker of the House, took him aside and said, "You're going to have lots of people around you. And they will tell you what a great man you are, Harry. But you and I both know you ain't." As it turned out, Truman became a truly great president.

Until you quit agreeing with those who've mistreated you, or bowing to the events that crippled you emotionally, you'll remain locked in a prison of your own making. When your critic's opinion becomes *your* opinion, you've built a prison inside your soul with only one prisoner—you. Are you prepared to accept that some of the people you've spent your life trying to impress, may never be impressed? And can you accept that from God's perspective—it doesn't matter? To succeed in life you must be able to work alongside people without allowing yourself to be controlled by their moods or governed by their opinions. This is what Paul was talking about when he said, "Am I now trying to win the approval of men, or of God? ...If I were still trying to please men, I would not be a servant of Christ."

ONE-ON-ONE TIME WITH GOD

When they were alone,
He explained all things to His disciples.

MARK 4:34 NKJV

A recent survey confirms what most of us suspect: stress is increasing as work encroaches more and more on our personal time. The electronic age hasn't slowed the onslaught of mail, memos, books and periodicals we must read just to keep up. A PR consultant who fields four hundred emails, a hundred phone calls and twenty text messages every day says, "I used to stop working when it got too late to make calls. Now I'm never finished." Now she lives in the country behind a mountain because there's no phone signal there, and if they ever erect a cell tower she says she'll move!

It's critical to schedule one-on-one time with God, otherwise it won't happen. Mark says, "When they were alone, [Jesus] explained all things to His disciples." There are things the Lord will reveal to you only when you "Meditate within your heart...and be still" (Ps 4:4 NKJV). In *High Call, High Privilege* Gail MacDonald writes: "The ancient Desert Fathers used to commit themselves to a disciplinary creed: silence, solitude and inner peace. Only after adequate amounts of time listening, did they consider themselves ready to speak...Among many Christian[s] today there's a strange...logic [suggesting] that spiritual resource and renewal are found in constantly seeking new voices, attending more meetings, listening to incessant music, and gathering to exchange half-thought-out opinions. How often do we fall into the trap of believing that God's most pleased when we've maximized our information, our schedules, and our relationships? Disengagement means silence before God...a time of heavenly discussion during which we listen more than we speak. And silence demands solitude." Bottom line: You need one-on-one time with God!

LET YOUR LIGHT SHINE

Let your light shine before men.

MATTHEW 5:16 NIV

A man is being tailgated by a woman who's in a hurry. He comes to an intersection and when the light turns yellow he hits the brakes. The woman behind him goes ballistic. She honks her horn, yells profanities and gestures with her finger. As she's ranting and raving someone taps on her window. To her horror she looks up and sees a policeman. He invites her out of her car and takes her to the station where she's searched, fingerprinted and put in a cell. After a couple of hours she's released and the arresting officer gives her her personal effects and says, "I'm very sorry for the mistake, ma'am. I pulled up behind your car while you were blowing your horn and using ugly gestures and foul language. I noticed the 'What would Jesus do?' bumper sticker, the 'Choose Life' license plate holder, the 'Follow me to Sunday School' window sign and the peace emblem on your trunk, so I naturally assumed you had stolen the car." Obviously he was following a Christian who wasn't doing a very good job at following Christ.

The world gets turned off by people who have Christian bumper stickers on their cars, Christian peace signs on their trunks, Christian books on their shelves, Christian stations on their radios and TVs, Christian jewelry around their necks, Christian videos for their kids, Christian magazines for their coffee tables, but who don't have the life of Jesus in their bones or the love of Jesus in their hearts. What's the answer? "Let your light shine before men, that they may see your good deeds and praise your Father in heaven."

KNOWING WHAT WE'RE UP AGAINST!

Take up the whole armor of God.

EPHESIANS 6:12 NKJV

In spite of a great spiritual awakening in Samaria, Simon the Sorcerer was still in business. The people "heeded him because he had astonished them with his sorceries for a long time" (Ac 8:9-11 NKJV). So, how do the apostles handle this situation? Sidestep it? Coexist peacefully with evil? No, they confronted him with the claims of Christ, saying: "Repent... [that] your heart may be forgiven" (Ac 8:22 NKJV). And Simon did. A good doctor identifies the problem then treats it. The forces of evil around us are real, and we must know how to deal with them. Remember the tortured man living in the tombs of Gadara whom Christ healed? The spirits within him did two things worthy of note. First, they introduced themselves as "Legion...for we are many" (Mk 5:9 NIV). A legion was a well-trained, fully-equipped division of the Roman army that took orders from Caesar. Second, they "begged Jesus...not to send them out of the area" (Mk 5:10 NIV). That's because they'd established a stronghold there. Can you see a spiritual parallel here? You can't fight spiritual battles with carnal weapons and hope to win. Blaming Satan for all your problems is a cop-out, but *failing* to see him at work in your situation renders you powerless.

To fight and win you must know what you are up against. You must be able to look beyond the obvious and see the actual! You are dealing with "principalities...powers...the rulers of the darkness...spiritual hosts of wickedness...Therefore take up the whole armor of God, that you may be able to withstand in the evil day" (Eph 6:12-13 NKJV).

TELL SOMEONE ABOUT JESUS

A woman of Samaria came to draw water.

JOHN 4:7 NKJV

John records, "A woman of Samaria came to draw water." After five failed marriages her trust levels are demolished and her self-worth is zero, so she approaches Jesus cautiously. Brick by brick He takes down the wall she's hiding behind. When He gets through, she leaves transformed. What a contrast: one chapter earlier, Nicodemus, a religious leader, came to Jesus by night, suggesting he didn't want to risk being seen with Him. After telling him he must be born again, Jesus said, "Whoever lives by the truth comes into the light" (Jn 3:21 NIV). At that point, Nicodemus has to make a choice. There are three lessons here: *(1) Christ sees potential in you when others don't.* "The Pharisees...complained, saying, 'This Man receives sinners and eats with them'" (Lk 15:2 NKJV). They were right! This woman was the first person Jesus introduced Himself to as the Messiah. Why didn't He do that when He called His disciples, baptized John, cleansed the temple, performed His first miracle, or interviewed Nicodemus? Because Jesus doesn't measure you by your past, He measures you by your potential. *(2) Christ will change you, then use you to change others.* Amazingly, she was the first person to preach the gospel in Samaria. "Many... Samaritans...believed in Him because of the word of the woman who testified" (Jn 4:39 NKJV). *(3) Christ doesn't need to be defended, just introduced.* "Many more believed because of His own word. Then they said to the woman, 'Now we believe, not because of what you said, for we ourselves have heard Him and we know that this is indeed the Christ, the Savior of the world'" (Jn 4:41-42 NKJV). Today, tell someone about Jesus.

BEGIN AGAIN!

You have heard of the perseverance of Job.

JAMES 5:11 NKJV

There are four faces of the man of God in the book of Ezekiel: a lion, an eagle, a man, and an ox. The last face, the ox, speaks of *perseverance*. The ox is a plodder. He will plow from sunup till sundown. Put him in a stall, feed him, and next day he'll plow and plod until the task is complete. He refuses to quit. Look at Job, attending the funeral of his ten children, losing his wealth and his health, listening to a wife with a tongue sharp enough to clip a hedge. Yet despite all her dour words he didn't quit. Learn from him! "You have heard of the perseverance of Job, and seen the end intended by the Lord." Job focused on the end-goal, not the immediate circumstance. Our problem is, we want it all *now*. A billboard reads, "Antiques manufactured while you wait." Life doesn't work that way!

There are times when quitting looks good, defeat inescapable and retreat the only option. The question is, how will you handle these times? David Ben-Gurion observed: "Courage is a special kind of knowledge; the knowledge of how to fear what ought to be feared and how not to fear what ought not to be feared. From this knowledge comes an inner strength that inspires us to push on in the face of great difficulty. What can seem impossible is often possible with courage." So whatever difficulties you're facing today, draw on God's grace and keep trying. Mountains only seem so high from the valley. The road to success runs uphill; don't expect to break any speed records. The thing to try when all else fails is—begin again!

STRENGTHEN YOUR MIND THROUGH THE SCRIPTURES!

Study to [show yourself]
approved unto God, a workman.

2 TIMOTHY 2:15

Our bodies don't work too well without adequate exercise; neither do our minds! Ever go back upstairs to remind yourself of why you originally went downstairs? Are names, numbers and appointments you remembered effortlessly in the past becoming increasingly elusive? Do you sometimes wonder if you're "losing it?" Doctors say that in most cases mindless hours in front of television, avoiding intellectual stimulation and exertion, result in the shrinking of our mind's capacity, including our memory. "Brain fitness" experts assure us that our brains don't grow old from working too hard, but from hardly working at all. "Brain plasticity"—the capacity of our mind to retain or regain flexibility—is a matter of exercise. When you just let your mind "veg" and don't stretch it with thoughtful reading, rational thinking, intelligent analysis and conversation, it loses plasticity and becomes old at any age. On the other hand, if you challenge your mind regularly, your brain gets younger as you get older. (The problem is not how old your brain is, but how old your thinking is.) Here's a great way to strengthen your mind: "Study to [show yourself] approved unto God, a workman...that needeth not to be ashamed rightly dividing the word of truth." The word "study" in Greek text means to exert yourself mentally, to push your mind to study God's Word. Like a "workman," *make it work!* God promises that if you meditate on His Word daily you'll become "like a tree planted by streams of water...which yields its fruit in season and whose leaf does not wither. Whatever he does prospers" (Ps 1:3 NIV). Don't let your mind "wither," exercise and strengthen it by studying the Scriptures!

THE PATH TO THE THRONE (1)

I have found David...
a man after My own heart.

ACTS 13:22 NKJV

Anytime God describes someone as "a man after my own heart," study them carefully. Let's look at the life of David.

He had a humble start but a great finish. David began as a shepherd and ended up as a king. The chances of that happening were slim to none. In those days shepherds were so low on the totem pole they couldn't testify in a court of law; their word wasn't considered reliable. Yet David ended up writing the most widely read and loved psalms of all time. When you invite God into your life He cancels the liabilities of your past and rewrites your future. But you must choose what He has chosen for you. There's an interesting contrast between Paul and David. Paul "sowed his wild oats" before he met Christ, then went on to live an exemplary life. David became king at thirty; yet during his forty years in leadership he experienced devastating failure. There are two lessons here: (1) Don't rush to judgment. It's not over until God says it's over. David's story is a warning to the transgressor, a rebuke to the self-righteous, a testimony to the justice of God that won't allow us to escape our consequences, and to His love that will never let go of us. (2) God can bring good out of it. He can take every experience you've been through, both positive and negative, and make it work for good, either your good or the good of others. When you seek to fulfill God's purposes in spite of your flaws, He makes "all things work together for good" (Ro 8:28).

THE PATH TO THE THRONE (2)

I have found David…
a man after My own heart.

ACTS 13:22 NKJV

David was anointed to be king in his teens, but he only ascended the throne at thirty. There's a pattern here: *(1) God calls the man.* In spite of being unappreciated by his family and overlooked by the prophet Samuel, God picked David. He also picked Deborah to lead the nation in a male-dominated society. Stop trying to figure God out, and stop comparing yourself to others! "Does not the potter have the right to make out of the same lump of clay some pottery for noble purposes and some for common use?" (Ro 9:21 NIV). We'd have rejected many of the people God used—which lets us know how much we don't know. *(2) God decides the plan.* "Being confident of this very thing, that He who has begun a good work in you will complete it" (Php 1:6 NKJV). Who decides it? Who performs it? Who should your confidence be in? God! God's plan for David involved years of ducking Saul's spears, living in caves and working with six hundred misfits who re-define the word "dysfunctional." God trains you in a small sphere so you can handle a bigger one. *(3) God knows the span of time required.* "Who through faith and patience [endurance] inherit the promises" (See Col 1:11-12). Endurance means standing firm under pressure. The prize belongs to the man or woman who's committed for the long haul. Joseph refused to let go of his dream; it's what enabled him to say no to the advances of Potiphar's wife and endure unjust imprisonment. But the day came when Potiphar and his wife knelt before Joseph. So keep your eyes on the prize and don't give up!

THE PATH TO THE THRONE (3)

I have found David...
a man after My own heart.

ACTS 13:22 NKJV

David knew Samuel was coming to his house looking for a king, and that he wasn't invited. That hurt. So how did he respond? By asking somebody to put his name in the hat? No! "Promotion comes from God" (See Ps 75:6-7). David knew that nobody could keep God from blessing him. Listen: "Then Samuel...anointed him in the midst of his brothers" (1Sa 16:13 NKJV). If you remain faithful, God will lift you up in the midst of those who overlooked and put you down.

Notice, when the Spirit of God left King Saul he was tormented by evil spirits and ended up consulting a witch. No wonder David prayed, "Take not thy holy spirit from me" (Ps 51:11). If God has called you to do the job He will give you all the grace needed; but if He hasn't called you to it, it'll torment you day and night.

But be prepared for trouble! Like Joseph's brothers, they'll say of you, "Let us...kill him and cast him into some pit...[and] see what will become of his dreams" (Ge 37:20 NKJV). Why would those who are supposed to love you say such a thing? Because they don't really know who you are, or recognize your God-given dream. Expect rejection in the early stages, especially when there's no evidence to validate your God-given dream. When David demonstrated the faith to take on Goliath, his oldest brother Eliab called him arrogant and resented him (See 1Sa 17:28). Why did God put such stories in the Bible? "These things happened to them as examples and were written down as warnings for us" (1Co 10:11 NIV).

THE PATH TO THE THRONE (4)

I have found David...
a man after My own heart.

ACTS 13:22 NKJV

Some of God's promises are fulfilled quickly. But others, like the one God gave to David telling him he'd be king, have to be fought for. The Jebusites controlled Jerusalem; they taunted David saying, "You will not get in here" (2Sa 5:6 NIV). And to make matters worse, Jerusalem was on an elevation hundreds of feet above David's army. The only way up was through a water cistern where they had to wade and climb through pitch-black darkness. "Nevertheless David took the strong hold of Zion" (2Sa 5:7). Understand this: if He has to, God will bring you up through the gutter to get you to the throne! Notice two words: "nevertheless" and "took." When you're up to your neck in problems and the enemy is saying, "You won't make it," stand on God's Word and declare "nevertheless." Rise up in faith and claim what God's promised you. "The people who know their God shall be strong, and carry out great exploits" (Da 11:32 NKJV). God can show you how to exploit the situation for your good and His glory.

But don't expect everybody to celebrate your success. "When the Philistines heard that they had anointed David king over Israel, [they] went up in search of David" (2Sa 5:17 NKJV). You'll have to fight to get to your destiny—and fight to hold on to it. You can't "coast" on old victories. With each new battle you have to get fresh instructions. "David inquired of the Lord, saying, 'Shall I go up against the Philistines?'...the Lord said ...'Go up, for I will...deliver the Philistines into your hand'" (2Sa 5:19 NKJV). Today, go forward knowing God is with you!

THE PATH TO THE THRONE (5)

I have found David...
a man after My own heart.

ACTS 13:22 NKJV

The Bible says: "And David said with longing, 'Oh, that someone would give me a drink of the water from the well of Bethlehem'...So the three mighty men broke through the camp of the Philistines, drew water from the well...took it and brought it to David. Nevertheless he would not drink it" (2Sa 23:15-16 NKJV). There are two important lessons here: *(1) You must surround yourself with the right people.* Unlike those who are only "in it for what they can get out of it," these men had only one thing in mind: to serve their king and promote his kingdom. No wonder David said, "I am a companion of...those who keep Your precepts" (Ps 119:63 NKJV). *(2) You must refuse to settle for less than God's best.* These men risked their lives to bring David a cup of water, yet he poured it out on the ground before the Lord. David was saying: "I refuse to settle for a cup, I want the well; I must be connected to the life source." Stop treating God like a janitor you call when you've made a mess and need someone to clean it up; or as your "go to" person when you need something you can't otherwise get. Don't go to God for a miracle, go for a relationship—and you can walk in His miraculous provisions every day. "He who dwells in the secret place of the Most High shall abide under the shadow of the Almighty" (Ps 91:1 NKJV). Note the words "dwells" and "abide." Instead of commuting in and out, stay in contact with God and all that He has will be available to you.

THE PATH TO THE THRONE (6)

I have found David...
a man after My own heart.

ACTS 13:22 NKJV

The life of David could be captioned in these words: "I love God supremely, and there's nothing He asks of me that I won't do." Can *you* say that?

Everybody dies, but not everybody fully lives. The Bible says, "These are the last words of David" (2Sa 23:1 NLT). A man's last words are considered to be some of his most important words. During his lifetime David's son raped his sister, one son killed another, his wife turned her back on him, his best friend betrayed him, they took his kingdom, his mentor tried to kill him, his family rejected him and he spent a lot of time hiding in caves. Now he's going to speak to us one last time. What will he talk about? Goliath, Saul, Bathsheba? No, listen: "David, the man who was raised up so high, David, the man anointed by the God of Jacob, David, the sweet psalmist of Israel. The Spirit of the Lord speaks through me; his words are upon my tongue. The God of Israel spoke. The Rock of Israel said to me: 'The one who rules righteously, who rules in the fear of God, is like the light of morning at sunrise, like a morning without clouds, like the gleaming of the sun on new grass after rain.' Is it not my family God has chosen? Yes, he had made an everlasting covenant with me. His agreement is arranged and guaranteed in every detail. He will ensure my safety and success" (2Sa 23:1-5 NLT). These words were recorded in Scripture for those of us who are less than perfect, but whose hearts never cease to hunger for God.

NOTHING ELSE WORKS

*Jesus showed Himself again
to the disciples at the Sea.*

JOHN 21:1 NKJV

The disciples, experienced fishermen, fished all night and caught nothing. We all know what that feels like, right? Next morning Jesus appeared on the shore and said to them, "Cast the net on the right side of the boat and you will find some" (Jn 21:6 NKJV). One hundred and fifty-three fish, to be exact! This story teaches us three things about Jesus:

(1) Usually, you find Him at the end of your struggle. As long as you think you can do it successfully on your own, He will let you try. And as long as what worked for you before is still working, you won't reach out to Him for help. It's only when you run out of answers that you discover it's "Not by might, nor by power, but by my spirit saith the Lord" (Zec 4:6). *(2) He never takes His eye off you.* "When the morning had now come, Jesus stood on the shore; and yet the disciples did not know that it was Jesus" (Jn 21:4 NKJV). They couldn't see Him but He could see them. In spite of your emotional upheaval, your disappointment in those you trusted, and the futility of your own efforts, you're never beyond His care—or His reach. *(3) He invites you to come and dine.* That night He fed them and had fellowship with them. As a result their doubts dissolved, their faith was renewed and they were empowered to go out and do His work. It's back to basics! The answers you seek and the strength you need can be found only by feeding on God's Word and fellowshipping with Him in prayer. Simply stated: nothing else works.

GUARD AGAINST LUST

Above all...guard your heart.

PROVERBS 4:23 NIV

Jesus said, "Anyone who looks at a woman lustfully has already committed adultery with her in his heart" (Mt 5:28 NIV). Why did Jesus say this? Because every lustful glance damages your marriage bond. The less you desire your mate, the more you'll look for things in them to justify your fantasies. And the saddest part is, you'll never know how good your marriage could have been.

To win, you must decide once and for all to be fully committed to God. Here are three Scriptures you need to live by: (1) "I have made a covenant with my eyes not to look lustfully" (Job 31:1 NIV). Before David got into trouble with Bathsheba we read: "He saw a woman bathing...inquired about the woman...and took her" (2Sa 11:2-4 NKJV). Pay close attention to the progression: "saw," "inquired," "took." If what you're looking at is not yours, pull your eyes away immediately. (2) "Take captive every thought...make it obedient to Christ" (2Co 10:5 NIV). Police your mind. Instead of giving in to your daydreams or the internet or magazines, etc. fill your mind with God's Word and memories of your best moments with your mate. "Thy word have I hid in my heart, that I might not sin against thee" (Ps 119:11). (3) "Above all...guard your heart." Work on strengthening your bond with your mate. Decide to love even when you don't feel like it, and your love will begin to blossom. And if you need to, find someone who can help you. "A brother is born for adversity" (Pr 17:17). Sometimes the difference between victory and defeat can be as little as five or ten minutes on the telephone, talking and praying with someone who understands.

TWO LESSONS YOU LEARN ONLY IN LIFE'S STORMS

Why are you so fearful?

MARK 4:40 NKJV

In the Gospel of Mark we read: "He said to them, 'Let us cross over to the other side'…And a great windstorm arose, and the waves beat into the boat, so that it was already filling. But He was in the stern, asleep on a pillow. And they awoke Him and said to Him, 'Teacher, do You not care that we are perishing?' Then He arose and rebuked the wind, and said to the sea, 'Peace, be still!' And the wind ceased and there was a great calm. But He said to them, 'Why are you so fearful? How is it that you have no faith?' And they…said to one another, 'Who can this be, that even the wind and the sea obey Him!'" (Mk 4:35-41 NKJV).

Here are two lessons you learn only in life's storms: *(1) You must trust what God has told you.* When Jesus said, "Let us cross over to the other side" there wasn't a big enough wave to take them under, no matter how threatening. What has God promised you? Standing on that won't keep you from getting scared or soaked, but it'll keep you from sinking. *(2) You must remind yourself who's in the boat with you.* If the Lord can calm a storm, He can prevent one. So when He permits you to go through storms it's to show you that you don't have a problem He can't solve; that you may be powerless in the situation but He's not; and that through this experience you'll come to know Him in a way you have never known Him before. So learn these lessons well and come out stronger on the other side.

IT-TAKES-ONE-TO-MAKE-ONE

Each according to its kind.

GENESIS 1:24 NKJV

In the book of Genesis ("beginnings"), God shows us how He intends things to work in life: "Let the earth bring forth the living creature...each according to its kind." Each one of us is a product of our DNA and our environment. Now, fast forward. How many giant killers were in Saul's army? Not one. When Goliath challenged Israel every soldier quaked with fear. Yet David, who came to bring food to his brothers, sized up the situation, recalled his experiences with God and went out and killed him. Now, after David became king, how many other giant killers arose in Israel? Lots: "Then Sibbecai...killed Sippai, one of the descendants of the giants, and they were subdued. And there was war with the Philistines again, and Elhanan ...killed Lahmi the brother of Goliath the Gittite, the shaft of whose spear was like a weaver's beam. Again there was war at Gath, where there was a man of great stature who had twenty-four fingers and toes, six fingers on each hand and six toes on each foot; and he also was descended from the giants. When he taunted Israel, Jonathan the son of Shimea, David's brother, killed him. These were descended from the giants in Gath [Goliath's home town], and they fell by the hand of David and by the hands of his servants" (1Ch 20:4-8 NAS). Why do you suppose there were no giant killers in Saul's day? Because Saul himself wasn't one! But under David's leadership they multiplied because David was a giant killer. This illustrates the "it-takes-one-to-make-one" principle that starts in Genesis and runs through the Bible.

So the word for you today is—be careful who influences you, and be careful how you influence others.

LISTEN TO GOD (1)

Your ears will hear a voice...
saying, "This is the way."

ISAIAH 30:21 NIV

Any time you step out in faith and try something, a voice within you will whisper, "You must be out of your mind. You're not capable of this. Those little accomplishments you had before were pure luck; you just happened to be in the right place at the right time. Now you're in over your head." That voice will waken you in the middle of the night, sick to your stomach. You can hear it in every boardroom, living room and sidewalk. It's the voice of fear, and it doesn't play fair. It pulls the file on your past failures and preys on your deepest insecurities.

But there's another voice—God's! It says: "Fear not, for I am with you; be not dismayed, for I am your God. I will strengthen you, yes, I will help you, I will uphold you with My righteous right hand" (Isa 41:10 NKJV). Attuning your ears to God's voice doesn't mean your problems are automatically solved or that the other voice just fades away. No, it's more like having an intimate conversation with a close friend in a noisy, crowded place. There may be other voices around you but you don't hear them because you're so focused on what your friend is saying. That's how it is with God's voice. Whether He speaks to you through the Scriptures, through a friend, or through your life's circumstances, He's *always* communicating with the heart that seeks Him. His promise to you is, "Your ears will hear a voice...saying, 'This is the way; walk in it.'" One word from God, just one, can change your entire outlook. So today, take time to listen to God's voice.

LISTEN TO GOD (2)

Fear not, for I am with you.

ISAIAH 41:10 NKJV

To be successful in anything God calls you to do, you must be sensitive to the Holy Spirit within you and learn to recognize when He speaks to you through the Scriptures.

When the pressure is on and you're tempted to move too quickly you'll hear His voice saying: "You shall not go out with haste...for the Lord will go before you, and the God of Israel will be your rear guard" (Isa 52:12 NKJV). God's got you covered—front and back. How good is that? When you're about to make a wrong turn or a bad decision He will remind you, "In his heart a man plans his course, but the Lord determines his steps" (Pr 16:9 NIV). When you don't have the ways and means to get the job done His voice will whisper: "The Lord will guide you continually, and satisfy your soul in drought, and strengthen your bones; you will be like a watered garden, and like a spring of water, whose waters do not fail" (Isa 58:11 NKJV). You have an unfailing supply. When you run out of answers and don't know what to do He will reassure you: "I will instruct you and teach you in the way you should go; I will counsel you and watch over you" (Ps 32:8 NIV). When the load becomes too heavy to carry you'll hear His voice saying, "Cast your cares on the Lord and he will sustain you; he will never let the righteous fall" (Ps 55:22 NIV).

Hearing God's voice may mean you have to sacrifice lesser things and tune out other voices, but you must do it. Nothing, absolutely nothing, is more important than learning to recognize God's voice when He speaks to you.

GOD IS PROTECTING YOU

He permitted no man to do them wrong.

1 CHRONICLES 16:21 NKJV

What would you be willing to do to protect your child from harm? Multiply that by infinity and you'll understand how much God cares for you.

Nebuchadnezzar took the sacred vessels from the temple in Jerusalem and placed them in a pagan temple in Shinar (See Da 1:1-2 NKJV). After his son Belshazzar became king, one night during a drunken feast, "They brought in the...goblets ...from the temple of God...and the king...and his concubines drank from them" (Da 5:3 NIV). Now if they'd mishandled some worthless old cup it might not have mattered, but God had too much invested in these sacred vessels to allow them to be mistreated. That night Nebuchadnezzar and his entire kingdom were destroyed because of this unchanging Bible principle: "He permitted no man to do them wrong; yes, He rebuked kings for their sakes, saying, 'Do not touch My anointed ones'" (1Ch 16:21-22 NKJV).

As God's redeemed child you are loved, valued and protected. So stand on that truth. You may have to fight in a foreign land or live and work in a difficult situation. You may have to endure great hardship for your faith. But understand— God's got too much invested in you to let you be destroyed. Any time Satan tries that, God will interrupt his party and say, "This vessel is off limits; it took me too long to teach this woman to pray. I've devoted too many hours to training this man how to overcome. They've learned how to stand amidst trials. They've suffered too much for My name's sake for Me to let you harm them. Take your hand off them, they're Mine!" Rejoice, today God is protecting you!

INTUITION

If a man's gift is...leadership,
let him govern diligently.

ROMANS 12:6-8 NIV

Good leaders have intuition. They "see it" when others don't; they "get it." We all fall into three intuition levels: (1) Those who will *never* see it. Putting these people into a leadership role is like putting a square peg in a round hole; you can keep hammering and driving it, but it won't fit. When someone's gifted to work in a support role, it's a mistake to put them into a leadership role. Besides, every orchestra needs a good second fiddle. We're only responsible for the gifts God gives us, not the ones we want—or other people think we should have. (2) Those who are *nurtured* to see it. These folks have the raw material; they just need to be nurtured and mentored. Dr. John Maxwell points out that the ability to think like a leader is "informed intuition." These people just need someone to inform, instruct and inspire them, and they'll become good leaders. The truth is, without intuition we're condemned to be blindsided by events and opinions all of our lives. (3) Those who *naturally* see it. These are the ones who are born with true leadership gifts. They instinctively understand people and know how to move them from point A to point B. Even as children they act like leaders. Watch them on the playground and you will see everyone else following them. People with such God-given intuition can build on it, become great leaders and bless others.

Now, if you want to see leadership in its finest form study the life of Christ, who said, "The Son of Man did not come to be served, but to serve, and to give His life" (Mt 20:28 NKJV).

DON'T FORGET YOUR CHILD

Joseph and His mother did not know it.

LUKE 2:43 NKJV

Jesus' parents got so busy with other things, they didn't notice they'd lost Him: "The Boy Jesus lingered behind in Jerusalem. And Joseph and His mother did not know...supposing Him to have been in the company" (Lk 2:43-44 NKJV). Fortunately for them they found Him again. But it doesn't always work that way.

One Christian leader tells of meeting a man at a conference. This man's daughter, who was in second grade, was asked by her teacher to draw a picture of her family. That evening she proudly brought her art work home and showed it to her parents. When her dad looked at the picture he said, "What is this picture of?" His daughter replied, "That's of us and our house. The teacher asked me to draw a picture of our family." He looked at the picture more carefully and saw that everyone was there except him. "Sweetheart," he asked, "am I in the picture?" "No," she replied. "Why not?" he asked. "Because this is a picture of us at home, and you are never there." It hit him like a ton of bricks. Without malice she'd stated a simple fact. It was a wake-up call to an absentee dad. That day he decided to turn around and go back to his family. The Psalmist said, "I need your help, especially in my own home" (Ps 101:2 TLB). Television, the internet, peer pressure; how are your children doing? If you've been traveling the road to success but neglected to bring your family along with you, make a U-turn. Go back and pick up the people who matter most. Commit yourself to making the journey, only if it includes *them*.

SEEING OTHERS THE RIGHT WAY

Take Mark...he is profitable...for the ministry.

2 TIMOTHY 4:11

When John Mark decided to take time off to visit his family, it didn't sit too well with Paul. Later when Barnabas wanted to take John Mark on their next mission's trip, Paul exploded! "The contention became so sharp...they parted from one another...Barnabas took Mark and sailed to Cyprus; but Paul chose Silas" (Ac 15:38-40 NKJV). But the story doesn't end there. Later, an older and wiser Paul who had learned to add grace to his grit, writes, "For Demas hath forsaken me, having loved this present world...[so] Take Mark, and bring him with thee: for he is profitable to me for the ministry" (2Ti 4:10-11). There are three important lessons here for you:

(1) Always be willing to give someone a second chance. After all, that's what God does for you. Now in extending grace you can get hurt and disappointed, but if you're going to be Christ-like it's a risk you must take. *(2) Don't measure everybody else by your standards and goals.* The truth is, they may not be called to do what you're called to do. Or they may have been called to do it in a different way. Don't make your personal preferences a precondition for loving, accepting and working with someone. *(3) When you look for the best in others you usually find it.* The Bible says, "We have this treasure in earthen vessels" (2Co 4:7). So every time you meet the treasure you'll bump into the earthen vessel. Don't allow that to devalue the treasure, or your responsibility to look for it. Motivated people will rise to meet your expectations.

SERVING GOD—AND YOUR MATE!

A married man...has to.

1 CORINTHIANS 7:33 NLT

Paul writes: "An unmarried man can spend his time doing the Lord's work and thinking how to please him. But a married man can't do that so well. He has to think about... how to please his wife." Gayle Urban tells of browsing in a bookstore and discovering a shelf with reduced-price items. Among the gifts was a little figurine with a man and woman, their heads lovingly tilted toward one another. "Happy Tenth Anniversary," read the inscription. It appeared to be in perfect condition yet its tag indicated "damaged." Examining it more closely, she found another tag underneath that read, "WIFE IS COMING UNGLUED!"

When you marry somebody, you marry everything they *are* and everything they have been *through*. It's a package deal! And if you ask God, He'll give you the grace to minister to your mate. You may not see immediate change. It takes time for even a small cut to heal. But if you allow Him, God will give you the oil of compassion and the wine of love to pour into their wounds. Never become so *spiritual* that you become *unavailable*. Your first calling is to your mate and your family. Your priorities should start there, then spread to your career, your vocation and other pursuits. Paul says, in effect, "I release those who are married from the level of consecration I expect from those who are single, so that they'll be able to spend time working on their relationship." You say, "But I need to spend time with the Lord." That's true, and the Bible doesn't release you from your responsibility to God, it just sets some priorities. You're called to serve the Lord—and your mate!

WHAT ARE YOU CALLED TO DO? (1)

You are the salt of the earth.

MATTHEW 5:13 NIV

Sometimes what a person contributes doesn't get noticed until they're no longer around to do it. The story's told of the husband who came home from work to find his house in a complete mess. The baby was crying, there were dishes piled up in the sink and dirty laundry on the floor. The TV was blaring, beds weren't made, carpets weren't vacuumed and dinner wasn't ready. When he demanded to know what was up, his wife said, "You know how you always ask what I've been doing all day? Well, today I didn't do it." The Bible says, "Each one should retain the place in life…to which God has called him" (1Co 7:17 NIV). This doesn't mean that we should not aspire to greater things. It just means that if we can't start where we *are*, we can't start at *all*.

One day Jesus healed a demon-possessed man who'd spent years separated from his family. After being set free, the man wanted to travel with Jesus. But Jesus said, "No, go back home and tell them what the Lord has done for you" (See Lk 8:39). In other words, start where you are, use what you've got, and do what you can. The Bible says: "You are the salt of the earth." Salt doesn't exist for its own pleasure. It must be poured into something bigger than itself; only then does it fulfill its purpose.

But be careful, don't be ego-driven. The quest for significance can be misleading. You can't do it *by* yourself *for* yourself, you must do it *with* God and for *His* purposes—then God will bless you!

WHAT ARE YOU CALLED TO DO? (2)

You are the salt of the earth.

MATTHEW 5:13 NIV

When God called Moses, one of the questions He asked him was, "What is that in your hand?" (Ex 4:2 NIV). Moses held his shepherd's staff. It represented his livelihood; it's what he was good at. It represented his income; his flock was his wealth and his family's security. God asked him to be willing to lay it down. God still asks, "What is that in your hand?" What has been given to you? Your gifts, your money, your temperament, your experience, your relationships, your mind, your education. God has given you what Dr. Martin Seligman calls "signature strengths." Seligman found that human abilities fall into certain categories. He defined them as: (a) Wisdom and knowledge (which includes abilities like curiosity, love of learning, sound judgment, and social intelligence). (b) Courage (perseverance and integrity). (c) Humanity (with capacities for kindness and the expression of mercy). (d) Justice (the ability to bring about fairness and leadership). (e) Temperance (qualities like self-control, prudence, humility). (f) Transcendence (the appreciation of beauty, the expression of gratitude, the ability of hope, the capacity for joy). We all have the capacity for each of these strengths, but a few resonate more deeply in you; they are your "signature strengths." Identify these, and you begin to understand your calling.

Sometimes we think God couldn't or wouldn't use us because of our weaknesses. No, the opposite is true. No one can speak to those who grieve, better than those who've suffered loss. Chuck Colson was the chief White House lawyer, until Watergate. But it wasn't until he was a convict that he was prepared to begin prison fellowship. Today, if you let him, God will use you.

WHAT ARE YOU CALLED TO DO? (3)

You are the salt of the earth.

MATTHEW 5:13 NIV

Observe: *(1) Your calling is often connected to what troubles you deeply.* For Moses it was the oppression of his people. So God used that, and called Moses to lead his people to freedom. For William Wilberforce it was slavery. He devoted his entire life to seeing it eradicated in England, which it finally was shortly before his death. For Dr. Martin Luther King, Jr. it was the injustice of a society that enslaved and oppressed African-Americans. So he dreamed and he preached and he marched and he organized and he boycotted, and the Civil Rights Movement was galvanized. If you want to discover your calling, begin praying about what troubles you deeply. Usually we try to avoid unpleasantness, but if you have a sense that your calling involves helping the poor, spend time around those in poverty. Allow your heart to be moved, carry within you the conviction that things must change, and keep praying, "Lord, make me a change agent."

(2) Your calling means God believes in you. When Jesus called His disciples they didn't look like winners. Generally, in their day if someone was going to be the follower of a rabbi it happened much earlier. Plus, rabbis didn't recruit, they took applications. But not Jesus. He picked a doctor, a tax collector and fishermen and said, "I believe in you. What I know I will teach you." He promised, "He who believes in Me, the works that I do he will do also" (Jn 14:12 NKJV). No wonder they left their nets! Jesus empowered His followers to go out to live as He lived. Today, that's what He is calling *you* to do.

KNOWING WHAT "IS ALSO WRITTEN"

Jesus answered…"It is also written."

MATTHEW 4:7 NIV

After the blessing comes the battle! And Jesus was no exception. Following His baptism "the Spirit sent him out into the desert" (Mk 1:12 NIV), and after fasting forty days He was hungry. That's when Satan showed up and said, "If you are the Son of God, tell these stones to become bread" (Mt 4:3 NIV). You can count on the enemy to show up at your most vulnerable moments. And when he does you'd better know what the Word of God actually says—not just selected snippets and quotes you've heard second or third hand. "All scripture is God-breathed and is useful for teaching…in righteousness" (2Ti 3:16 NIV). We pick the parts of Scripture that fit our lifestyle and bolster our theology, but when the enemy manipulates God's Word and uses it against you, you need to be able to say, "It is *also* written." You need to know what *else* God has to say. The Bible says Satan "will speak against the Most High…oppress his saints and try to change…times and…laws" (Dan 7:25 NIV). Satan knows the Word of God is "a double-edged sword" (Heb 4:12 NCV), but he'll still try to engage you in a swordfight!

But "Jesus answered…'It is also written: Do not put…God to the test.'" He knew what His Father had *actually* said, and refused to allow Satan to dictate His responses, including what He should eat. Whose menu are *you* eating from today? Are you like the prodigal, settling for pig-swill while your Father has a feast prepared for you? Tell Satan, "Get thee behind me" (Mt 16:23), and stop letting him bamboozle you with lies and half-truths! Get into God's Word and get it into you!

HE CHOSE TO SAVE YOU!

He saved others; himself he cannot save.

MATTHEW 27:42

When the pastor introduced the visiting speaker, an elderly preacher walked to the pulpit and told this story: "A father, his son, and his son's friend were sailing off the Pacific coast when a storm overturned their boat sweeping all of them into the ocean. Grabbing a rescue line, in a split second the father had to make the most excruciating decision of his life —which boy to throw the other end to and which one to sacrifice. He knew his son had accepted Christ and his friend hadn't. Anguished, the father yelled, 'I love you, son,' and threw the rope to his son's friend. By the time he'd pulled the boy back to the capsized boat his son had disappeared beneath the waves. His body was never recovered. The father knew his son would step into eternity with Jesus and couldn't bear the thought of his friend facing eternity without Christ." At the end of the service a teenage boy approached the old man and said, "That's a nice story, but what father in his right mind would sacrifice his son's life in hopes that the other boy would become a Christian?" "You've got the point," the old preacher replied, "It's not realistic. But I'm standing here today to tell you that story gives me a glimpse into what it must have been like for God to sacrifice His only Son for us. You see...I *was* that father, and your pastor was my son's friend."

The Pharisees who watched Christ die said, "He saved others; himself he cannot save." And they were right; He couldn't do both, so He chose to save you. Today will you accept His offer of salvation?

EIGHT PRINCIPLES TO LIVE BY

Good planning and insight...
bring...you honor and respect.

PROVERBS 3:21-22 NLT

People who set goals accomplish much more than people of equal education and ability who don't. With that in mind, build these eight principles into your life. *(1) Decide what you want.* But first consult God. "Many are the plans in a man's heart, but it is the Lord's purpose that prevails" (Pr 19:21 NIV). *(2) Think on paper.* Writing your goals down gives them a sense of permanency, plus it energizes you. "Good planning and insight... bring...you honor and respect." Wishy-washy objectives won't get you where you want to go. *(3) Establish a deadline.* Without a definite beginning and ending it's easy to procrastinate and get nowhere. *(4) Make a list of what you need to do to.* Keep it before you at all times; it'll give you a track to run on. *(5) Convert your list to a plan.* Decide what you need to do first and what you can do later. An organized plan is always better than trying to carry stuff around in your head. *(6) Act immediately.* "Be very careful, then, how you live—not as unwise but as wise, making the most of every opportunity" (Eph 5:15-16 NIV). Do something! A mediocre plan that's implemented beats a brilliant one that's not. *(7) Do something every day to move you forward.* Build it into your schedule. For example, read systematically through your Bible, call a specific number of clients, engage in physical activity for a given time. *(8) Have a goal you're willing to devote your life to.* And keep your eye on that goal at all times. "Teach us to number our days aright, that we may gain a heart of wisdom" (Ps 90:12 NIV).

"LAY IT ASIDE"

Let us lay aside every weight,
and...run with endurance.

HEBREWS 12:1 NKJV

The Bible says, "Do you not know that those who run in a race all run, but one receives the prize? Run in such a way that you may obtain it" (1Co 9:24 NKJV). In life you only get to run once, so run to win. To avoid stumbling or losing your place, don't look back. You can't change the past, but thank God you can learn from it and leave it behind. Don't be anxious about the next lap, focus only on the next *step.* If you miss that you may fall and not get up again. Before you know it you'll soon have more laps behind you than ahead of you, so make every lap count: "Let us lay aside every weight, and the sin which so easily ensnares us, and let us run with endurance the race that is set before us." Many of us carry the weight and worry of burdens that older and wiser people understand are of no real importance. We spend our strength extinguishing fires that, if left alone, would burn out on their own. Time is your most valuable resource. Save it and you've increased your assets and decreased your liabilities. Get rid of the baggage of old relationships, pointless fears, and false indebtedness to those who seek to manipulate you. There are enough painful trials in life; why endure the ones you can lay aside?

When blind Bartimaeus heard that Jesus was within reach he threw off his coat lest it trip him up, and ran toward Him. And his faith paid off: "Immediately he received his sight and followed Jesus" (Mk 10:52 NKJV). Today, "lay it aside" and run!

THANK GOD FOR THE CROSS!

*God...reconciled us to Himself
through Jesus Christ.*

2 CORINTHIANS 5:18 NKJV

Tim Miller writes: "My nine-year-old daughter Jennifer was looking forward to our family vacation. But she became ill, and a long-anticipated day at Sea World was replaced by an all-night series of CT scans, X-rays and blood work at the hospital. As morning approached the doctor told my exhausted little girl that she would need to have one more test, a spinal tap. The procedure would be painful, they said. The doctor then asked me if I planned to stay in the room. I nodded, knowing I couldn't leave Jennifer alone during the ordeal. The doctor gently asked Jennifer to remove all her clothing. She looked at me with child-like modesty as if to ask if that were alright. They had her curl up into a tiny ball. I buried my face in hers and hugged her. When the needle went in, Jennifer cried. As the searing pain increased, she sobbed repeatedly, 'Daddy, Daddy, Daddy,' her voice becoming more earnest with each word. It was as if she were saying 'Oh Daddy, please, can't you do something?' My tears mingled with hers. My heart was broken, I felt nauseated. Because I loved her, I was allowing her to go through the most agonizing experience of her life. In the middle of that spinal tap my thoughts went to the Cross. What unspeakable pain both the Son and the Father went through—for our sake."

But because of the Cross of Christ we have: *(1) Reconciliation.* "God...reconciled us to Himself." *(2) Regeneration.* "Having been born again" (1Pe 1:23 NKJV). *(3) Resurrection.* "Everyone who...believes...I will raise him up at the last day" (Jn 6:40 NKJV). Thank God for the Cross!

JESUS CONQUERED DEATH FOR YOU! (1)

He has given us...a living hope.

1 PETER 1:3 NIV

Ernest Becker wrote a book called *The Denial of Death*. In it he said we live our lives ignoring, avoiding and repressing the truth that we are mortal, and sooner or later we are all going to die. He pointed out that it's the reason for our workaholism, approval addictions and obsession with money and security. Becker published his book in 1974 with great acclaim, won the Pulitzer Prize and became famous. That year he found out he had cancer. That year he turned to God. That year he died. It's said that Arizona has the largest cryonics foundation in the world. For a healthy fee your blood can be filled with anti-coagulants, your body frozen and stored in a capsule of liquid nitrogen at minus 320 degrees until you can be reheated later. At that point advanced medical technology can cure whatever disease killed you and you can live again. Or if you don't like being cold, another company offers "eternity in a paperweight." For a small fee your DNA is put in a little box for the next ten thousand years so that you can be cloned whenever it's convenient. They also offer a ten-thousand-year money-back guarantee, though it's hard to say who will collect if things go wrong. John Ortberg writes: "We try to outsmart death in more subtle ways; health clubs, skin creams, surgical techniques, new diets, warmer climates, better medications, smarter doctors and more. Perhaps science will help us live forever, like Gulliver's toothless, hairless, memoryless race of Struldbrugs." Rejoice, Jesus conquered death, and His resurrection guaranteed yours: "He has given us...a living hope through the resurrection... into an inheritance that can never perish" (1Pe 1:3-4 NIV).

JESUS CONQUERED DEATH FOR YOU! (2)

He has given us...a living hope.

1 PETER 1:3 NIV

Mount Auburn, America's first cemetery, was so beautiful it became the number-one tourist attraction in Boston. When they created Central Park in New York they modeled it after Mount Auburn. The rallying cry was, "Why not have it all, but without the graves?" We keep trying to have it all, but without the graves! But we can't. We live only a heartbeat from eternity. So here are two truths you must keep in mind: *(1) God put you on this earth for a specific purpose.* Have you found yours yet? Are you pouring your life into it and making every moment count? Paul did, and he ended up writing: "The time of my departure is at hand. I have fought the good fight, I have finished the race, I have kept the faith. Finally, there is laid up for me the crown of righteousness, which the Lord, the righteous Judge, will give to me on that Day, and not to me only but also to all who have loved His appearing" (2Ti 4:6-8 NKJV). *(2) When you know Christ as your Savior, the best is yet to be.* It is said that on his deathbed, D.L. Moody suddenly sat upright, opened his arms as though embracing something wonderful, declared that earth was receding, heaven was near, and that it was his coronation day. What a way to go! You don't need to fear death because Jesus said, "I am the resurrection and the life. He who believes in Me, though he may die, he shall live. And whoever lives and believes in Me shall never die. Do you believe this?" (Jn 11:25-26 NKJV). Believe it, it's true!

"ABOVE AND BEYOND"

If someone forces you to go one mile, go...two.

MATTHEW 5:41 NIV

In Roman times soldiers could make Jewish citizens carry their gear for a mile. But Jesus says: "If someone forces you to go one mile, go...two." Max Lucado writes: "We've a second-mile servant in our church. By profession he's an architect; by passion, a servant. Prior to each worship service he does his rounds through the men's restrooms...wipes sinks, cleans mirrors, checks toilets and picks up paper. He tells no one and requests nothing in return...Let me tell you how to spot [second-milers]. They don't wear badges or uniforms; they wear smiles. They've discovered...joy in the extra effort...satisfaction in helping others...that the real reward rests at the base of the second milepost...Why? Liberation! They've passed from slave to volunteer. When 'Mary anointed Jesus' feet,' one-milers like Judas criticized the deed as wasteful. Not Jesus. He received the gesture as a demonstration of love, a friend surrendering her most treasured gift. There's an elderly man in your community who just lost his wife. An hour of your time would mean the world to him. Some kids in your city have no dad to take them to movies or baseball games. Maybe you can. They can't pay you back but they'll smile like a cantaloupe slice at your kindness. How about this one? Down the hall is a person who shares your last name. Shock them with kindness...your homework done with no complaints...coffee served when they awake...a love letter written for no special reason. Alabaster poured out 'just because.' Jesus chose the servants' quarters. Can't we?" John Gardner said, "When people are serving, life is no longer meaningless." You're not called to "get by," you're called to go "above and beyond."

SUCCEEDING AT HOME

Through wisdom a house is built.

PROVERBS 24:3 NKJV

Building a good relationship at home is like building a wall: It's done brick by brick. And the mortar that holds it together is unconditional, un-condemning, unselfish love. The only way you'll know how good a job you've done is when it's tested by the storms of life. One of the most important keys to succeeding at home is—communication. So:

(1) Become creative. Spend time together as a family. Call your mate during the day and try to meet sometimes for lunch. Drive your kids to school or soccer practice so you can talk to them. Communication can happen anywhere, but it won't happen unless you make it a priority. *(2) Identify communication killers.* Internet, cell phones and TV are the chief culprits. The average couple spends less than one hour a week in meaningful communication; they spend five times more each day watching television. This is a "screen test" you'll have to pass if you want to succeed at home. *(3) Encourage every member to speak their mind.* And when they do, don't criticize or retaliate. Differences of opinion are healthy. Handled right, they can make things better. *(4) Be conscious of how you interact with your family.* You may have unwittingly adopted a style that stifles communication. Stop and consider; do you: (a) retaliate—that has a degrading effect; (b) dominate—that has an intimidating effect; (c) isolate—that has a frustrating effect. (d) cooperate—that has an encouraging effect. If you're in the habit of using any communication style other than a cooperative one, start working immediately to change it. You'll have to, if you want to build a good relationship with your family.

FIND SOMETHING TO PRAISE GOD FOR

If there is anything praiseworthy—
meditate on these things.

PHILIPPIANS 4:8 NKJV

General Robbie Risner described the seven years he spent as a prisoner of war as "the essence of despair." He said, "If you could have squeezed the feeling out of the word *despair*, it would have come out lead-colored, dingy and dirty." What's amazing is how he survived. He pried the cover off a floor drain in his cell and lowered his head into the opening. There he noticed a solitary blade of grass, the only smidgeon of color in his colorless world. Calling it a blood transfusion for the soul, Risner began each day in prayer, lying on the floor of his cell with his head down the vent, focused on that single blade of grass.

Jesus said, "Your eye...provides light for your body. When your eye is good, your whole body is filled with light. But when your eye is bad, your whole body is filled with darkness" (Mt 6:22-23 NLT). What are you looking at? Each day you get to decide where you'll focus. And you won't have to look hard to find things to complain about: war, gas prices, the economy, global warming, and crime. God gave Adam and Eve everything they needed in the Garden of Eden, but they chose to focus on the one thing they *couldn't* have. He divided the Red Sea, sent signs to guide the Israelites in the wilderness and provided food so they'd never go hungry. Initially, "They...sang his praise. But...soon forgot what he had done" (Ps 106:12-13 NIV). Don't be like that. The Bible says, "If there is anything praiseworthy—meditate on these things." Surely you can find *something* to praise God for today!

HAVING A PEACEFUL STATE OF MIND

I have stilled and quieted my soul.

PSALM 131:2 NIV

One of the greatest stress inducers we face daily is *noise*. We live in a noisy world. To enjoy a more peaceful atmosphere—we must create one! So find a place where you won't be interrupted and learn to enjoy simply being quiet for a while. If you're a high-energy, time-conscious, results-oriented individual with too much to do and not enough time to do it, you'll discover this is not easy. And before you start thinking, "This is not very spiritual," take a moment and consider these four Scriptures:

(1) "The fruit of righteousness will be peace; the effect of righteousness will be quietness and confidence forever" (Isa 32:17 NIV). (2) "Better one handful with tranquility than two handfuls with toil and chasing after the wind" (Ecc 4:6 NIV). (3) "Make it your ambition to lead a quiet life, to mind your own business" (1Th 4:11 NIV). (4) "Be still, and know that I am God" (Ps 46:10 NIV). You can't live a continually noisy life and expect to walk in peace.

Jesus made sure He had seasons of peace and time alone. Nobody had a greater life's purpose or more incessant demands placed upon Him than He did. Yet the Bible says, He "often withdrew to lonely places and prayed" (Lk 5:16 NIV). Surely if Jesus needed this type of lifestyle, you do too. Spending quiet time with God is essential to restoring your body, your mind and your emotions. The truth is, you need it regularly, so insist on having it and don't let anyone take it from you. Work your schedule around God—don't try to work God in around your schedule.

COMING CLEAN WITH GOD

When I kept silent about my sin...
Your hand was heavy upon me.

PSALM 32:3-4 NAS

A therapist who graduated thirty-four years earlier called the University of Oregon and admitted she'd cheated on a final exam. Instead of revoking her degree the University asked her to write an article on integrity. A woman who completed a walk around the world confessed she traveled part-way in a support truck. "I shouldn't be remembered as the first woman to walk round the world when I cheated," she said. How many of *us* would even have admitted our deception?

The Psalmist said, "When I kept silent about my sin...Your hand was heavy upon me." Confessing your sins: *(a) Lets you experience God's forgiveness:* He already knows about them anyway, but He won't forgive you while you're busy making excuses and blame-shifting. John says, "If we confess...he will forgive our sins" (1Jn 1:9 NCV). The first move is up to you. *(b) Restores your emotional and physical energy:* Nothing's more draining than denial and nothing's more invigorating than a clean slate. David said, "My strength...failed because of my iniquity" (Ps 31:10 NAS). Reflecting on his affair with Bathsheba, he said, "When I kept silent...my vitality was drained...I acknowledged my sin...and You forgave the guilt" (Ps 32:3-5 NAS). *(c) Allows you to move on:* Confession allows you to hit the "reset" button and start again. It's also important to draw a line between the past and the future in case you're tempted to repeat your behavior. *(d) Lets you grow:* Thomas Edison said failure taught him over a thousand ways not to make a light bulb! Making your mistakes work for you instead of against you, starts with confessing them to God and accepting His forgiveness.

STILL WANNA BE FIRST?

If anyone wants to be first.

MARK 9:35 NIV

A s Dan Mazur led his team of climbers up Mount Everest the conditions were ideal for reaching the summit. Then two hours from the top they came across Lincoln Hall, a climber who'd collapsed the day before on his way down. Alone and hallucinating, he had no equipment and was suffering from frostbite and dehydration. (They later learned Hall's team leader had called his wife to say he was dead!) Without hesitation they gave Hall their oxygen, food and water, and by the time help arrived, reaching the peak was out of the question. They sacrificed years of planning, weeks of climbing, and their lifelong dream to save another climber. Not surprisingly, today Mazur helps build schools and hospitals in parts of Nepal without roads, electricity, phones and running water. That's the kind of person he is.

Would *you* give up your dream to save another person? Ordinary people do it every day: moms and dads working two jobs to feed and clothe their kids; parents who turn down job transfers rather than uproot their families; round-the-clock caregivers whose loved ones are depending on them. Jesus said, "If anyone wants to be first, he must [put himself] last." In God's kingdom, things are different. The least are considered the greatest (See Lk 9:48). The most honorable seat in the house is for the one we overlook (See Lk 14:8-9). We esteem others more highly than ourselves (See Ro 12:10 & Php 2:3). We give up our coat and go the extra mile (Mt 5:40-41). John the Baptist said of Jesus, "He must become greater and greater, and I must become less and less" (See Jn 3:30). Still wanna be first?

LEARNING TO STAND

And having done all...stand.

EPHESIANS 6:13 NKJV

Don't allow the conflict-free seasons of your life to lull you into a false sense of security: "Be vigilant...the devil walks about like a roaring lion, seeking whom he may devour" (1Pe 5:8 NKJV).

What should we do when the Devil comes along? "And having done all...stand." Indeed, "God is able to make [you] stand" (Ro 14:4 NKJV), not in your own strength, but the strength of Jesus Christ. By yourself you're an easy target, but in the strength of the Lord you can stand and not give in. So today when Satan shows up with his temptations, announce that you're going to stand in Christ. Let him know you're going to stand until the shaking stops, until the wave of loneliness passes, until your marriage is restored, until you come out of debt, until the struggle is over, until the tempter loses his power to trap or topple you. When you do the standing—God does the strengthening!

Paul said, "I can do all things through Christ which strengtheneth me" (Php 4:13). Note the word "strengtheneth." He won't just strengthen you once, He'll do it again and again. He'll strengthen you every time you face a difficult challenge, every time a memory comes back to torment you, every time you're reminded of your imperfect past, every time you face a difficult situation. Drawing from God the strength you need to stand up to the enemy will take effort. It will take your praise, your prayer, your getting into His Word with an intensity you never had before. But the truth is—you can stand if you want to!

HOW TO LEAVE A LASTING LEGACY

Those who turn many to righteousness
[shall shine] like the stars forever.

DANIEL 12:3 NKJV

An unsavory character passed away and a eulogy was delivered by a pastor who'd never met him. Hoping to comfort the family the reverend got carried away, describing the departed as a caring son, a dedicated father and a loving husband. After the service the widow nudged their son and said, "Go up to the casket and make sure it's your father he's talking about!" Seriously, if *your* life was measured by its donation instead of its duration, how would people remember you?

D. James Kennedy wrote: "Consider the Great Pyramid of Giza, one of the world's most massive structures. Someone built it as a memorial to himself...King Khufu, not exactly a household name! The Shah of India built the Taj Mahal as a tribute to his wife, yet he too built in vain; after all who knows the name of Arjumand? And how about the Great Wall of China? Astronauts can see it from space, yet no one remembers Qin Shi Huang, the man initially responsible for the largest man-made structure in the world. While these people are all forgotten, *we* can make a permanent imprint on the world. God placed a desire in our hearts for significance and permanence, because we're bound for eternal life. So how can we make a name for ourselves for eternity? *By bringing others to Christ!* Do you know somebody who needs salvation? They'll be forever grateful you took the time and made the effort to introduce them to Jesus." The Bible says by bringing people to Him you'll "shine ...like the stars forever and ever."

SEEING GOD IN YOUR SITUATION

*I pray also that the eyes
of your heart may be enlightened.*

EPHESIANS 1:18 NIV

When you are in a crisis it's easy to lose perspective. It happened to Jesus' disciples on the Emmaus Road. Discouraged about His death, they were "going over all these things that had happened. In the middle of their…questions, Jesus came up and walked along with them. But they were not able to recognize who he was" (Lk 24:15-16 TM). When you take your eyes off Jesus, you begin to feel helpless about things. Dr. Michael Youssef says: "Facing a major crisis…I tend to be the kind of person whose vision becomes blurred…my perceptions are shot…my contemplations one-sided…and I often shut out the very people who can deliver me…just like these two disciples…Their vision was blurred about the very person who was walking with them and talking to them. The One whose death they were mourning was alive…but they didn't realize it because their focus was on the wrong thing."

But everything changed the minute they recognized Him. "Within the hour they were on their way back to Jerusalem. There…the two…told…how Jesus had appeared to them as they were walking along the road, and how they had recognized him as he was breaking the bread" (Lk 24:33-35 NLT). Notice the words "within the hour." In an instant they went from fear to courage, pain to joy, and despair to hope. And that's the story of Easter. No matter how bad things may appear to be, when you set your eyes on Jesus He will fill you with hope. So Paul writes: "I pray also that the eyes of your heart may be enlightened."

WHEN THINGS LOOK BAD

Happy is he...whose hope is in the Lord.

PSALM 146:5 NKJV

F.B. Meyer says: "The education of our faith is incomplete [till] we learn that God's providence works through loss... that there's a ministry to us through the failure and fading of things. The dwindling brook where Elijah sat is a picture of our lives! 'Some time later the brook dried up' (1Ki 17:7 NIV) is the history of our yesterdays and a prophecy of our tomorrows...learn the difference between trusting in the gift and trusting in the Giver. The gift may last for a season but the Giver is eternal. If the Lord had led Elijah directly to the widow at Zarephath, he'd have missed something that helped make him a better man—living by faith. Whenever our earthly resources dry up it's so we may learn that our hope and help are in God."

One author writes: "Sometimes there's not enough money to make ends meet; people tell us to budget and we chuckle. We look at the situation and say 'No way.' That's the time to trust God. Your possibilities are not limited by past or present circumstances. If there's not enough to pay legitimate expenses, do your best then let go. Trust God to supply your need, then look beyond your wallet. Look to your source. Claim a divine ...unlimited supply...Do your part. Strive for financial responsibility in thought and action. Ask for wisdom and listen to God's leadings. Then let go of your fears and your need to control. 'Trust in the Lord with all your heart; do not depend on your own understanding' (Pr 3:5 NLT). We all know money is a necessary part of living—and so does God."

RULES FOR HANDLING ANGER (1)

Let each one of you speak truth.

EPHESIANS 4:25 NKJV

Two forceful personalities in a relationship are like two rivers flowing into one; there's going to be a strong current. Anger can be instant like a flash of lightning, or prolonged like the rumble of thunder. Sometimes we clash painfully, other times we distance and silently abandon the relationship. But anger handled the right way doesn't have to destroy. Here are God's rules for handling your anger. *Rule 1: Keep it honest.* "Stop telling lies. Let us tell...the truth...don't sin by letting anger control you" (Eph 4:25-26 NLT). When you're angry don't deny it. Anger can be constructive. We're right to get angry when people are mistreated and wrongs are not made right. Saying, "I've been feeling angry and because I value our relationship I'd like to talk about it," is honest, non-threatening and invites resolution. Observe: (a) Ignoring, stifling, suppressing, or pretending you're not angry is basically dishonest. (b) Another form of lying when you're angry is exaggeration. "You *never* listen to what I say." "You *always* ignore my wishes." "*Nobody* does anything around here except me." Such generalizations are untrue and serve only to aggravate and polarize, guaranteeing the real problem gets obscured and goes unsolved. (c) Another way to lie when you're angry is blaming. "If you'd arrive on time I wouldn't have to nag you," or "If you'd quit nagging so much, maybe I'd start being on time." Blaming is a way of evading your own responsibility while pointing the finger at others. It angers others, perpetuates your own anger and never produces the result you want. God's way is, "Let each one of you speak truth," and it works when you do it in love.

RULES FOR HANDLING ANGER (2)

Let each one of you speak truth.

EPHESIANS 4:25 NKJV

Rule 2: *Keep it non-lethal.* Paul writes: "In your anger do not sin" (Eph 4:26 NIV). What do Paul's words mean? Don't let your anger escalate to the point of doing damage. Don't use your words as a weapon or a control mechanism. It's okay to express your emotions in a healthy way, but keep them in check. Your goal must be to resolve the problem and strengthen the relationship, not "sound off" and wound the other person. Is this easy to do? No. You'll need a good strong dose of grace to do it. Words spoken in jest, sarcasm, self-righteousness or "righteous indignation" wound people, sometimes permanently. "Perverseness [of the tongue] breaks the spirit." (Pr 15:4 NKJV). "A crushed spirit who can bear?" (Pr 18:14 NIV). "The tongue can bring death" (Pr 18:21 NLT). Angry words, once unleashed, can: "Go down into a man's inmost parts" (Pr 26:22 NIV). Your words can live in the heart and memory of a person and go all the way to the grave with them. We say, "Sticks and stones may break my bones, but names will never hurt me," but it's not true. A person can die of a crushed spirit, and the one who spoke the words can live to regret the damage they inflicted and never get a chance to undo it. On the other hand, anger properly handled never needs to be repented of. So learn to differentiate between the anger you feel and the words you speak. Anger, carefully thought through, can reveal important information about needed changes. Focus on that, and ask God to show you what needs changing in the other person—and you!

RULES FOR HANDLING ANGER (3)

Let each one of you speak truth.

EPHESIANS 4:25 NKJV

Rule 3: *Keep it current.* Storing anger in your hard drive only hurts you. When you download old resentments you start to rehearse them and grow bitter. "The good man brings good things out of the good stored up in his heart, and the evil man brings evil things out of the evil stored up in his heart. For out of the overflow of his heart his mouth speaks" (Lk 6:45 NIV).

When you're angry deal with it quickly. Don't passively allow time to decide your options, or sit around hoping the other person will see the light and apologize. "If your brother sins against you, go [to] him" (Mt 18:15 NIV). Try to resolve it and restore the relationship. When you repress it you add one more skeleton to your closet. Sooner or later, doctors say, it'll be at your stomach lining, attack your immune system, and predispose you to heart problems, cancers and other physical, social and emotional disorders. Meantime, it'll preoccupy you, dissipate your energy, cripple your creativity, and hinder your fellowship with God, your friends and fellow believers; not to mention that it denies the offender the opportunity to clear their conscience, repent and get right with God and you. Stop dragging up the past, trying to blackmail the guilty by hauling skeletons out of closets at "auspicious" moments, plotting revenge, and passing down resentments for the next generation to carry. Ask God for the humility and courage to deal with today's problems—today. When your head hits the pillow tonight, know that your issues are current, up-to-date with God and everyone else, and sleep well!

RULES FOR HANDLING ANGER (4)

Let each one of you speak truth.

EPHESIANS 4:25 NKJV

Rule 4: Keep it solution-focused. Someone has said that fellowship is like two fellows in a ship: one can't sink the other without sinking himself. By seeking to gain the upper hand you both lose. By seeking to save and strengthen the relationship you both win. So when you speak, be sure it's "helpful for building others up according to their needs" (Eph 4:29 NIV). Try to understand what the other person needs. Don't bring up previously confessed offenses; don't drag in other people; don't use wisecracks about people's weight, height, color, IQ, physical, mental and emotional limitations; don't bring up unrelated things that cloud the issue and keep you from finding a solution. And don't raise the volume in order to intimidate and manipulate. God made you with a capacity for anger because, when handled the right way, it's the fuel that brings needed change and the medicine that heals. So:

(a) Seek a solution, not a "victory." Name-calling and "diagnosing" others only makes things worse. Your focus should not be on what they did, but on what you can do together to resolve it. *(b) Admit your own flaws and ask for forgiveness.* Since it takes two to tango, acknowledging your own imperfections makes it easier for someone else to acknowledge theirs. *(c) Every time you take a "swing" at someone, offer them a positive "stroke."* "If there be any virtue…think on these things" (Php 4:8). For each of the difficulties you address, give a compliment. "I'm sure this wasn't easy for you to hear. Thanks for listening to me so graciously." Being solution-focused gives people something positive to live up to, not down to!

RULES FOR HANDLING ANGER (5)

Let each one of you speak truth.

EPHESIANS 4:25 NKJV

R*ule 5: Keep it in the laundry room.* "Don't treat each other with malice" [ill will, spite] (See Eph 4: 31 NIV). When you're angry, spreading gossip is hard to resist. But malicious talk is like wildfire; it consumes those who spread it and those who listen to it. Don't display your dirty wash; keep it in the laundry room. Dirty laundry gets aired in two ways: (1) Open embarrassment. You say it where you know others are going to hear it. (2) Subtlety. You make jokes about their figure, family members and friends, etc. in order to belittle them. This results in embarrassment for the person you're angry at, widens the gap between you and makes reconciliation impossible. Solomon writes: "He that is of a faithful spirit concealeth the matter" (Pr 11:13), and "Love covereth all sins" (Pr 10:12). Paul writes: "In malice be babes, but in understanding be mature" (1Co 14:20 NKJV).

Rule 6: Be part of the clean-up crew. We say, "They brought it on themselves. Let them get over it." They may have deserved it, but we can't walk away and leave open wounds to become infected. We "forgive, even as Christ...has forgiven" us (See Eph 4: 32). How did Christ forgive us? After we'd acknowledged, confessed and repented of our sins? No. "When we were enemies, we were reconciled to God by the death of his Son" (Ro 5:10). God took the initiative, so forgive, before the other person asks for forgiveness. And should they remain your enemy for life, forgive them anyhow. That's mopping up after the war. Only then are you yourself forgiven, the wounds you inflicted healed, and your record before God expunged!

TRUSTING GOD WHEN
THERE ARE NO ANSWERS

The secret things belong to the Lord.

DEUTERONOMY 29:29 NIV

Life's losses leave us hurting and wondering. Cancer takes a young mother or father. Divorce strikes your happy home. Financial ruin devastates your retirement plans. A child goes to jail, is killed or commits suicide. Such times raise questions which are difficult, if not impossible to answer. We examine the circumstances again and again. We speculate about the details, searching for clues that might make some sense and make it easier for us to bear. We turn the spotlight on ourselves, others, even God, wondering what could or should have been done differently that might have prevented this. We turn to friends, fellow believers and pastors only to hear what sounds like religious platitudes and inadequate attempts to minimize our pain. When answers don't seem forthcoming and the heavens are silent, what should you do?

Here are two Scriptures to help you in such times: (1) "The *secret things* belong to the Lord our God, but those things which are revealed belong to us" (Dt 29:29 NKJV). When it comes to understanding things, we have our territory, God has His. And ours is limited to what He decides to reveal. At that point you must "Trust in the Lord with all your heart, and lean not on your own understanding" (Pr 3:5 NKJV). (2) "And we know that *all things* work together for good to them that love God" (Ro 8:28). God may explain it to you, or He may not. But He's "the Alpha and the Omega, the Beginning and the End" (Rev 22:13 NKJV), which means, He has a plan and He's working it out for our good and His glory. So trust Him!

MOVE FORWARD!

The glory of the Lord appeared...
before all the children of Israel.

NUMBERS 14:10 NKJV

People once thought the world was flat and that you would sail off the edge. They thought man would never walk on the moon. In 1899 the U.S. patent office almost closed because the CEO said, "Everything that can be invented already has been." In retrospect his statement is ridiculous. But some of us have bought into the same philosophy about our lives. We stop learning because we're "too old." We're afraid to change careers in case we "jeopardize our pension." We don't pursue our dreams in case we fail or get ridiculed. We're so accustomed to self-imposed limitations that we tell ourselves, "I can't do *that,* so I can't do *anything.*" In essence we're building a box, crawling inside, then looking for something to blame for our lack of faith. God didn't box you in, *you* did, and you need to take the initiative for breaking out!

When you get down to it, there's very little difference in people. But the little difference amounts to a big difference, and the little difference is *attitude;* it determines whether you see life through the eyes of faith or the lens of fear. When others around him saw only giants and wanted to turn back, Caleb said, "If the Lord delights in us, then He will bring us into this land and give it to us" (Nu 14:8 NKJV). At that point two things happened. First, "All the congregation said to stone them" (v. 10). Second, "The glory of the Lord appeared in the Tabernacle." Caleb's critics said "no," but God said "yes." All you need is God's approval. When you have it, disregard the nay-sayers and move forward!

THREE QUESTIONS FOR LEADERS

We who teach will be judged more strictly.

JAMES 3:1 NIV

If you're a leader in God's work you must constantly ask yourself three questions:

(1) Am I accountable to anybody? If not, you're on dangerous ground. Only God can handle unquestioned authority. Who knows you well enough to pray with you, advise you and strengthen you in your vulnerable areas? We keep discovering that authority without accountability leads to disaster. *(2) Are my priorities in order?* Priorities have a way of sneaking out of position when we're not paying attention. Too many of us become successful only at the cost of broken homes or failing health because our priorities shifted somewhere along the line. *(3) Is my personal walk with God up to date?* If that doesn't prompt a quick yes, you're too close to the edge. A disciplined daily walk with God is your best protection. "Your word I have treasured in my heart, that I may not sin against You" (Ps 119:11 NAS). If you're not spending time with God, you're spending it on whatever has become more important to you than Him. Pay attention to that word "treasured." It means to protect something, to let nothing threaten it. You must discipline yourself to spend time in God's Word and guard that time from interruptions. Give God your mind each day when it's fresh. Pastor, your first calling is not the building project, the board meeting or the budget, it's: "Feed my sheep" (Jn 21:16). If Saturday finds you anxious because you've nothing prepared for Sunday, make some changes. Start delegating. "Seek out from among you...men...whom we may appoint over this business; but we will give ourselves continually to prayer and to the ministry of the word" (Ac 6:3-4 NKJV).

HOW TO MOVE THE MOUNTAIN

Say unto this mountain,
Be thou removed.

MARK 11:23

How can you move the mountain in your life? By: *(1) Using God's Word:* In the wilderness Satan tempted Jesus in three ways: (a) Put your temporal needs ahead of your spiritual ones: "Turn these stones into bread." (b) Use your power for the wrong reasons: "Throw yourself down from the pinnacle of the temple." (c) Take the easy way, not the cross: "The world is yours, just submit to me." Each time Jesus overcame Satan by saying, "It is written" (See Mt 4:1-11). Your most powerful weapon is God's Word—learn to use it!

(2) Being persistent: Jeremiah said that God's Word is "like a hammer that breaks a rock in pieces" (Jer 23:29 NKJV). Ever wonder how a hammer can hit a rock ninety-nine times, but on the one-hundredth blow it shatters? That's because all the previous blows kept weakening it. Live in God's Word, keep speaking it over your situation and it will work.

(3) Forgiving: The story's told of a pastor who asked his congregation, "How many of you are willing to forgive your enemies?" Everybody was except one old guy. "Why not?" the pastor asked. He replied, "Cause I have none—I've outlived them all!" After speaking about mountain-moving faith and prayer that bring results, Jesus said, "Whenever you stand praying, if you have anything against anyone, forgive him, that your Father in heaven may also forgive you your trespasses" (Mk 11:25 NKJV). Your mountain can't be moved or your prayers answered if you're harboring un-forgiveness. So ask yourself, "Is it worth it?" Whether you think the offender deserves forgiveness or not, for your own sake, forgive it and let it go.

STOP COMPLAINING!

Do all things without complaining.

PHILIPPIANS 2:14 NKJV

If somebody gave you a dollar every time you complained and collected one every time you showed gratitude, would you be rich or poor? You say, "If you had my problems you'd complain too." The Bible says: "Do all things without complaining," because the more you complain the worse things get. Notice: *(1) Complaining is addictive.* The cycle goes: You've a problem; you complain and remain stuck in it; you feel bad, so you complain even more and you end up with stress, not solutions. How foolish is that? *(2) Complaining robs you of God's blessing.* Instead of committing it to God, you're doubting His wisdom and His provision. God put twenty-three thousand Israelites to death for doing that. "Do not grumble, as some of them did—and were killed…These things…were written down as warnings for us" (1Co 10:10-11 NIV). Don't just check your attitude, change it! *(3) Complaining affects your health.* "A calm and undisturbed mind and heart are the life and health of the body" (Pr 14:30 AMP). Be honest, how many calm, undisturbed complainers do you know? Instead of complaining, work on your attitude. Start counting your blessings. A wise man once said, "I complained that I had no shoes until I met a man who had no feet." Consider what author Barbara Johnston speaks about: "A hand-lettered sign nailed to a telephone pole said, 'Lost dog with three legs, blind in left eye, missing right ear, tail broken, and recently castrated. Answers to the name of Lucky.'" The Bible says: "In everything (notice, it doesn't say *for* everything, but *in* everything) give thanks; for this is the will of God" (1Th 5:18 NKJV).

ONE STEP AT A TIME

Blessed are those who have learned to…
walk in the light of your presence.

PSALM 89:15 NIV

In ancient European monasteries monks walked dark corridors with candles on the toes of their shoes, giving them just enough light to see the next step. That's how God leads us.

Educator Verdell Davis's faith was challenged when a plane crash killed her husband of thirty years. Facing a mountain of letters, insurance forms and bills, she spread them on the table and threw a sheet over them. "Out of sight, out of mind," she thought. She writes: "I knew the monster under the sheet was going to attack me if I didn't attack it first. I sat down and cried tears of anger…frustration…loneliness. Eventually I raised my head and said, 'Okay, Lord. I'm a fairly bright girl. I'm going to open one envelope. If I can make sense of what's inside I'll open another. If not, I'm putting this sheet back…and going back to bed.'…Even that bit of levity was a little extra light for that particular step. Back then I wanted to *already* know how to take care of all the details…feel confident about the monumental daily decisions I had to make…have some clue that the steps in front of me were surmountable. I wanted the path flooded with light…yet, it was with small flickers of candle glow that God gently reminded me, 'My grace is sufficient for you, for my power is made perfect in weakness' (2Co 12:9 NIV). The Psalmist said, 'Blessed are those who have learned to… walk in the light of your presence' (Ps 89:15 NIV). I only needed light for one envelope, one conversation, one decision, and one step at a time." So do you!

WHAT YOU SOW, YOU REAP

Let us not become weary in doing good...
we will reap a harvest if we do not give up.

GALATIANS 6:9 NIV

The name Corrie ten Boom is widely recognized in Christian circles, but few people know about her nephew Peter who was also instrumental in saving Jews from Nazi persecution. When Dutch patriots heard SS troops were sending Jewish orphans to concentration camps, they smuggled kids out of orphanages and brought them to the ten Boom house till they could be placed for adoption. At sixteen, Peter, a committed Christian, defied the Germans by pulling out all the stops on the church organ and playing the Dutch national anthem while the congregation stood up and sang. He was imprisoned for his defiance. After World War II he traveled the world with the same message as his aunt—that forgiveness is the only answer to hatred. On tour in Israel Peter had a heart attack and needed surgery. Talking with him the night before his operation the cardiologist asked, "Are you by any chance related to the ten Booms of Holland?" Peter replied, "Yes, that's my family." The doctor responded, "I'm one of the babies your family saved!" Next day the man whose life had been saved forty years earlier, repaid the debt by saving Peter ten Boom's life.

The Bible says when you, "Cast your bread upon the waters...after many days you will find it again" (Ecc 11:1 NIV). What you sow—good or bad—comes back to you. So, "Let us not become weary in doing good...at the proper time we will reap a harvest if we do not give up." Remember, God is no man's debtor, and no matter how long it takes He will honor His Word.

RESPECT YOUR TEMPLE (1)

God bought you with a high price.
So...honor God with your body.

1 CORINTHIANS 6:20 NLT

At the resurrection, "Our earthly bodies...will be raised to live forever" (1Co 15:42 NLT), but in the meantime you must "honor God with your body" by observing a few basic principles like: *(1) Exercising regularly:* Half of us who start exercise programs abandon them within six months. The secret is to start slowly. Take the stairs instead of the elevator, park the car and walk, play ball with the kids instead of watching TV. God designed your body to move, and strolling from the car to your desk every morning doesn't cut it! Exercising thirty minutes three or four times a week reduces blood pressure and stress, and boosts your sense of well-being. *(2) Eating right:* Many of us eat for the wrong reasons, like fatigue, anger, and low self-esteem. Eat to live, don't live to eat. Insufficient fruit, veggies and fiber and too much fast food can wreak havoc with your health. Practice self-control. Remember, "Those who belong to Christ...have given up their old selfish feelings and... things they wanted to do" (Gal 5:24 NCV). *(3) Getting enough sleep:* Pastor Tony Jenkins consulted his doctor about his wife's snoring. "Does it really bother you that much?" he asked. "It's not just *me,*" Jenkins replied, "It's bothering the whole congregation!" Seriously, we live in a sleep-deprived society but most of us require seven to nine hours shut-eye. You can probably get by on less, but do you just want to "get by?" The Psalmist said, "It is no use...to get up early and stay up late...The Lord gives sleep to those he loves" (Ps 127:2 NCV). So turn off the TV and the computer and turn in at a reasonable hour!

RESPECT YOUR TEMPLE (2)

God bought you with a high price.
So...honor God with your body.

1 CORINTHIANS 6:20 NLT

Dr. Kenneth Cooper's name is synonymous with fitness, but his commitment to health goes beyond simply looking good. Cooper believes your body is a temple and you owe it to God to keep it in shape. Now in his seventies, his physical condition is that of a forty-nine-year-old. How did he go from being an overweight med student living on junk food and caffeine, to the wiry man who power-walks every day? On a waterskiing trip his heart started hammering at 250 beats a minute and he thought he was dying. It was a wake-up call. God was telling him something—and He didn't have to speak twice! Cooper developed what we call *aerobics,* dropped thirty-five pounds and ran a marathon. Fitness became his passion, but speaking and traveling took a spiritual toll on him. So he decided to start feeding his inner man by reading, praying, integrating spiritual lessons into his lectures, and getting involved in church again. As a result he's helped thousands of people. He says his greatest motive for staying in shape is spiritual.

So, how do you counteract a frenetic lifestyle and work-related stress? *First:* recognize that "Your body is the temple of the Holy Spirit" (v. 19 NKJV) *Second:* get into a fitness program...eat right...practice moderation...and prioritize your schedule. If you think taking care of yourself physically isn't "spiritual," think again! It's just as harmful to let yourself become run down through bad habits as it is to abuse drugs and alcohol. Instead of saying, "I don't have time," *make* time. It could save your life! In the meantime you'll feel better *and* be a lot easier to live with.

TURNING STUMBLING BLOCKS INTO STEPPING STONES (1)

We are more than conquerors.

ROMANS 8:37 NKJV

How would you describe somebody who was an accomplished pianist at ten, a professional organist at eleven, had compositions published at thirteen, and was a member of the royal court musical staff at fourteen? Privileged? Born with a silver spoon in his mouth? Hardly! Ludwig van Beethoven was a black-haired, swarthy-complexioned, pockmarked boy who endured taunts and name calling in his hometown along the Rhine River, an area of mostly blond, fair-skinned children. His alcoholic father decided that Ludwig would support him, so he made him a slave to the keyboard. Looking back, Beethoven couldn't recall a single moment of childhood happiness. His life was comprised of work, tears, beatings and angry tirades. In his twenties he encountered another more insidious enemy—deafness. When he could no longer play publicly he put all his energies into composing. His years of deafness were his most prolific. Although at the time his works weren't well received, he influenced many of the great composers like Brahms, Wagner and Schubert. Nearing death and recognizing that the world had never fully understood or appreciated him and his music, he said with a smile, "I shall hear in heaven."

When life knocks you down don't stay down, bounce back! Everybody stumbles or gets knocked off their feet from time to time; the winners are just the ones who keep getting back up! That's what Paul meant when he said, "In all these things we are more than conquerors." If you pray and look hard enough, you'll find the seed of good in every adversity (See Ge 50:20). The difference between winners and losers, is their ability to turn stumbling blocks into stepping stones.

TURNING STUMBLING BLOCKS INTO
STEPPING STONES (2)

None of these things move me.

ACTS 20:24

We don't hear much about Abraham Lincoln's defeats because his victories were so notable. But for much of his life the odds were against him. His mother died when he was nine. In 1832 he lost an election to the Illinois State Legislature. In 1849 he was rejected as Commissioner of the General Land Office. He lost Senate races in 1855 and 1858, and in between failed to win a vice-presidential nomination. However, his most painful losses were the deaths of his four-year-old and twelve-year-old sons. Born in the backwoods of Kentucky, Lincoln had only a few months of "blab school"—one without books where students repeated the teacher's words. He taught himself mathematics, read the classics and worked on his writing and speaking skills using the Bible as his model. His philosophy was, "I'll study and prepare, and when the time comes I'll be ready." He told a friend, "Bear in mind, your own resolution to succeed is more important than any other one thing." His Gettysburg Address is one of the most notable speeches in history. During the darkest days of the Civil War he said, "I do the very best I know how…and I mean to keep on doing it to the end."

Paul didn't say, "None of these things *hurt* me," he said, "None of these things *move* me." Big difference! Paul refused to let life's problems derail him. He understood that what happens *in* you is more important than what happens *to* you. He also understood that when you look to Jesus as your role model and draw strength from Him each day, He'll give you all that's needed to overcome in life.

LET IT GO (1)

Forget the former things; do not dwell on the past.

ISAIAH 43:18 NIV

What do you do when your memory drags the "there and then" into the "here and now," immersing you in the same old pain? The Bible answers, "Forget the former things; do not dwell on the past. See, I am doing a new thing! Now it springs up; do you not perceive it?" Your past can infect your present and influence your future unless you decide to let it go. For the next few days, let's think about it.

First, *let go of what God has forgiven!* God's only response to confessed sin is to forgive and forget it. If it comes up again, you, not He, brought it up. "If we confess our sins he is faithful and just to forgive us…and to cleanse us from all unrighteousness" (1Jn 1:9). Two things make letting go difficult. (1) Your feelings. "I just don't feel forgiven!" you say. You're forgiven by God's grace obtained through Christ's sacrifice—regardless of emotions. Don't wait to feel it before you accept it; accept it and you'll start to feel it! (2) A wrong concept of God. You say, "My dad says he forgives me, but each time I fail all my old offenses are thrown in my face again." Your heavenly Father doesn't operate that way. "I, even I, am he who blots out your transgressions, for my own sake, and remembers your sins no more" (Isa 43:25 NIV). God doesn't bring them up—because He doesn't remember them. All your sins were judged and paid for at Calvary. Once confessed, you'll never again be charged with them, so rejoice and let them go. The Court of Heaven has ruled you "not guilty."

LET IT GO (2)

God has made me forget all my trouble.

GENESIS 41:51 NIV

Second, *let go of what others have done to you!* Thorns come with roses, and hurts come with human relationships. And few hurts go as deeply as those inflicted by friends and family. Ask Joseph, who was sold out by his brothers and locked up in a foreign prison for a crime he never committed. It's the stuff bitterness, depression, despair and defeat are made of. And who'd have blamed him? But Joseph knew that he, not his abusers, had the last word; that he, not they, would decide his future. Others can wound you, but no one can destroy you without your permission and cooperation. It's not what *they* do to you that determines your outcomes, it's what *you* do next. Joseph decided to let the offenses go and accept responsibility for his own reactions. When you do that you take back your power, open yourself to new options, and make choices that position you to come out of it stronger, wiser and more blessed.

Notice: (a) Joseph saw it from God's perspective. "You did not send me here...God did...to keep you alive by a great deliverance" (See Ge 45:8). (b) He released his resentment. He moved beyond it and ministered to the needs of those who had hurt him. (c) He refused to become a victim of other people's actions. As a result God made him "ruler over all...Egypt" (v. 8). (d) He prepared for the future. How? By excelling in his prophetic and administrative gifts, even though imprisoned (See Ge 41:39). So, choose to see it God's way. Let it go. Do what you've been called to do, and watch God vindicate you royally!

LET IT GO (3)

I persecuted the church.

GALATIANS 1:13 NIV

Third, *let go of what you have done to others!* The wounds we've inflicted on others can weigh us down like a ton. The drunk-driving accident. The family shattered by divorce. The child abused in anger. The abortion following an affair. The faithful partner infected by HIV. We can't wound others and remain whole ourselves, so the "ghost of failures past" dogs our days, fills our nights with remorse and steals our peace of mind. How do I live with the things I've done? Enter Saul of Tarsus, a man with a record. "I violently persecuted God's church. I did my best to destroy it" (Gal 1:13 NLT). He'd torn believers from their families leaving traumatized children watching their parents carried off to flogging, imprisonment and death. Now, a convert to Christianity and a preacher of the gospel, he meets the widows and orphans in the churches he once persecuted. How do you handle such a situation? A crucial decision faced him. He could shoulder the guilt until it broke him and maybe even made him an addict or a suicidal wreck. Or he could roll it onto shoulders big enough to carry it and walk away free. He calls out, "O wretched man that I am! Who will deliver me from this body of death?" (Ro 7:24 NKJV). The answer follows instantly, "Thank God! It has been done by Jesus Christ our Lord" (Ro 7:25 TLB). The result? "Even though I was...a persecutor and a violent man, I was shown mercy" (1Ti 1:13 NIV). Today that same mercy is yours for the taking. Make amends where possible, trust God to heal the hurts you've caused, and let it go!

LET IT GO (4)

I will make up to you
for the years that the…locust has eaten.

JOEL 2:25 NAS

Fourth, *let go of what you failed to do!* "If I could just go back, I'd…" The poet said, "The saddest words of tongue or pen, are these, we hear, 'It might have been.'" Not one of us escapes the long shadow of "opportunity missed." We fail more frequently by what we *didn't* do than by what we *did*. We could have helped, healed, blessed, or changed things for the better. But by pursuing our own interests we left words of love and gratitude unspoken. Avoiding unwanted consequences, we left the awkward truth unacknowledged. Evading the label, "religious nut," our witness remained mute: a responsibility unfulfilled, a decision sidestepped, an aging parent neglected, a child crowded out, a spouse excluded. "How different my life could have been if I'd pursued my education, accepted that promotion, made that investment, relocated, or taken a chance on love." When the door is closed, the person's gone and the opportunity missed, it's time for:

(a) Letting it go. The same cross that cancels your sins of commission, cancels your sins of omission too. Confession, not remorse, brings God's forgiveness and cleansing from "all sin" (See 1Jn 1:9). (b) Renewing your faith in the God of second chances. He can "make up to you for the years that the locust has eaten" (See Joel 2:25). Believe Him; He can place you where you'd be, had the opportunity never been lost. (c) Asking God for a new dream, then "forgetting those things (old, sabotaged dreams) which are behind and reaching forward to those things (new dreams)…which are ahead, press forward," to a life of restored opportunity and fulfillment (See Php 3:13).

BECOME AN "IN EVERYTHING" PRAY-ER!

In everything, by prayer...
present your requests to God.

PHILIPPIANS 4:6 NIV

One Christian author writes: "Often when I pray, I don't talk to God about things that I'm really thinking about because they just don't sound very spiritual. So I'll pray about world peace, or the missionaries, or something like that. But my mind keeps wandering back to what's really on my heart. The solution to this wandering-mind problem is contained in this phrase: 'In everything.' I must pray what is *in* me, not what I *wish* was in me. Praying what's really in my heart is an 'in everything' kind of prayer. I don't wait to clean up my motives or try to sound more spiritual than I am. I pray what's really in me. If you're going to grow in prayer and overcome worry, you must begin by becoming an 'in everything' pray-er. Whether your request is large or small, whether your motives are mixed or pure, whether what you ask is wise or foolish, God can sort it all out. You can trust Him to respond wisely. He's not going to give you something foolishly. But you've got to learn to hold your prayer loosely and trust that if God doesn't answer it the way you want it to be answered, He knows what He's doing; He has very good reasons. It's such a simple thing to go through your day asking God, 'What's the one thing needed that you have for me in this moment?' And when He reveals it to you, you need to do it!" Don't debate, don't rationalize, don't postpone. Whoever you are, whatever your background, starting this moment you can do it. You can become an "in everything" pray-er.

START A TREND!

Jesus...laid aside His garments.

JOHN 13:3-4 NKJV

John records that: "Jesus...rose from supper and laid aside His garments, took a towel and girded Himself...poured water into a basin and began to wash the disciples' feet, and to wipe them with the towel with which He was girded. Then He came to Simon Peter. And Peter said to Him, 'Lord, are You washing my feet?'" (Lk 13:3-6 NKJV).

Jesus didn't wait for His disciples to make the first move, He went first. He taught that in order to serve God you must be willing to lay aside your image, your comfort and your agenda. And He dramatized it in a way His disciples would never forget. By laying aside His garments He showed them God has no time for form or fashion. Real ministry is not image conscious; it's done with a complete loss of distinction. God incarnate clothed Himself in humility. Amazing! But Peter didn't get it. He was embarrassed to think that His Lord would allow Himself to be seen in such demeaning light. So Jesus said, "You call Me Teacher and Lord...If I then, your Lord and Teacher, have washed your feet, you also ought to wash one another's feet. For I have given you an example, that you should do as I have done to you...If you know these things, blessed are you if you do them" (Jn 13:13-17 NKJV). If you want to be blessed, don't join the "spiritual elitists" who are impressed by their own speeches and display their own accomplishments. Lay aside everything you privately glory in and pick up the towel of servant-hood. And don't wait for others. Somebody at your table needs to start a trend. Today let it be you!

WHEN FEELINGS AND FAITH ARE IN CONFLICT

My soul is overwhelmed with sorrow
to the point of death.

MARK 14:34 NIV

Ever hear the words: "You shouldn't feel that way. If you trusted God more you wouldn't be emotionally down and feel like quitting. A good dose of faith and prayer is what you need!" When the bottom falls out of your world well-meaning friends think such words ought to pick you up instantly. But they don't; they can actually make you feel worse. Remember Job's friends?

So, what should we do when we experience these troubling, anxious, discouraging feelings? *(1) Understand that feelings are neither right nor wrong.* Having them doesn't make you un-spiritual and not having them doesn't make you spiritual. They're just human emotions we all have. No one experienced greater emotional pain than Jesus: "My soul is overwhelmed with sorrow to the point of death." He felt like he was going to die on the spot. Such deep feelings threatened His very life! Yet He didn't hide or deny His feelings, or condemn Himself for having them. Denial only amplifies emotion. Jesus openly acknowledged His feelings, processing them in a healthy way. In the throes of anguish, He prayed twice, "Father...Please take this...suffering away from me" (Mk 14:36 NLT). The Father didn't scold or rebuke His plea to avoid His circum-stances or His feelings, and He won't scold or rebuke you either. *(2) Understand that your feelings don't dictate your options or invalidate your choices.* You can have bad feelings and still make good choices! Crushed with grief, Jesus said, "Yet I want your will, not mine" (Mk 14:36 TLB). Choose God's will re-gardless of your feelings and He'll strengthen you to handle the tough times.

DON'T SETTLE FOR LESS

Run in such a way that you...win.

1 CORINTHIANS 9:24 NRS

Have you ever moved into a new house and made a list of all the little jobs you wanted to do, like touching up the paintwork or planting a garden? Chances are, six months later they're still not done and you are okay with it. Complacency is part of the human psyche. Incredible as it may sound, the children of Israel got so used to living in slavery that they were *angry* when Moses wanted to free them. Here is what they said to him: "We hope the Lord will punish...you for making [Pharaoh] and his officials hate us" (Ex 5:21 CEV). When you get so used to living with your problems and hang-ups that you lose your desire to overcome them, the enemy has you exactly where he wants you.

Ever wonder why some of us go on to experience higher heights and deeper depths in our walk with God, while others go in circles or never make it out of the starting gate? That's because the first group *committed* themselves to pursuing God till His presence became a reality in their lives and as a result God honored their commitment. Paul says: "Run in such a way that you...win." If you've grown lukewarm and half-hearted about running the race, God wants to reenergize you and get you back on track. His word says, "Return to Me...and I will return to you" (Zec 1:3 NKJV). In this Scripture God is saying to us, "Turn around. Come back, you'll find me where you left me." Don't settle for less than a living, breathing, walking, talking relationship with the King of Kings Himself, when it's part of your inheritance.

"BEATITUDES FOR PARENTS"

Children...learn...from their parents.

EPHESIANS 5:1 TM

A mathematics teacher who agreed to baby-sit while her friend went shopping, left her this note: "Dried tears eleven times...tied shoelaces fifteen times...blew up balloons, five per child...warned kids not to cross the street twenty-six times...kids insisted on crossing the street twenty-six times. Number of Saturdays I'll volunteer to do this again—Zero!" The following "Beatitudes for Parents" were written forty-five years ago by Marion E. Kinneman when her daughters were raising her six grandsons. They're still spot-on!

Blessed are those who make peace with spilled milk and mud, for of such is the kingdom of childhood. *Blessed* is the parent who engages not in the comparison of his child with others, for precious unto each is the rhythm of his own growth. *Blessed* are those who have learned to laugh, for it's the music of a child's world. *Blessed* and mature are those who without anger can say "No," for comforting to a child is the security of firm decisions. *Blessed* is the gift of consistency, for it brings heart's-ease in childhood. *Blessed* are they who accept the awkwardness of growth, for they are aware of the choice between marred furnishings and damaged personalities. *Blessed* are the teachable, for knowledge brings understanding and understanding brings love. *Blessed* are the men and women, who in the midst of the unpromising mundane, give love, for they bestow the greatest of all gifts to each other, to their children, and—in an ever-widening circle—to their fellowmen." One successful entrepreneur said, "I may be a self-made man, but the blueprints came from my mom and dad." Bottom line: "Children...learn... from their parents." What're you teaching *yours?*

THE SIN OF SLANDER

These things ought not to be so.

JAMES 3:10 NKJV

The Bible says: "With [our tongue] we bless our God...
and with it we curse men...these things are not to be so"
(Jas 3:8-10 NKJV). It displeases God when we praise Him in
church on Sunday then tear someone down at work on Mon-
day. "But what I'm saying is true," you say. "All a man's ways
seem innocent to him, but motives are weighed by the Lord"
(Pr 16:2 NIV). Slander begins with pride; it says, "When I'm
right and you're wrong, I've the right to say so." No, people
flock to church altars for healing from wounds inflicted by
Christians. Gossip broke their spirits. One lady writes: "I went
through a period of trying to overcome gossip but I'd still tell it
to my husband. Although I knew he wouldn't repeat it, I realized that by exposing him to it I was poisoning his spirit. That's
when I decided to change what was coming out of my mouth."

What you say about someone colors how others see them.
One pastor tells all his new members, "If you hear another
member slandering somebody, stop them right away and say,
'Excuse me, who hurt you, ignored or slighted you? We'll pray
together about it so that God can restore peace to this body,
but we won't let you talk about people who aren't around to
defend themselves.'" Ninety-nine times out of a hundred the
issue dies right there—or the offender leaves. "Be...gentle, and
patient, accepting each other in love" (Eph 4:2-3 NCV). Since
none of us are infallible and all of us need to be treated gently,
patiently and with love, let's make it a habit of treating each
other that way.

GOD'S WAY, OR YOURS

He gave them their request,
but sent leanness into their soul.

PSALM 106:15 NKJV

When you insist on wanting something that God in His wisdom is withholding, sometimes He steps back and says, "Okay, have it your way." After God brought His people through the Red Sea and delivered them from the hand of Pharaoh, we read, "They believed His words; they sang His praise" (Ps 106:12 NKJV). That sounds good. But notice what happened next, for it happens to *us:* "They soon forgot His works; they did not wait for His counsel, but lusted exceedingly in the wilderness and tested God in the desert. And He gave them their request, but sent leanness into their soul" (vv. 13-15). Wanting our own way can lead to spiritual emptiness.

When God called Moses to deliver His people from Egypt, Moses decided to do it his own way. He saw an Egyptian beating a Hebrew slave, but instead of consulting God he took matters into his own hands. The Bible says, "He looked this way and that way, and when he saw no one, he killed the Egyptian and hid him in the sand" (Ex 2:12 NKJV). Obviously Moses was more concerned with the opinions of people than how God felt about it. So God had to teach Moses that his orders came from *Him.* After Moses dug a hole and tried to hide the work of his flesh, God allowed it to be exposed. He showed Moses that by doing things his own way he couldn't keep a single soldier buried in the sand. Whereas, by doing things God's way, a whole army could be buried in the depths of the Red Sea. So today, make up your mind to do it God's way.

DEBUNKING MARRIAGE MYTHS (1)

Know the truth,
and the truth shall make you free.

JOHN 8:32

A lot of us are "myth-informed" about love and marriage. The myth of "a perfect marriage" is widespread and dangerous among us. By setting up unrealistic expectations, impossible dreams and magic thinking, it misinforms, misleads and disillusions us, preparing us to walk away the moment our fantasy clashes with reality. Only the truth can make us free to find fulfillment in our marriage. For the next few days let's explore a few of these myths.

Marriage myth 1: *The myth of "viral love,"* insists that love is caught, much like a virus. "Some enchanted evening" when you happen to be in the right place at the right time, it will zap you. You'll "catch the bug" and enter a lifetime of unending bliss! The trouble is, when we're worn out taking care of three kids, two jobs and a second mortgage, the "virus" subsides. In the whirlwind of dishes, diapers and daily routines, something has to give. So romance vacates center stage and reality takes over. When it does, we confuse romance for true love and mistakenly think it has moved out and that we need to follow it. The truth is, love does not die because romance bows to reality. If two people who once "fell" in love are willing to "stand" together in love through the challenges and opportunities of family life, romance can grow again, stronger and more resilient than ever. Love based solely on romance doesn't work when "for better" meets "for worse." Romance based on a decision to love "till death us do part" is the only love that's dependable, consistent and trustworthy. Romance *brings* us together, this kind of love *keeps* us together!

DEBUNKING MARRIAGE MYTHS (2)

Know the truth,
and the truth shall make you free.

JOHN 8:32

Marriage myth 2: *The myth of the "right person,"* suggests happiness in marriage depends entirely on finding the right person. It's said to be a matter of luck, Cupid, the alignment of the stars, the moon hitting your eye like a big pizza pie, etc., occasionally even God. Just find the right person and they'll make your life supremely happy, romantic, excited, fulfilled, blissful. They will become, as the song says, "that old black magic" that holds you in its spell, leading you into the enchanted land of endless love. It's all up to *them.* And nothing ever felt more convincingly real or right! Despite the advice of friends and family, we'll "give away the farm" and turn ourselves inside out to keep this addictive magic happening. When it stops (and it does), three things happen:

(1) We cry, manipulate, bribe, and later blame, vilify and consider them phonies for changing on us and making us miserable. "He's not the man I married," we complain. He may not be the person you *expected* him to be (that person doesn't exist outside your myth) but he *is* the one you married and the problem isn't all *his*. (2) We label him "the wrong person" and either search for the right one or give up on the opposite sex as being false, faithless and fickle. (3) We learn the truth: there is no right person to make us happy always. At that point we're set free to find happiness by *becoming* the right person, the one God created us to be, giving generously, allowing others to be real, limited, changeable humans, and looking to God for our joy!

DEBUNKING MARRIAGE MYTHS (3)

Know the truth,
and the truth shall make you free.

JOHN 8:32

Marriage myth 3: *The myth of "the full box,"* suggests that when we marry we inherit a big box filled with self-replacing good things, guaranteeing effortless unending marital bliss. This box is supposed to contain romance, physical fulfillment, generosity, true love, and being served "in the style to which we've become accustomed." Ideally, we can dip in and take what we want from a never-depleted supply. Instant, low-maintenance satisfaction guaranteed! And it seems to work initially, so we believe the myth. Till one rainy day we dip into the box and come up empty. At that point we feel shock, disappointment, anger, despair and hopelessness and conclude that our partner failed, fooled or forsook us. Why else would the box be empty? At that point the myth suggests, "It's time to find another box!" Or you could listen to the liberating truth:

(a) Marriage *is* a big box, an *empty* one. Your job is to make enough deposits to guarantee sufficient withdrawals for a rich relationship. Jesus said: "The amount you give will determine the amount you get back" (Lk 6:38 NLT). (b) You must start by asking, "*What* would I like to have in the box? Then you deposit that into the box. Then you ask, "How *much* of it do I want in the box? Then you deposit enough to generate that amount. You see, the box is only a container; it didn't fail and you didn't get a bad box. You are the owner of the box, not its victim. Accepting this truth frees you to make your marriage rich and rewarding by becoming a giver, not just a taker!

DEBUNKING MARRIAGE MYTHS (4)

Know the truth,
and the truth shall make you free.

JOHN 8:32

Marriage myth 4: *The myth of the "marriage-go-round,"* says you can hop on and off marriages when you're bored, discontented, stressed out, or get a better offer. Today we're conditioned to instant gratification. If we don't like the rules we'll take our ball to another playground. We're a "disposable" society; whatever doesn't perform satisfactorily will be replaced rather than repaired. Tragically, we transfer this mentality to our relationships and replace the people in our lives who don't play the game our way. Each generation becomes less likely to be tolerant, patient, hard-working, flexible and creative in marriage, and more likely to trade in what they're unwilling to work on. The myth of the marriage-go-round tells us we don't have to grapple with our marital issues. Just replace it!

But the truth reveals that the myth doesn't work. Over 50 percent of first marriages end in divorce, 65 percent of second ones, and better than 70 percent of third ones. Clearly, when it comes to marriage, the more we do it the *worse* we get at it! In fact, with few exceptions, the painful numbers indicate that statistically you have a better chance of finding happiness in your current marriage with all its challenges than if you move on to another one. God's way is your best option. Always! When He says, "[Whom] God hath joined together, let no man put asunder" (Mt 19:6), He intends that in working and growing through the obstacles and opportunities of your marriage, you'll become a better partner and end up building a happier marriage!

KEEP STRIFE OUT OF YOUR LIFE!

Let nothing be done through strife.

PHILIPPIANS 2:3

Strife is defined as "conflict...struggle...rivalry," and God's Word says to avoid it at all cost: "Let nothing be done through strife...but in lowliness of mind let each esteem [the] other better than themselves." Strife is custom-designed to play havoc in marriages, churches, businesses and relationships. It stems from our self-centered ego and leads to comparing, competing and condemning. The Word of God says: "Where envying and strife is, there is...every evil work" (Jas 3:16). Keeping strife out of your life means recognizing and uprooting it *before* it grows; "See...no root of bitterness springing up, causes trouble, and...many be defiled" (Heb 12:15 NAS). And Paul adds, "Complete my joy by living in harmony...being of the same mind...having the same love" (Php 2:2 AMP). Enjoying God's blessings requires doing all we can to live in harmony with one another. Is that easy to do? No, but the sooner you learn it, the better things will be.

When David saw Goliath he didn't stop to consider the odds or listen to the opinions of others. Instead, he "ran quickly toward the battle...to meet him" (1Sa 17:48 NIV). Rapid response is required here. When God prompts you to turn the other cheek or take the short end of the stick, draw on His grace and do it. In fact, when you do it on *your* timetable you end up doing it in your own strength. So: (a) forgive those who hurt you; (b) pray for them; (c) bless them by speaking well of them and wanting only good things for them. Your commitment to walk each day in love and forgiveness (yes, it's a daily commitment!) will open the door to God's blessing in your life.

TAKE CONTROL IN SMALL THINGS

Daniel purposed in his heart.

DANIEL 1:8 NKJV

Daniel was a victim of circumstances far beyond his control. King Nebuchadnezzar had conquered his homeland and carried him off into exile in Babylon. He lost his freedom, his home, his culture, his friendships and his status as one of Israel's nobility. He had to learn to speak a foreign language and live in a place he never wanted to be. If you'd been Daniel, wouldn't you have been tempted to focus on the things you couldn't control, like complaining what a bad leader Nebuchadnezzar was, blaming exile for your unhappiness and feeling sorry for yourself? Not Daniel! He "determined that he would not defile himself by eating the king's food" (See Da 1:8). He spent time thinking about what he most deeply valued and decided to honor God and live by his convictions—even in small things.

Small battles train us to win big ones. If Daniel hadn't taken action early on, he wouldn't have had the strength to say "no" to idol worship and face the lion's den without fear or compromise. Maybe you can't do anything right now about the house you live in or the job you work at, but you can change your life by taking action in small things. Maybe like Daniel it will involve what you eat, what you feed your mind, or what comes out of your mouth. You can refuse to allow your boss or your spouse the power to dictate what kind of mood you'll be in based on how they treat you. Like Daniel, you can choose. When you "purpose in your heart" to honor God, He blesses you and becomes involved in your life in ways you never thought possible.

CONCEPTION, FORMING, PUSHING

Until Christ is formed in you.

GALATIANS 4:19 NKJV

There are three stages to spiritual growth: *(1) Conception:* It results from intimacy between two people. God's love for you is clear and compelling; the question is, how much do you love Him? (See Jn 21:15). *(2) Forming:* Paul writes: "My little children, for whom I labor in birth again until Christ is formed in you" (Gal 4:19 NKJV). God knows the experiences required to produce in us the character of Christ and He'll do whatever it takes to bring it about. *(3) Pushing:* When you commit to bringing forth what God has placed within you, you'll have to push against everything everybody ever did to you or said about you. Now God will help you to bring it out, but it's up to you to push. In fact, it may not happen if you don't. You'll have to push against satanic attacks in all their debilitating forms such as bad memories, low self-esteem and feelings of worthlessness. The Devil may have spent years pushing you aside, pulling you back and putting you down, but today God is saying to you, "I want to open you up, I want to empower you to give birth to what I've placed within you."

When a baby is born everything in the family changes. The same is true for you. When you give birth to what God's placed within you, everything in your life will be affected. God's blessing is an overflowing blessing that will touch every area of your existence. A mother knows when she's pregnant; the same is true in the spiritual realm. So don't fail to give birth to what God has put within you. Now is the time for you to bring it forth!

DON'T GET "HOOKED" BY YOUR TEENAGER

Be clear minded and self-controlled.

1 PETER 4:7 NIV

Teenagers can test your sanity. They're neither adult nor child, and can become either without notice. Flooding hormones and exploding neurons spark biochemical reactions in their heads and bodies. Words like, "What in the world were you thinking?" form involuntarily on your lips. In response come sullen teenage shrugs, followed by the incomprehensible, "I don't know." And they don't! What can you do? "Lock them up?" Sorry, that's illegal. But here are two things that will help. *(1) Back off and slow down.* "Be clear minded and self-controlled." One of the biggest mistakes parents make is over-reacting, which triggers an escalating battle of wills you're unlikely to win. Decibel levels rise, wisdom fails, your teen concludes you're the crazy one, and suddenly there's no adult present and nobody's "minding the store." You've become part of the problem, leaving your child angry and insecure, without a rational role model. Pray, breathe deeply and count to ten! For your child's sake, it's time for the clear minded and self-controlled parent to prevail. *(2) Remember, anger begets anger.* "An angry person starts fights; a hot-tempered person commits all kinds of sin" (Pr 29:22 NLT). No one can infuriate you like a teenager trying to grow up. A look, a word, an attitude, and you're "hooked;" you're in a shouting match with your own child. How crazy is that? Emotionally charged exchanges hard wire your teenager's brain for automatic, long-term anger reactions. What's the answer? Use the carrot and stick approach of Scripture: "Provoke not your children to wrath: but bring them up in the nurture [love and encouragement] and admonition [character building discipline] of the Lord" (Eph 6:4).

STAND UP STRAIGHT!

She could stand straight.

LUKE 13:13 NLT

The ability to stand up straight and hold your head high has less to do with the color of your skin and more to do with the contents of your heart. "But my ancestors came to America on the Mayflower," you say. That's impressive, but "there is neither slave nor free...you are all one in Christ." In God's kingdom social status doesn't count. And gender doesn't either; "there is neither male nor female...you are all one in Christ" (Gal 3:28 NKJV). And your moral background doesn't either. Rahab was a harlot until she exercised faith in God's Word. Once that happened she never returned to her old profession. In fact, she's mentioned alongside Sarah, Abraham's wife, because she believed God and was blessed (See Heb 11:31). *Faith in Christ* creates true equality; when you have it you can walk with your head high in spite of your past. It doesn't matter what people say; what God says about you—and what you believe about yourself—are what matter.

Luke records: "One Sabbath day as Jesus was teaching in a synagogue, he saw a woman who had been crippled by an evil spirit. She had been bent double for eighteen years and was unable to stand up straight. When Jesus saw her, he called her over and said, 'Dear woman, you are healed of your sickness!' Then he touched her, and instantly she could stand [up] straight" (Lk 13:10-13 NLT). When you commit your life to Christ He will change you. He will deal with that thing which has crippled you spiritually, mentally and emotionally, and cause you to stand up straight.

PRAYER IS—AMAZING!

Through faith...we may approach God
with freedom and confidence.

EPHESIANS 3:12 NIV

One Bible teacher writes: "I read an interesting book by an unbeliever who attempted to 'do in' the Christian faith. Despite his lack of belief, I found insightful something he said regarding prayer. He called it 'the most incredible conceit in the history of humankind,' arguing that if you worked for General Motors as a lowly employee and wanted to see the boss, you wouldn't have the remotest chance...Think about it. What would happen if a citizen tried to speak to the President of the United States? I've thought about putting in a person-to-person call just to see what would happen. I'd probably speak to an undersecretary to an assistant to somebody, but not likely the President...'And so,' says my skeptical friend in his book, 'what an incredible conceit to suppose that at any moment we can talk to the boss of 'the whole shebang.' And indeed the concept of prayer *would* be an incredible conceit...if it weren't true. But it is...and it's the most incredible condescension on the part of a gracious God. You could probably never speak to the highly placed people in this world, yet the most highly placed Person in the universe—'the Boss of the whole shebang'—waits patiently to hear what you have to say. 'We can come before God with freedom and without fear...through faith in Christ' (NCV). Don't you find that amazing? This day and every day you have the great privilege of prayer. You can talk to the Boss, tell Him your worries and cares, share with Him your triumphs and joys—and He *always* has time to listen." Prayer is—amazing!

STICK TO WHAT YOU KNOW!

Who are you to judge someone else's servant?

ROMANS 14:4 NIV

Our brain doesn't like blank spaces, so when it encounters questions without answers it searches for something to put in the blank spaces. And because we're driven by our own perceptions, needs and prejudices, we're not always objective. We're blind to our blind spots and think we "know," and the results can be disastrous for our relationships. "I know what your real intentions are. You think I don't know what's going on in that head of yours? I can tell by the look on your face exactly what you're thinking." Such words indicate we've got the other person "pegged," and feel no need to consider the situation further because we couldn't possibly be wrong. Case closed. What about such Scriptures as, "He who answers a matter before he hears the facts—it is a folly and shame to him" (Pr 18:13 AMP). Or, "Be quick to hear, slow to speak" (Jas 1:19 NAS). Or, "Even a fool is counted wise when he holds his peace; when he shuts his lips, he is considered perceptive" (Pr 17:28 NKJV).

Before you "sound off," consider three things: (1) "No one can know a person's thoughts except that person's own spirit" (1Co 2:11 NLT). You may suspect, guess, even feel strongly, but you don't know their thoughts or intentions. (2) "Who art thou that judgest another man's servant?" (Ro 14:4). Much of our "knowing," is merely our own judgmental spin on things. (3) If you think you know and need to deal with the issue, try saying, "I have some impressions (concerns, observations, etc.) I'd like to talk about." Then discuss your observations, feelings and impressions as *your perceptions,* not "gospel truth," leaving judgment to God.

GOD WILL BRING YOU THROUGH

The God of all comfort.

2 CORINTHIANS 1:3 NIV

God can bring you through situations you think you won't survive, or feel you'll be stuck in forever. He can make you comfortable in the most uncomfortable places, and give you peace in the midst of trauma. Before your life is over you'll live, love, and experience loss. Losing some things will actually help you to appreciate the things you still have. It's the taste of failure that makes success sweet. You'll live each day not knowing what tomorrow holds, but confident that God has your tomorrows all planned out. They're not in the hands of your boss or your banker or your mate or anybody else. Nor are they in your own hands to manipulate and control. No, all your tomorrows are in God's hands.

Just because you don't recognize the path you're on doesn't mean that God's not leading you. He promises, "I will lead them in paths they have not known. I will make darkness light before them, and crooked places straight. These things I will do for them, and not forsake them" (Isa 42:16 NKJV). So get to know God—you'll need Him. And He'll be there for you. He'll be there when everybody and everything else has failed you. He'll be there for you in the dark places. "Weeping may endure for a night, but joy comes in the morning" (Ps 30:5 NKJV). However long the night, morning always comes, and with it His joy. As you look back you'll realize that His grace protected you, provided for you, secured you, calmed you, comforted you and brought you through. Times and seasons change, but not God. He's always "the God of all comfort."

BE OPEN TO CHANGE—AND PURSUE IT!

Let patience have its perfect work.

JAMES 1:3 NKJV

A letter was returned to the Post Office. Handwritten on the envelope were the words, "He's dead." Through an oversight the letter was inadvertently sent to the same address again. Again it was returned to the Post Office with yet another message: "He's still dead!" Let's be honest; most of us resist change. We desire improvement, but we don't want to pay the price for it. And that's a problem, because we will never become what God intends us to be by remaining what we are. It's not enough to be *open* to change, we need to *pursue* it.

If you're serious about changing your life, Dr. John Maxwell says: "Don't just change enough to get away from your problems—change enough to *solve* them. Don't change your circumstances to improve your life—change *yourself* to improve your circumstances. Don't do the same old things expecting different results—get different results by doing something *new*. Don't see change as something hurtful that must be done—see it as something helpful that *can* be done. Don't avoid paying the immediate price tag of change—if you do, you will pay the *ultimate* price of never improving." James writes: "When your faith is tested, your endurance has a chance to grow. So let it grow, for when your endurance is fully developed, you will be perfect and complete, needing nothing" (Jas 1:3-4 NLT). Character building is a slow process; it happens day-by-day. Whenever we try to escape life's difficulties we short-circuit the process, delay our growth, and end up with a worse kind of pain—the worthless type that accompanies denial and avoidance. So, be open to change—and pursue it!

WHEN YOU DON'T GET WHAT YOU WANT (1)

Grow in grace.

2 PETER 3:18

Psychologist Henry Cloud does a lot of corporate consulting. Sometimes he asks executives this question: "When in your business training or education, did you ever take a course on how to lose well?" Losing is an inevitable part of life. It gives us an invaluable window into the development of our character. How do we do when we're part of a team that makes a decision that's opposed? How do we handle it when the promotion we applied for, goes to somebody else? How do we do when our idea, proposal, or invitation for a date gets rejected? To live is to lose. But to lose badly, gracelessly, can be lethal.

The president of an organization has an agenda for change that is dead in the water. No one wants it. But he's stubborn and won't take no for an answer, so he gets malicious compliance instead. People don't resist him openly, but they sabotage his agenda. He loses their respect and their loyalty. He could not stand to lose on his agenda, so instead, he loses what matters far more.

A pastor wants his church to change in ways that the people don't embrace. He wants it to look like *his* ideal of what a church should be. So he preaches angry sermons that chastise them for not following his leadership. He tries to pressure the elders. He threatens, he whines, he manipulates. Eventually the elders ask him to leave the church. Because he cannot learn from his losses, he loses everything. Peter, who was known for being bull-headed, had grown wiser and more mature, so he writes, "Grow in grace." When you don't get what you want— be gracious!

WHEN YOU DON'T GET WHAT YOU WANT (2)

Grow in grace.

2 PETER 3:18

Samuel and Susanna Wesley (John Wesley's parents) were at evening prayer one night when Susanna didn't say "amen" to her husband's prayer for William of Orange, then King of England. When he asked her why, she explained that her sympathy lay with the deposed James the Second. It turned into a game of "you do what I say" which he couldn't win. She wrote about what happened next: "He immediately kneeled down and invoked the divine vengeance upon himself and all his posterity if he ever touched me again or came to bed with me before I had begged God's pardon, and his, for not saying amen to a prayer for the king." The stalemate lasted six months and was broken only when a tragic fire destroyed two-thirds of their home.

People who cling to resentments, who don't know how to handle disappointment with grace, who have long memories, who choke on the words, "I'm sorry," or who sulk and pout and whine, always finish up on the short end of the stick. Losing well is an art that requires all the grace we can muster. It means having the humility to face reality with no excuses, but with the confidence not to allow losing to define our identity or make us feel "less than." It means no excuses, no blaming, no self-pity— but no self-condemnation either. It means having the discernment to know when to quit and when to persevere. It means learning how to say "congratulations." It means letting go of an outcome we cannot change, but holding on to the will to live fully and well, and seeking to glorify God in all that we do.

WHEN YOU DON'T GET WHAT YOU WANT (3)

Grow in grace.

2 PETER 3:18

Winning gracefully can be harder than losing gracefully. When we win we're tempted by arrogance, power, insensitivity, gloating, and wanting to relive our success long after everyone else is bored by it. Gracious winners always remember what it feels like to lose. They are caught up in something bigger than their own wins and losses.

Abraham Lincoln had the wisdom to place the good of the country above his own ego, appointing his worst political critic, Edwin Stanton, to run the War Department. Stanton, a brilliant legal mind, could be brusque and condescending. As Frederick Douglass put it, "Politeness was not one of his weaknesses." Lincoln, on the other hand, was keenly aware of his looks and his uneducated background. (When someone charged him with being two-faced during a campaign, he responded: "If I had two faces, do you think I'd be wearing *this* one?"). As outgoing attorney general of the losing party, Stanton had belittled Lincoln as "the original gorilla." How Lincoln treated Stanton is Civil War history. Lincoln trusted in him, confided in him, leaned on him, depended on him. And Stanton responded with unfailing loyalty and affection. On the morning of April 14, 1865, Abraham Lincoln died after having been shot the night before at Ford's Theatre. The most famous words ever spoken after the death of a president were spoken that morning: "Now he belongs to the ages." The speaker was Edwin Stanton. Robert Lincoln, Abraham Lincoln's son, said that after his father died he was visited in his room each morning for two weeks by Stanton who "Spent the first ten minutes of his visits weeping without saying a word." When nothing else works, showing grace does!

DON'T LOSE YOUR PEACE

You will keep him in perfect peace,
whose mind is stayed on You.
ISAIAH 26:3 NKJV

One of the greatest promises in the Bible is, "You will keep him in perfect peace, whose mind is stayed on You, because he trusts in You." Who are you trusting to solve the problem, God or yourself? You need to live by the principle "Do your best, then let God do the rest." Too many of us have the idea that it's wrong to enjoy ourselves while we have problems. We grow up believing that if we can't do anything else, the least we can do is worry, act stressed out and be miserable. The Bible addresses this: "Do not [for a moment] be frightened…for such [constancy and fearlessness] will be a clear sign…from God" (Php 1:28 AMP). This Scripture teaches us that when adversity comes (and it will) we must stay in peace. Satan doesn't know what to do with us when he can't get us upset; we've taken a powerful weapon out of his hands. "For such [constancy and fearlessness] will be a…sign…from God." Keeping your peace doesn't exempt you from life's difficulties, it just allows God to have the last word. By trusting Him completely you are no longer at the mercy of circumstances, other people, or your own emotions and limitations.

Somebody quipped, "In times like these it's helpful to remember that there have *always* been times like these." The question is not will trouble come, but how will you handle it? The writer to the Hebrews says, "We which have believed do enter into rest" (Heb 4:3). When things go wrong—do what God leads you to do, then rest in Him and watch Him work on your behalf!

THINKING ABOUT CUTTING CORNERS? (1)

Set an example...in life.

1 TIMOTHY 4:12 NIV

Writer Kathryn Lay learned about honesty when she was vacationing in Texas. She and her husband were having lunch at a little restaurant when a lady walked in, handed her a dollar bill and said, "I'm sorry, but I short-changed you earlier." Recognizing her as a sales assistant from a store she'd been in earlier Lay asked, "How'd you know I was here?" Amazed, she learned that the woman had gone from store to store looking for her. Lay also tells about another man who returned a TV to the store and got his money back. Later, after realizing the amount had also been credited to his Visa he did nothing. Lay writes: "Does God want us to be just a little honest...or only in certain situations...or only when someone's looking? How much dishonesty is too much? Sometimes I'm the only person who knows whether I'm being honest or not. Do I keep the extra change, cheat on my taxes, ignore the double credit on my statement? Do I tell my daughter a white lie is still a lie, but later tell the police officer my accelerator stuck? When did honesty become an endangered species? Somewhere out there is a man who's proud of the $700 he cheated a department store. He probably laughs about it with everyone, including his daughter. And somewhere in Texas there's a truly honest woman, whose story I rejoice in sharing with *my* daughter."

Dostoyevsky said, "When we lie we lose respect for ourselves and for others. And when we've no respect for anyone we end up yielding to our impulses and indulging in the lowest forms of pleasure." So, "Be an example...in the way you live" (1Ti 4:12 NLT).

THINKING ABOUT CUTTING CORNERS? (2)

Set an example...in life.

1 TIMOTHY 4:12 NIV

In 1994 golfer Davis Love III called a one-stroke penalty on himself during the second round of the Western Open. He moved his marker to get it out of another player's putting line and later he couldn't remember if he'd moved his ball back to its original spot. Since he wasn't certain he gave himself an extra stroke, and that one stroke caused him to miss the cut. He was eliminated from the tournament. (Ironically, if he'd made the cut, even if he finished last he'd have earned $2,000 that week). At year's end Love was $590 short in winnings to automatically qualify for the Masters and needed to win a tournament in order to get into one of golf's most coveted events. Fortunately, the story ends well. The week before the big event he qualified by winning a tournament in New Orleans, and went on to earn $237,600 by finishing second in the 1995 Masters. Later when Love was asked how he'd have felt if he'd missed the Masters because of calling a penalty on himself, he replied, "The real question is how I'd have felt if I'd won and spent the rest of my life wondering if I'd cheated."

It's easier to maintain your integrity than to try and recover it. Paul instructed Timothy: "In everything set...an example by doing what is good...show integrity...and soundness of speech that cannot be condemned, so that those who oppose you may be ashamed because they have nothing bad to say" (Tit 2:7-8 NIV). It may cost you to do the right thing, but it'll cost you more when you abandon your principles and do the wrong thing.

UNANSWERED PRAYERS

You ask but do not receive.

JAMES 4:3 NKJV

Pastor Jerry Sittser writes: "What would happen if all our prayers were answered? I thought about my early years when I was ready to conquer the world, with or without Christ. The group I led grew, I was riding a wave of success, everything I touched turned to gold. Eventually the ministry leveled off and lost momentum. Thank God it did...I'd become insufferably proud, a self-appointed expert. What would've happened if my prayers had been answered, our group had continued to grow and our program had continued to receive recognition?"

James says, "You ask but do not receive, because you ask with wrong motives." There are certain prayers God won't answer for your own good. Sittser continues: "Your cause may be right, but you may still be wrong—manifesting pride, gloating in victory, punishing wrongdoers with excessive severity and excusing sin. The great hazard for people on a crusade is...they become blind to their own faults. They fight for civil rights but treat...janitors like second-class citizens. They uphold standards of biblical sexuality, but show little grace towards their spouse. Unanswered prayer is God's gift...it protects us from ourselves. If all our prayers were answered we'd abuse the power...use prayer to change the world to our liking, and it would become hell on earth. Like spoiled children with too many toys and too much money, we'd grab for more. We'd pray for victory at the expense of others...intoxicated by power ...we'd hurt people and exalt ourselves. Isaiah said, 'The Lord longs to be gracious to you...therefore He *waits*' (Isa 30:18 NAS). Unanswered prayer protects...breaks...deepens...and transforms. Past unanswered prayers which left us hurt and disillusioned, act like a refiner's fire to prepare us for future answers."

STAY IN FORMATION!

Let us not give up meeting together.

HEBREWS 10:25 NIV

Ever wonder why geese in the Fall fly in a "V" formation and not just randomly? Remember that old United Airlines ad, "Fly the friendly skies of United"? Geese know that to complete the long trip south, they have to fly united. Scientists tell us that flying in formation increases their flight range by 71 percent. Airwaves created each time a bird flaps its wings provide an uplift for the next one in formation, supporting it, decreasing its work load and conserving its energy. A solo goose could never complete the trip, but in formation the youngest, the oldest, and even the weakest get there. In other words, they do collectively what they could never do alone.

When God said, "Let us not give up meeting together, as some are in the habit of doing, but let us encourage one another," He was saying, "Stay in formation, children! Enjoy the uplift!" You weren't designed to fly solo no matter what your rank, calling, gifting, or maturity level. You're a part of the body of Christ, created to function in concert with all the other parts. "The eye cannot say to the hand, 'I don't need you!' And the head cannot say to the feet, 'I don't need you!'" (1Co 12:21 NIV). Occasionally a goose, disoriented or over-confident, goes on autopilot and finds itself adrift. Soon, however, its wings become heavy from exhaustion and it loses altitude. It begins to feel the drag of increasing wind resistance, and it pulls its weakened body back into formation alongside its feathered fellow pilgrims. Jesus said, "Look at the birds" (Mt 6:26 NIV). So get back in formation (and fellowship) and stay there!

BE EXTRAVAGANT

She has shown me much love.

LUKE 7:47 NLT

Luke writes, "One of the Pharisees asked Jesus to have dinner with him, so Jesus went to his home...a certain immoral woman...heard he was...there [and]...brought a beautiful alabaster jar filled with expensive perfume. Then she knelt... at his feet, weeping...she kept kissing his feet and putting perfume on them" (Lk 7:36-38 NLT). Some of us, who have been hurt by religion, wouldn't consider eating dinner with a Pharisee. And some of us are so religious we don't know how to reach out to a real sinner. But not Jesus. He accepted the invitation of the Pharisee, and extended grace to the sinner. And we must do the same. Jesus said, "Her sins—and they are many—have been forgiven, so she has shown me much love. But a person who is forgiven little shows only little love."

There are three important lessons here: *(1) Others may know what you've done, but Jesus knows what you can become.* Simon the Pharisee saw this woman as a weed. Jesus saw her as a potential rose and watered it. *(2) Remembering what God saved you from, will make you extravagant in your love and your giving.* Look at her, anointing His feet with expensive ointment. When you fall in love with Christ the first thing He opens is your heart, the next is your pocketbook. You begin to look for opportunities to give to His kingdom. *(3) Don't be afraid to show your emotions.* Some of us are traditional "Be still and know that I am God" people. Others are "Shout to the Lord" people. Be what you are, but be extravagant in your love for Jesus!

BULLDOGS AND POODLES

Draw near to God and He will draw near to you.

JAMES 4:8 NKJV

The story's told of a bulldog and a poodle who were arguing one day. The bulldog was making fun of the poodle, calling him a weak little runt who couldn't do anything. The bulldog said, "I challenge you to a contest. Let's see who can open the back door of their house the fastest and get inside." The bulldog was thinking he would turn the doorknob with his powerful jaws, while the poodle was too small to even reach the knob of his back door. But to the bulldog's surprise the poodle said, "I can get inside my house faster than you can. I accept the challenge." So with the poodle watching, the bulldog ran to the back door of his house and jumped up to the doorknob. He got his teeth and paws around it and tried to turn it, but he couldn't get enough grip on the knob to do it, so he finally quit in exhaustion. Now it was the poodle's turn. He just did what he'd been doing every day for the last several years. He went up to the door and scratched a couple of times, then waited patiently. Within a few seconds his master not only opened the door, but picked him up in his arms, patted him on the head affectionately and carried him inside.

The difference was in the *relationship*. Some of us are bulldog Christians. It's all grunting, growling and working to try and please God. Give it up! All God asks us to do is, "Draw near to Me and I will draw near to you."

GOD NEVER GIVES UP ON YOU

You have laid your hand upon me.

PSALM 139:5 NIV

A London bus driver was assigned to shuttle passengers to special crusade services with Billy Graham at Wembley Stadium. When one of them invited him in to listen he declined. The following year he moved to New York, and when Billy was speaking at Madison Square Garden the man's job again was shuttling people to the meetings. As he got off the bus a lady asked if he'd like to join them. Once more he politely declined. He married an Australian lady and eventually ended up working in Sydney, where surprisingly, he was again assigned to drive people to the stadium where Billy was preaching. This time when he was invited he figured there was no escape, so he gave in. Looking back he says, "No matter where I went I was confronted with Billy Graham, so I went to hear him and committed my life to Christ. It was the best decision I ever made."

The Psalmist said, "You hem me in…you have laid your hand upon me…Where can I go from your Spirit? Where can I flee from your presence? If I go up to the heavens, you are there …in the depths, you are there…on the far side of the sea… your hand will…hold me fast" (Ps 139:5-10 NIV). Isn't grace amazing? Peter said, "God is patient…he wants everyone to turn from sin and no one to be lost" (2Pe 3:9 CEV). God will follow you to the ends of the earth to give you another opportunity to surrender your life to Him. How many opportunities has He already given *you?* Isn't it time you stopped running and surrendered your life to Him?

WHEN THERE'S NO LOGICAL EXPLANATION

[God] rides across the skies to...help us.

DEUTERONOMY 33:26 CEV

When Steve Anderson's mother-in-law developed cancer, his wife flew out to see her. Steve wanted to go too, but money was tight, so he prayed and his friend Joe offered to fly him in his two-seater Cessna airplane. Approaching their destination, they encountered thick fog, and after contacting the tower they learned that the airport was closed. The controller recommended they turn back, but fuel was low, so Steve prayed again. Finally a voice said, "Okay, we're readying the ground crew. Come in on emergency landing." Then as they descended the controller shouted, "Pull it up! Pull it up!" Through a break in the fog they saw that instead of approaching the airport they were over a busy highway and had narrowly missed an overpass! The controller continued, "Listen to me and I'll get you down," and calmly issued instructions till they landed safely. Picking up the radio, Joe told the tower, "We'd never have made it without you. Thanks, you saved our lives." The controller replied, "What're you talking about? We lost contact with you right after we told you to turn back. In fact, we were stunned when you broke through the clouds over the runway for a perfect landing!"

So, if the controller didn't guide them in, *who* did? There's no natural explanation, but on a supernatural level, "[God]... rides across the skies to...help us...he carries us in his arms!" The Psalmist wrote, "God will command his angels to protect you wherever you go" (Ps 91:11 CEV). Steve Anderson agrees, "I believe God sent an angel to bring us in safely." *And He'll do the same for you!*

IN THE SHADOW!

In the shadow of his hand he hid me.

ISAIAH 49:2 NIV

Isaiah says three notable things about how God works in our lives: *(1) "In the shadow of his hand he hid me."* Before Elijah called down fire from heaven at Mount Carmel, God instructed him to go and hide himself at the brook Cherith where he would be supernaturally fed and strengthened (See 1Ki 17:3). Before every "showing" there's a "hiding." God gets us alone and does a work in us that cannot be accomplished any other way. *(2) "He made me into a polished arrow...concealed...in his quiver."* The archer takes a rough tree branch, cuts it down and makes it into a highly polished arrow capable of hitting the mark. Next, he puts it into his quiver. What a wonderful place to be, tied securely to Him, within easy reach when the moment to use you comes. Such words make us think differently about being in the shadow, don't they? *(3) "You are my servant...in whom I will display my splendor."* After visiting the Balkans, Canadian reporter James Creelman wrote, "I learned that the world's supply of rose oil comes from the Balkan Mountains. The thing that interested me was that the roses had to be gathered during the darkest hours. Initially this seemed to be a relic of superstition. But as I investigated I learned that a full 40 percent of the fragrance disappears in the light of day." Without speaking a word, your life gives off an aroma. Through your influence, others are lowered or lifted. Do you want to have impact? Embrace the shadows, discover God and grow in them, then emerge with something to say that's worth listening to!

BILLY

God chose things the world considers foolish.

1 CORINTHIANS 1:27 NLT

Writing about his time as a counselor at a teen Bible camp, Tony Campolo says, "Teenage boys have a tendency to pick on some unfortunate kid. That summer it was thirteen-year-old Billy, a kid who couldn't walk or talk right. When the kids from his cabin were assigned to lead devotions, they voted Billy in as the speaker. It didn't seem to bother him. He dragged himself up to the pulpit amid sneers and snickers, and it took him a long time to stammer, 'Je–sus loves...me... and...I...love Je–sus.' There was stunned silence, and when I looked around there were boys with tears streaming down their cheeks. We'd done many things to try to reach these boys, but nothing had worked. We'd even brought in famous baseball players whose batting averages had gone up since they started praying, but it had no effect. It wasn't until a special needs kid declared his love for Christ that everything changed. I travel a lot and it's surprising how often I meet people who say, 'You probably don't remember me. I became a Christian at a camp where you were a counselor, and do you know what the turning point was for me?' I never have to ask. I always know I'm going to hear—*Billy!*"

The Bible says, "God chose things the world considers foolish in order to shame those who think they are wise." So when you find yourself focusing on what you *can't* do, remember His "power works best in [your] weakness" (2Co 12:9 NLT). Just do what you *can,* and God will do the rest! He'll crown your efforts with success.

CHEERFUL GIVING OR FEARFUL GIVING?

God loves a cheerful giver.

2 CORINTHIANS 9:7 NIV

The Bible says, "Whoever sows generously will also reap generously. Each man should give what he has decided in his heart to give, not reluctantly or under compulsion, for God loves a cheerful giver. And God is able to make all grace abound to you, so that in all things at all times, having all that you need, you will abound in every good work...You will be made rich in every way so that you can be generous on every occasion" (2Co 9:6-11 NIV).

Are you a cheerful giver or a fearful giver? It's not that we're greedy or opposed to supporting God's work, we're just concerned that if we don't look out for our own interests, they might not get looked out for at all. But such fear is irrational! It's like a farmer, who, out of fear of losing his seed, refuses to plant his fields. Don't hoard the seed God intends to be sown, for the harvest He wants you to have. God's promise to you is, "If you sow generously you'll reap generously." When you make giving to God your first priority, you don't have to fear. Jesus said, "Put God's work first and do what he wants. Then the other things will be yours as well" (Mt 6:33 CEV). When you strive to be a faithful conduit for His kingdom, God promises to "increase your store of seed." And it gets better: "You will be made rich in every way." When you partner with God, He rewards you abundantly for every good deed.

When you view your money from God's perspective, the thing to fear isn't giving away too *much*, but sowing too *little!*

HEALING WOUNDED RELATIONSHIPS (1)

*He heals the brokenhearted and
binds up their wounds.*

PSALM 147:3 NIV

It happens every day. Maybe it's happening right now in your once-happy home: unrealistic expectations, infidelity and broken promises destroying the dream of life-long love and trust. Thankfully, God is the Healer of broken relationships and violated trust. When someone you love is hurting:
(1) *Give it time.* Healing is a process, not an event. Wounds of the heart heal slowly. Maybe you're thinking, "But I've apologized over and over. How long will it take them to let it go and start trusting me again?" It takes as long as it takes! Demanding the other person to heal on your schedule only delays the process. "But if they really forgave me they wouldn't keep bringing it up." Not so. When your loved one can bring it up without your getting upset, healing will happen faster. *(2) Don't expect things to be normal for now.* They won't be—and that's normal! Ever notice how you automatically protect an injured limb against knocks and bumps? It's a natural, instinctive reaction. The fact is, the one who caused the pain may be ready for business as usual, but for the wounded, "normal" feels way too vulnerable right now. By lowering your expectations and giving them space, you'll hasten and promote the healing process. *(3) Remember, people heal at different rates.* God said, "There is a time...to weep...a time to laugh...a time to embrace and a time to refrain" (Ecc 3:4-5 NIV). Be sensitive. Let God teach you patience and growth as you give your loved one time to heal.

HEALING WOUNDED RELATIONSHIPS (2)

I have heard your prayer
and seen your tears; I will heal you.

2 KINGS 20:5 NIV

Just sitting waiting for healing to happen doesn't help; it only lengthens the process. Working to become a positive influence is what moves things forward. If you want to help: *Listen.* When your loved one needs to talk, listen without trying to defend, explain, rationalize or excuse your behavior. Don't try to correct their "misperceptions" or lessen their pain by minimizing it. *Validate.* Don't tell somebody, "You shouldn't feel that way." When people talk about their pain, often they're doing the work necessary to help them heal. By letting them know their feelings are legitimate rather than making them feel weak or silly, you enable them to work through the negative emotions. *Apologize.* Yes, again! Whoever said, "Love means never having to say you're sorry," didn't know much about human relationships. Every genuine apology promotes healing. A heartfelt "I'm so sorry" is medicine to a wounded soul. So apply it till it's no longer needed—and your loved one will let you know when that is. *Repair.* Offer to help repair the hurt you've caused. "I know I've wounded you, and I really want to know what I can do to help heal the damage." Genuinely spoken, those words realign and make you part of the solution, not just the cause of the problem.

God said, "I have heard your prayers and seen your tears; I will heal you," and the sooner you become actively engaged in promoting the healing process, the sooner you'll get out of the penalty box and back on the field.

HEALING WOUNDED RELATIONSHIPS (3)

I will restore.

JEREMIAH 30:17 NIV

There are no painless, foolproof guarantees; healing a relationship involves shared effort and risk. I have to trust that ultimately *you'll* forgive me and put the offense behind you, and you have to believe that *I'm* sincere about changing. Healing wounded relationships is a two-person job. Your job is to work at trusting me again, and mine is to provide you with evidence that I'm trustworthy. When we do that we invite one another's cooperation, encourage each other and shorten the distance that separates us. Making a relationship work means deciding you have real and positive options, and both partners committing to them.

If your betrayal caused the wounds, you can make your own job easier by becoming more accountable. By voluntarily keeping your partner in the loop about your schedule, without their having to quiz you, you graduate from being the bad guy to becoming a full-fledged team member, pursuing a mutual game plan so you can both win. By agreeing to self-police you also remove the resentment one partner feels when the other one monitors them. In other words, it relieves them of the dirty work of micromanaging you, and spares you the humiliation of feeling like you're always under the microscope.

On the other hand, if you are the wounded party you can make your mate's job easier by letting them know you value the relationship enough to make it work by keeping up your end. Tell them you appreciate their efforts. When healing a relationship becomes the main focus of both partners, and you include God, who said, "I will restore," it will happen!

HEALING WOUNDED RELATIONSHIPS (4)

I will heal my people and let them enjoy...
peace and security.

JEREMIAH 33:6 NIV

The "surgery" stage of confession and apology can happen quickly. The more complex "recovery" stage of forgiveness, healing and restoration takes time. Remember the last time you took your car to the mechanic? You brought it in for one problem and he found others you weren't aware of that needed attention. In the same way, the healing process brings into focus issues related to the original one: communication, finances, time, parenting, and intimacy issues. If you want a healthy relationship there are no shortcuts; you have to deal with them. If you try to cheat the process, your unfinished business will keep undermining your hopes for a whole and happy relationship. So if you haven't already guessed it, restoration work isn't for the cowardly or lazy. But the rewards are well worth it, so roll up your sleeves!

Reinforce each other's efforts. God said, "Render...honour to whom honour is due" (Ro 13:7) because it's a principle that works. We routinely thank the waiter, the taxi driver and the checkout clerk. It's an ingrained, invaluable courtesy—and one we'd do well to take home. People working on relationships need the healing power that comes from regular doses of courtesy. You'd be amazed at the restorative mileage you get from simply expressing your appreciation. The "principle of reinforcement" says you get more of what you acknowledge, so remember to thank your partner for even the smallest effort to improve things. Not only will you be honoring them, you'll be inviting more of the same, and making interest-bearing deposits in your relationship account.

HEALING WOUNDED RELATIONSHIPS (5)

He has sent me to bind up the brokenhearted.

ISAIAH 61:1 NAS

When you violate your partner's trust, you send your "relationship account" into deficit! Intimacy is replaced by painful emotional and physical distance. As the offender, you feel that, in spite of your apology and repentance, your wounded partner is still exacting their pound of flesh and making you pay. But they are not! They are simply out of surplus emotional resources. Their tank is empty. It's taking all they have just to "keep it together." Expecting them to be their old self is like asking a legless man to hurry up and walk! It's not going to happen.

What can you do to help? The same thing you do when you have a deficit in your bank account. *(1) Stop making withdrawals!* Don't ask or expect from your partner all they normally do for you. Don't wait to be served. Pick up your dirty dishes. Iron your own clothes. Surrender your sense of entitlement. Practice the Christ-like art of denying yourself. For now, lean on God and your Christian friends and family to help meet your temporarily unmet needs. *(2) Start making deposits!* Make them small and often. "If you give, you will get! Your gift will return to you...pressed down, shaken together...running over" (Lk 6:38 TLB). Consistent deposits can eventually cancel the deficit, moving the relationship into surplus! Quietly find ways to make your partner's life easier: small courtesies, thoughtful deeds, little considerations that serve and salve. These are the things that invite your partner to feel like it's safe to push "defrost," start taking small risks, reconnect, and test the waters again!

CHOICES

Choose for yourselves.

JOSHUA 24:15 NIV

Our lives are like icebergs. Only 15 percent is visible; that's reputation. The rest, our character, is below the surface, hidden. Character is what we think but never share. It's what we do when no one's watching. It's how we react to everyday aggravations. It's how we handle failure—and success. The thing that has made us what we are is our *choices*. At the end of a successful career, Joshua challenges the people of Israel: "Choose for yourselves this day whom you will serve...But as for me and my household, we will serve the Lord." So the choice is yours!

French writer François de la Rochefoucauld asserted, "Almost all our faults are more pardonable than the methods we think up to hide them." Ever notice that people with the weakest character tend to place blame on their circumstances? They talk a lot about poor upbringing, financial difficulties, the unkindness of others, or other circumstances that have made them victims. Your circumstances may be beyond your control, but your *character* is not. You can no more blame your character on your circumstances, than you can blame the mirror for your looks. Developing character is always your choice. Every time you make a character-based decision, you take another step forward in your spiritual growth.

Take a moment and jot down times when you have faced temptation and adversity. Next to each, note your choice: escape, excuses, capitulation, avoidance, perseverance, or victory. What problem areas do you see? How will you learn to do better? If many of the things you list are due to circumstances beyond your control, then choose to take greater control of your life.

TODAY, SAY "YES" TO JOY

The joy of the Lord is your strength.

NEHEMIAH 8:10

Lenny was desperate to lose weight, so his doctor told him, "Eat normally for two days, then skip a day. Repeat this pattern for six weeks and you'll lose ten pounds." Amazingly, after two weeks he dropped twenty! "How'd you do it?" the doctor asked. "Honestly, Doc, I thought I'd die!" he replied. "Were you *that* hungry?" the doctor asked. "No!" Lenny exclaimed, "But that third day of skipping and jumping all day nearly wrecked me!" Life doesn't have to be so hard! We make it that way by saying no to joy because we don't think we deserve it. Feeling deprived and "virtuous" doesn't make points with God, nor does acting like a martyr hoping somebody will rescue you.

A little boy asked his mom if he could sleep over at his friend's house. "Why?" she asked. "Just for fun," he replied. "But you slept over last night," she said. "Who says you can't have fun two nights in a row?" he reasoned. Beware of imposing so many rules and regulations on yourself that you're like the Pharisees who became slaves to the very laws they created. How long has it been since you said yes to a little lighthearted fun? Paul says, "Be full of joy now!" What are you waiting for? If you pride yourself on always being structured, steadfast and serious, it's time to balance the scales and start building some spontaneity into your life. The Bible says, "Let those...who love Your name be joyful...and be in high spirits" (Ps 5:11 AMP); "Be happy...rejoice and be glad-hearted continually" (1Th 5:16 AMP). Today, say "yes" to joy!

SAFE IN GOD'S ARMS

Underneath are the everlasting arms.

DEUTERONOMY 33:27 NIV

During World War II, when Jill Briscoe was six, her family was evacuated to the English Lake District. Recalling a particularly scary night, she writes, "A storm had broken over our heads. Rain, like giant tears, slashed against the window and thunder grumbled. I didn't like storms, and I was old enough to understand that an even bigger storm was raging, a war involving the entire world. But it seemed far away. The fire was warm and my father was relaxed in his big chair. Suddenly, aware that I needed reassurance, he put down his paper and smiled, 'Come here, little girl' he said in his quiet but commanding voice. And then I was safe in his arms, lying against his shoulder and feeling the beat of his heart.

"Looking back, I realize how my Heavenly Father shelters me from the storms of life. When sorrow swamped me at my mother's funeral, I sought reassurance in my Father's presence. When the winds of worry whipped away my confidence as I faced gangs of young people in street evangelism, I glanced up to see my Father's face. When floods of fear rose as I waited in hospital for the results of frightening tests, I sensed my Heavenly Father say, 'Come here, little girl.' I climbed into His arms, leaned against His shoulder and murmured, 'Ah, this is a grand place to be.'" The Bible says, "The eternal God is your refuge, and underneath are the everlasting arms." If life's storms are overwhelming you, climb up into your Heavenly Father's arms, feel the beat of His heart, and rest assured He's bigger than the storm you're facing.

LESSONS FROM THE TEN LEPERS

Thy faith hath made thee whole.

LUKE 17:19

Luke writes, "There met him ten…lepers, which stood afar off: And they lifted up their voices, and said, Jesus, Master, have mercy on us. And when he saw them, he said…Go shew yourselves unto the priests. And…as they went, they were cleansed. And one of them…turned back, and…glorified God …Jesus…said, Were there not ten cleansed? but where are the nine?…And he said unto him, Arise, go thy way: thy faith hath made thee whole" (Lk 17:12-19). Observe three things in this story:

(1) When people reject you, you start thinking God does too. Because of their problem, these men were rejected by society. So when they met Christ they expected more of the same. But no, the Bible says, "When you draw close to God He will draw close to you" (see Jas 4:8). So come, bring your problem to Him. He's the great problem-solver! *(2) Sometimes you have to "walk it out."* We read, "As they went, they were cleansed." Sometimes change takes place quickly, but most times it happens slowly, step-by-step. You don't know exactly which step will bring victory, so you need to keep walking in faith. Before a leper was welcomed back into society the priest had to pronounce him "clean." How wonderful; Jesus saw the change in these men before it ever took place. That's because He has the power to make it happen. So keep walking! *(3) Gratitude and praise are so important to God.* This story reminds us how quickly we forget God's goodness, how much our praises mean to Him, and that only one in ten of us will pass the gratitude test. But that one becomes "whole."

ARE YOU PREPARING YOURSELF?

And their net brake.

LUKE 5:6

It's wise to have "safety nets" such as savings, insurance and investments. Rainy days come unexpectedly. But—what are you doing to prepare for success? God says He can "Open the windows of heaven and pour out blessings so great, you won't have enough room to take them in" (See Mal 3:10). If God pours out His blessings on you, will you be ready to handle them? Are you preparing yourself for greater things, or just settling for the status quo?

After fishing all night without success, Jesus told Peter, "Launch out into the deep, and let down your nets" (Lk 5:4). Explaining that the fish weren't biting, Peter says, "Nevertheless at thy word I will let down the net" (Lk 5:5). Observe; Jesus said, "Let down your nets" (plural). Peter responded, "I will let down the net" (singular). Clearly, Jesus was thinking bigger than Peter! That night they caught so many fish, "their net brake." Next we read, "They beckoned unto their partners, which were in the other ship, that they should come and help them. And they came, and filled both the ships, so that they began to sink. When Simon Peter saw it, he fell down at Jesus' knees" (Lk 5:7-8). Peter needed more than *one* net and *one* boat to handle what God had in mind. Getting the idea?

If you're praying for greater success, are you taking steps to prepare yourself for it? Are you furthering your education? Are you sharpening your skills and developing new ways of doing things? Are you open to working with others? Are you willing to fall at the feet of Jesus, acknowledging Him as the source of all blessing, and sovereign Lord of your life?

MEETING "THE MAN"

Come, see a man.

JOHN 4:29 NIV

When the woman at the well met Jesus, unlike all the other men she'd met, He addressed her *real* need. "[He said,] 'Go...get your husband'...'I don't have a husband,' the woman replied. Jesus said...'you have had five husbands, and you aren't...married to the man you're living with'" (Jn 4:16-18 NLT). Because we're weak, we keep getting into situations that leave us wounded. And those wounds can't be healed by going from relationship to relationship. After meeting Jesus this woman ran to tell everybody, "Come...meet a man who told me everything!" (TLB). Her answer wasn't another man; she'd already tried that! Her answer was meeting *the* Man, and asking Him to fill the void in her life.

The Bible refers to this as putting "on the new self, which is being renewed in...the image of its Creator" (Col 3:10 NIV). If you're sick of the way you're living and want to change, remember, the woman at the well couldn't "put off the old man" till she met the new One. When you're attached to certain habits and relationships, it's hard to break free in your own strength. You'll only be able to disengage when you acknowledge Jesus as Lord of your life. Only by embracing the new, will you find strength to say goodbye to the old. So what does all this mean for *you?* It means coming to Christ as you are, asking Him to save you, and entering into a relationship with Him. James says, "Surrender to God...Resist the devil, and he will run from you" (Jas 4:7 CEV). When you do that, God will give you the strength to forsake those old patterns and begin a new life!

HONORING FATHERS

Like a father...whispering encouragement,
showing you... how to live well before God.

1 THESSALONIANS 2:11-12 TM

With typical humor, journalist Paul Harvey writes: "A father is forced to endure childbirth without anesthesia. He growls when it feels good and laughs when he's scared. He's guilty of giving too much time to his business when his kids are growing up. He never feels entirely worthy in their eyes. He lectures them when their grades aren't as good as he thinks they should be—although secretly he knows it's really the teacher's fault! Dads have tough exteriors and sometimes their hearts must be broken, otherwise nobody would know what's inside. They work hard smoothing rough places in the road for their sons, and give their daughters away to men who aren't nearly smart enough, so they can have grandkids who are smarter than anybody else's. Fathers get old faster than other people. Every day they enter the arena of work where they tackle the three-headed dragon of work, stress and monotony. They make bets with insurance companies about who'll live the longest, and although they know the odds, they keep on betting until one day they lose...and the bet is paid off to the part of them they leave behind."

When Paul needed an example of a positive influence, he talked about "a father with his child, holding [his] hand, whispering encouragement, showing [him]...how to live... before God." If your dad distinguished himself as a good role model, remember to thank him. If you weren't blessed with that kind of influence, or you grew up without a dad, let today be an occasion to honor the spiritual fathers who *did* nurture and inspire you.

THE SOVEREIGNTY OF GOD (1)

From him...are all things.

ROMANS 11:36 NIV

Acknowledging God's sovereign control in all things doesn't make us helpless pawns, or free us from responsibility. No: *(1) It takes away our anxiety.* When you rest in the loving character of God you can say, "Surely goodness and mercy shall follow me all the days of my life" (Ps 23:6). That's a "surely" you can't get from your banker, your broker, your insurance man, or anybody else.

(2) It frees us from explanation. We're liberated from the tyranny of having to have all the answers. We can say, "I don't know, but I trust the One who does." The danger of knowing a little theology is that we start thinking we can fathom the unfathomable. Even the great Apostle threw up his hands and said, "How unsearchable are His judgments and His ways past finding out" (Ro 11:33 NKJV). Face it, we can't explain why God closes some doors and opens others, or how He can take evil and use it for good. But He does, and He usually doesn't explain it to us.

(3) It keeps us from pride. Paul writes, "From him and through him and to him are all things." If you want to make God's sovereignty temporal or limited, then you have to get rid of the "all things," in this Scripture, just as you must do in Romans 8:28: "And we know that in all things God works for the good of those who love him" (NIV). If God says "all things," He means it! It comes down to a simple choice: either we trust God, or we play God. And it's an easy choice to make!

THE SOVEREIGNTY OF GOD (2)

Therefore...in view of God's mercy.

ROMANS 12:1 NIV

There are two sides to God's sovereignty: on one side is *God's initiative*, on the other side is *our response*. Paul writes in Romans 12:1, "Therefore...in view of God's mercy" we are responsible to: (a) Resist the pressures of a world system that pulls us in the wrong direction. (b) Renew our minds each day through prayer and reading God's Word. (c) Recognize His will for us and live according to it.

But Paul doesn't stop there. He continues: "Hate what is evil; cling to what is good. Be devoted to one another in brotherly love. Honor one another above yourselves. Never be lacking in zeal, but keep your spiritual fervor, serving the Lord. Be joyful in hope, patient in affliction, faithful in prayer. Share with God's people who are in need. Practice hospitality. Bless those who persecute you; bless and do not curse. Rejoice with those who rejoice; mourn with those who mourn. Live in harmony with one another. Do not be proud, but be willing to associate with people of low position. Do not be conceited. Do not repay anyone evil for evil. Be careful to do what is right in the eyes of everybody" (Ro 12:9-17 NIV).

God's sovereignty doesn't mean that we're released from responsibility, have no interest in today's affairs, need not be bothered about decisions, have no desire to strive for personal excellence, or show concern for a lost world. The songwriter captured the essence of God's sovereignty in these words: "Were the whole realm of nature mine, that were an offering far too small. Love so amazing so divine, demands my soul, my life, my all!"

YOUR HEAVENLY HOME

I am going...to prepare a place for you.

JOHN 14:2 NIV

All that stuff you see in the movies, like fog banks and dis-embodied spirits floating around in some nether world to the eerie sounds of Celtic music—forget it! Heaven will be:

(1) A home built just for you. Are you worried about where you go when you die, or where your loved ones have gone? Don't be! Jesus said, "Do not let your hearts be troubled. Trust in God; trust also in me. In my Father's house are many rooms; if it were not so, I would have told you. I am going there to prepare a place for you. And if I go and prepare a place for you, I will come back and take you to be with me that you also may be where I am" (Jn 14:1-3 NIV).

(2) A city you'll love! "I John saw the holy city, new Jerusalem" (Rev 21:2). It's an exact square of 1,400 miles. It stretches from the Carolinas to California, and from Canada to Mexico. It's forty times the size of England, ten times the size of France, and larger than India. And that's just the ground floor; it's as tall as it is wide; 600,000 stories, more than enough space for billions of people to come and go. And come and go they will. The gates never close. Why shut them? The enemies of God will be banished, leaving only a perfect place of per-fected people.

(3) With Christ, the One you love most! Paul, who had the privilege of visiting heaven, wrote, "I desire to depart and be with Christ, which is better by far" (Php 1:23 NIV). So don't get too comfortable here on earth!

STICK TO THE PLAN (1)

I know the plans I have for you.

JEREMIAH 29:11 NIV

Today God is saying to you, "While in process, stick to the plan!" Nothing takes God by surprise. He's a master planner. Joseph discovered that when your family turns against you, your friends let you down and you finish up in trouble, God still has a plan. Looking back Joseph could say, "You intended to harm me, but God intended it for good" (Ge 50:20 NIV). When your situation seems too hard to handle and downright impossible to explain, remind yourself that God said, "I know the plans I have for you."

Some of us are not sure God has made up His mind about us, so we keep trying to earn His favor. Give it up! Receive the truth that God, for Christ's sake, has *decided* to bless you. And when God decides, temporary situations or the actions of others don't change His decision. There's nothing the enemy devises against you that God hasn't already made "a way of escape" for. Paul writes, "God is faithful, who will not suffer you to be tempted above that you are able; but will with the temptation also make a way to escape, that ye may be able to bear it" (1Co 10:13). Observe:

(1) In times of testing you discover how faithful God is. (2) He knows what you can handle. (3) He will "make a way" so you can exit this season stronger, and ready for what He has next. So stick to the plan. The fact that you have a problem is a sign that you have a promise. It's only a matter of time before God reveals the solution.

STICK TO THE PLAN (2)

My God, why have you forsaken me?
MATTHEW 27:46 NIV

Jesus knew that Judas would betray Him, yet He didn't stop him. He could have summoned twelve legions of angels to help Him, yet He didn't call on them. Under the weight of our sins He cried from the cross, "My God, why have you forsaken me?" That's because He understood it was all part of God's plan for Him. His words, "God, where are you?" teach us that:

(a) You can be in God's plan, yet at times feel overwhelmed and alone. (b) When God doesn't answer, you must stand on the Word He has given you. (c) The pain of this season will eventually give way to the joy God has awaiting you on the other side of it. So stick to the plan; that's what disciples do.

The word "disciple" means to be disciplined. It means sticking to the plan when you're under attack. It teaches you how to function when you don't feel like it. The enemy will come against the plan of God in your life, because that plan is like a hedge of protection around you. As long as you stay in God's plan, nothing that the enemy does can destroy you. So, when you feel like you've reached the end of your rope and you can't go another step, do what Jesus did—pray, "Father, into your hands I commit my spirit" (Lk 23:46 NIV). Give it to God! Look up and say, "Lord, I'm trusting You to do what I cannot do. Bring me through this. Here it is; I'm turning it over to You. My life, my future, and my all are in Your hands!"

STICK TO THE PLAN (3)

Then Peter got...out of the boat,
walked on the water... toward Jesus.

MATTHEW 14:29 NIV

Peter proved that as long as you keep your eyes on Jesus and stick to the plan, you won't go under. Notice: *(1) Before you get into something, make sure it's God's will for you!* Peter said, "Lord, if it's you, bid me to come to you on the water" and Jesus said, "Come." Before you take on something like water-walking, pray and be sure God's in it. In other words, get God's plan and stick to it. *(2) Don't expect everybody in the boat to go with you.* Water-walking is a lonely calling; it sets you apart from those who are timid and security-minded. It also tends to bring criticism from those who think you're making them look bad by contrast. *(3) If you wait for good weather you'll miss your moment.* When Jesus said, "Come," they were in the middle of a storm. Face it; we'd all like the stars to line up, or some big donor to underwrite the whole project before we make a move. But how often does that happen? Peter wasn't walking on the water; he was walking on the Word! What has God told you to do? Stop waiting for ideal conditions and start doing it! *(4) Don't expect a mistake-free performance.* Nobody walks without fluctuation. The Bible describes its heroes in one sentence: "Whose weakness was turned to strength" (Heb 11:34 NIV). All the great men and women of God you admire, go through sinking spells when they cry out, "Lord, save me." And do you know what? He does! And He'll do the same for you.

STICK TO THE PLAN (4)

Peter replied, "Tell me to come to you on the water."

MATTHEW 14:28 NIV

Peter didn't walk on the water all by himself, he did it with Jesus. Today Christ invites you to walk with Him and experience His miracles. Why don't we see more of them in our lives? Because:

(1) We don't pray and believe God for them. Jesus said, "If you abide in Me, and My words abide in you, you will ask what you desire, and it shall be done for you" (Jn 15:7 NKJV). Your prayers give God an invitation, an entry point and a channel through which His miraculous power can flow to change your circumstances. But you have to pray and believe Him to do it! *(2) We think the day of miracles is past.* The Scriptures declare, "Jesus Christ is the same yesterday, today, and forever" (Heb 13:8 NKJV). In reality there never has been "a day of miracles," there's only a God of miracles, and He never changes. So don't limit Him! *(3) We allow sin to sabotage our confidence.* John writes, "If our hearts do not condemn us, we have confidence before God and receive from him anything we ask, because we obey his commands and do what pleases him" (1Jn 3:21-22 NIV). *(4) We look at the situation instead of the Savior, and our faith falters.* When Jesus asked Peter, "Why do you doubt?" He was saying, "Don't allow this storm to overwhelm you. I'm right here with you. Your problem is under My feet, therefore it's under your feet too. Just keep your eyes on Me, keep walking by faith and stick to the plan!"

DON'T KEEP SCORE

Forgive as quickly and completely
as the Master forgave you.

COLOSSIANS 3:13 TM

Jimmy drank too much at the party and embarrassed his wife Lisa. Next morning he felt bad and asked her to forgive him. She said she would, yet she kept bringing it up. One day in discouragement he said, "I thought you were going to forgive and forget." She said, "I have, I just don't want you to *forget* that I have forgiven and forgotten." Do you forgive like that?

Keeping score only works in competitive sports; it's disastrous in relationships. There's so much good in the worst of us and so much bad in the best of us, that we'll spend much of our lives learning to forgive and forget. And forgetting is harder when the offence is great. Small offences can be forgiven quickly; big ones require a healing process. But until you make the decision to forgive, the process can't even begin.

How can you "Forgive as quickly and completely as the Master forgave you"? Paul answers, "Clothe yourselves with tenderhearted mercy, kindness, humility, gentleness, and patience. Make allowance for each other's faults, and forgive anyone who offends you. Remember, the Lord forgave you, so you must forgive others" (Col 3:12-13 NLT). To practice this kind of forgiveness you must focus on a person's worth, not their weaknesses. You must turn your heart away from what *was,* to what *can* be. You say, "Why should I forgive and forget?" (1) Because God's Word tells you to. (2) Because you yourself will continue to need forgiveness. (3) Because you weren't built to carry the stress that goes with resentment.

WHAT'S CHOKING YOU?

Desires for...things...choke the word.

MARK 4:19 NIV

In the parable of the sower Jesus said, "Still others, like seed sown among thorns, hear the word; but the worries of this life, the deceitfulness of wealth and the desires for other things come in and choke the word, making it unfruitful" (Mk 4:18-19 NIV). Notice, the problem is not the sower or the seed, it's the soil. Jesus said they "hear the word," so we're talking about church folks with a pre-existing mindset that chokes every Scripture they hear, read, or try to apply. Jesus describes these thorns as: "The worries of this life, the deceitfulness of wealth and the desires for other things." Do you remember the time when you thought the house you now live in, the career you now enjoy, and the investments you now have, would make all your worries go away? But no, the more you have, the more you have to lose, to protect, to maintain, and to worry about. That's "the deceitfulness of wealth." If your significance as a person or your sense of security is tied to anything other than your relationship with God, worry will choke the life right out of you. True happiness lies in trusting God for what you need, knowing if it's right He'll provide it, and if not He'll give you something better.

Chuck Swindoll writes, "We live among thorns because we've a quiet, respectable, secret love for them. I know. I've got the ugly scars to prove it. Each one a mute reminder of years trapped in the thicket; periodically I still have to yank a few." How about you—do you have some thorns you need to pull?

DO IT WHILE YOU STILL CAN

You will be missed, because your seat will be empty.

1 SAMUEL 20:18 NIV

When you lose a loved one, you realize that *relationships* are much more important than *possessions*. But we forget that in our scramble to the top of the heap. Being told you've only a short time to live puts you into shock, then re-orders your priorities. It makes you want to fill each precious moment with the words you've left unsaid and the things you've neglected to do. Don't allow self-centeredness, masquerading as ambition (or religious zeal!), to keep you from showing love to those who need it. Make that call. Send that email. Buy those flowers. Say, "I love you." In other words, "be there." Most of the time people don't need our wise analysis or brilliant answers, they just need our love—and support—and they'll find their own answers.

If you are a leader, you're particularly at risk. Don't sacrifice your family on the altar of your career, or you'll end up with regrets you can't resolve. The son of a well-known missionary stood at his dad's grave without shedding a tear. He told someone, "You never miss what you never had. My dad loved people on the other side of the world, but I'm not sure he loved me." Wake up! The clock's ticking and the days are flying by. Yes, you must fulfill your God-given assignment in life, but not at the cost of the people who matter. Take a moment and think about these words: "And Jonathan had David reaffirm his... love for him...Then Jonathan said to David...You will be missed, because your seat will be empty."

DEAL WITH IT!

But the thing that David had done displeased the Lord.

2 SAMUEL 11:27 NKJV

When David committed adultery with Bathsheba and she became pregnant, he tried to cover his tracks by having her husband Uriah killed, then marrying her before the baby was born. It looked like David was home free, except for one important detail. "The thing that David had done displeased the Lord." And you can't silence the voice of an angry God! Now, while David was "a man after [God's] own heart" (1Sa 13:14 NLT), the Bible says, "Be sure your sin will find you out" (Nu 32:23). God told David, "I made you king...freed you from the fist of Saul...gave you...Israel and Judah. And...I'd have gladly thrown in much more. So why have you treated the word of God with...contempt?" (2Sa 12:7-9 TM). Then He passed sentence: "Because you despised me...I am going to bring calamity upon you...before all Israel" (2Sa 12:10-12 NIV). And from then on tragedy and turmoil plagued David's family.

"The way of transgressors is hard" (Pr 13:15) on many levels, not least of which is—God takes away our peace in order to take away our sin. It took an unplanned pregnancy, the murder of an innocent man, the death of a child, the persuasion of a prophet and the conviction of the Holy Spirit before David's heart finally softened and he admitted, "I have sinned against the Lord" (2Sa 12:13 NKJV). And when he did, God treated David's sin the same way He treats ours: "If we confess our sins, he is faithful and just to forgive...and...cleanse us from all unrighteousness" (1Jn 1:9). Is there a "sin" in your life you need to deal with today? Deal with it!

THE WAY UP WHEN LIFE GETS YOU DOWN (1)

Elijah was...just like us.

JAMES 5:17 NIV

There are times in life when we all feel down. But God's Word shows us the way to get back up. Look at Elijah, who "was just like us." How come he got so far down? *(a) It happened on the heels of a great victory.* He didn't start out in the doldrums, and he didn't fall into sin. No, he'd just called down fire from heaven and slain 450 false prophets (See 1Ki 18:22-39). But that's hard work! So he went from exhilaration to exhaustion. Weary, defenses down and vulnerability up, he fell into a natural depression because fatigue strips us of our courage. *(b) Fear caused him to lose perspective.* The man of God who'd just faced down an evil multitude, ended up running from one woman, Jezebel (See 1Ki 19). Fear made him forget God's power; it skewed his perspective and left him feeling suicidal. Exhaustion coupled with fear is a dangerous combination. It invites hopeless, wrong thinking, and creates the illusion that your options are gone. *(c) He became isolated.* Elijah left his servant at Beersheba and journeyed into the wilderness alone (1Ki 19:3-4). When you most need support, anxiety, a sense of inadequacy and fear of failure, will push you into isolation. At that point you're in the worst possible company—your own. Elijah thought, "I am the only one left, and now they are trying to kill me" (vv. 10, 14 NIV). Translated: "It's bad and I can't see it getting better!" When you're down isn't the time to isolate. That's when you need to reach for God, and the people who love you and can help you back up.

THE WAY UP WHEN LIFE GETS YOU DOWN (2)

Elijah was...just like us.

JAMES 5:17 NIV

What was God's prescription for getting Elijah back on his feet? A lecture on the prophet's faltering faith? No, just rest and nourishment! God recognizes our limitations, even when we don't. "A bruised reed he will not break, and a smoldering wick he will not snuff out" (Is 42:3 NIV). When we neglect our own legitimate needs, it shows up in our attitude.

God understands that being down is a "perspective" problem, and getting back up requires adjustment in four crucial areas. So: *(1) He adjusted Elijah's God-perspective.* "Get in the presence of God and he'll meet with you" (See 1Ki 19:11 NIV). The One who gave Elijah victory on Mount Carmel, could also sustain him in the desert of Jezreel. But first Elijah had to spend time with Him, otherwise he was running on an empty tank. Hello! *(2) He adjusted Elijah's world-perspective.* Elijah said, "God's covenant is broken, His altar destroyed, His prophets murdered, and I'm the only one left" (See v. 14). But God showed Elijah that He still had the necessary resources and strategies to accomplish His purposes, even in a hostile environment. *(3) He adjusted Elijah's self-perspective.* The prophet saw himself as helpless and inadequate: "Lord, let me die, for I am no better than those who preceded me" (See v. 4). But God showed him there were still kings to anoint, battles to win, and that Elijah had an important role to play (See v. 16). *(4) He provided a helper.* He sent Elisha to minister to him (See v. 21). You're not supposed to carry it all alone! Allow yourself to need help, and watch who God puts in your life to support you.

NEEDED—SPIRITUAL BLACKSMITHS!

There were no blacksmiths in the land.

1 SAMUEL 13:19 NLT

The Bible says, "There were no blacksmiths in the land of Israel in those days. The Philistines wouldn't allow them for fear they would make swords and spears for the Hebrews… none of the people of Israel had a sword or spear, except for Saul and Jonathan" (1Sa 13:19-22 NLT).

To keep the Israelites in slavery, the Philistines removed all the blacksmiths. It was a devastating blow. Blacksmiths made swords to be used in battle and sickles to be used in the harvest field. Can you imagine the effect that would have on a nation? Satan's tactics haven't changed. His goal is still to silence the molders and shapers of a new culture—a kingdom culture. Why do we need spiritual blacksmiths? Because they understand how to shape raw material into something God can use. They not only shape it, they sharpen it. All great leaders have emerged from raw material. And tomorrow's leaders are walking around today in raw form just waiting for a spiritual blacksmith to come along. Unfortunately many ministry leaders are so busy "running the show," they don't take the time to work with raw material. Spiritual blacksmiths aren't only needed in the local church, they're also needed in the nation to reshape our culture. We need "influencers" who can reform the ranks of business, education, government and media. Any volunteers?

It's time for the spiritual blacksmiths in the land to break free from the constraints of the Philistines and return to the ancient craft of shaping men and women for God's service. The battle is too big for Saul and Jonathan to handle alone!

PEACE COMES BY FORGIVING

Forgive anyone you are holding a grudge against.

MARK 11:25 NLT

A lady was upset because her mother in law forgot to ask her to a family picnic. So when her son called on the morning of the event to invite her, she replied angrily, "It's too late—I've already prayed for rain!" When we're hurting we want someone to pay, so we lash out at the wrong people. One lady writes, "I was so angry I spent years trying to collect what I thought was due, from people who'd nothing to do with my hurt. Finally God caused me to realize that I was trying to collect a debt from my husband that he didn't owe. When I accepted this, God began to bless me beyond anything I could ever have imagined."

One night after preaching about forgiveness, Corrie Ten Boom recognized that the man approaching her was a former guard from Ravensbruck, the Nazi prison camp where she was tortured and her sister Betsie starved to death. When he asked her to forgive him, Corrie thought about Betsie, and felt she couldn't do it. Nevertheless she knew she must, otherwise everything she'd preached would be meaningless. So she told God, "I can extend my hand, I can do that much, but You'll have to supply the feelings." Taking the man's hand she felt God's power rushing through her, enabling her to whole-heartedly say, "I forgive you, brother." Corrie never experienced God's love so intensely as she did that night. Although she'd been badly tortured, she let God heal her, and then went on to help others. The truth is—forgiveness is the *only* way to have peace!

SUPPORT YOUR PASTOR!

Hold them in highest regard.

1 THESSALONIANS 5:13 NIV

Phil Hines tells a humorous imaginary story about Jesus walking along the road one day and seeing a man crying. When He asked what was wrong, the man replied, "I'm blind," so Jesus healed him. Further along He met another man in tears and asked him the same question. He replied, "I'm lame," so Jesus healed him. Then He encountered a third man weeping. In response to Jesus' question he replied, "I'm a pastor." So Jesus sat down and wept right along with him! Pastoring can be a thankless job; that's why the Bible says, "Hold them in highest regard."

Somebody has described the "Perfect Pastor" as one who preaches twenty minutes and sits down. Condemns sin without offending anybody, works sixteen-hour days doing everything from preaching to sweeping, makes $400 a week and gives $200 back to the church, wears nice clothes, has a model family, supports good causes and helps panhandlers who stop by the church. He's thirty-six and he's been preaching for forty years. He has a burning desire to work with the youth, and spends all his time with the senior citizens. He smiles all the time while keeping a straight face, because he has a keen sense of humor that finds him seriously dedicated. He makes twenty visits a day, spends every waking moment evangelizing, and is always in his office in case he's needed. The bad news is, he burned out and died at thirty-seven! Paul writes, "Appreciate...pastoral leaders who gave you the Word" (Heb 13:7 TM). "Honor those...who work so hard for you, who have...the responsibility of...guiding you...Overwhelm them with appreciation and love!" (1Th 5:12-13 TM). In other words, support your pastor!

BE PREPARED (1)

Work hard so you can...receive his approval.

2 TIMOTHY 2:15 NLT

Moses spent eighty years preparing for a job that would last forty. That's a two-to-one ratio of preparation to execution. The greater the goal, the greater the preparation! Much of your life can be spent getting ready for what seems like a brief season and assignment. But to be able to say at the end, "I have finished my course" is to have lived successfully. And that's so whether you are called to run a marathon or a 100-yard dash. Before passing the torch to Timothy, Paul says, "Work hard so you can...receive his approval." Who does God use? People who prepare well. Whether you're called to business, education, politics, art, medicine or ministry, this principle remains—God uses prepared people. The price tag required for long-term success cannot be lowered. We all want what successful people have, we're just not all willing to pay the price they paid to achieve it. You must be prepared when your opportunities come. Abraham Lincoln said, "I will prepare and some day my chance will come." Benjamin Disraeli said, "The secret of success in life is for a man to be ready for his time when it comes." When the fate of the Jews hung in the balance, Mordecai told Esther that her experience in the king's palace had prepared her, "For such a time as this" (Est 4:14). She responded and the Jews were saved. All these people had talent, prepared themselves and made the most of their opportunities when they arose. *So your greatest challenge is not lack of opportunity, but being ready when it comes.*

BE PREPARED (2)

Hold on to instruction...
guard it well, for it is your life.

PROVERBS 4:13 NIV

It's not enough to get prepared, you must stay prepared. We're being told that knowledge is doubling every five years. So if you don't keep growing, you'll end up with coping skills that no longer match the challenge you face in the world you live in. It's estimated that many doctors are so busy taking care of patients, they're years behind the latest developments in their field. If you or a loved one gets ill, that could become a real concern for you. *Preparation doesn't begin with what you do, it begins with what you believe.* If you believe that success tomorrow depends on what you do today, you'll treat today differently. A wise sailor studies the weather before he goes to sea, because he knows that avoiding a storm is easier than getting out of one. Howard Coonley of the American National Standards Institute stated, "The leader of the future will be rated by his ability to anticipate problems, rather than to meet them as they come." *Preparation is not merely an event, it's a lifestyle.* Abraham Lincoln said, "If I had eight hours to chop down a tree, I'd spend six sharpening my axe." As a young man Lincoln had split rails with an axe, so he knew the value of staying sharp. Wisdom always prompted him to prepare—whether he was getting ready to cut wood, study law on his own to pass the bar, or lead the nation. This is why your Bible says, "Hold on to instruction, do not let it go. Guard it well, for it is your life."

BE PREPARED (3)

In all thy ways acknowledge him,
and he shall direct thy paths.

PROVERBS 3:6

One of the most important questions you must ask yourself is, "What am I supposed to prepare *for?*" You don't want to be like the Miss America contestant who recently told a late-night TV talk show host, "My goal is to bring world peace— and get my own apartment." Ask God what you're supposed to do, and keep asking till you get clear instructions as to your next step (or for that matter, your *first* step!).

There are timeless principles in the Bible that work, whether you're walking with God or going your own way. So be careful that you are not using God, rather than allowing God to use you. "In all thy ways acknowledge [consult, listen and submit to] him, and he shall direct thy paths." What ultimately matters most will not be what others say about your life, but what God says.

The humbling truth is, all achievements will eventually be surpassed, records will be broken, reputations will fade, and tributes will be forgotten. In college Dr. James Dobson's goal was to become the school's tennis champion. He felt very proud when his trophy was prominently placed in a display cabinet. Years later someone mailed him that trophy—they had found it in a trash can when the school was remodeled. Dobson says, "Given enough time, all your trophies will be trashed by someone else." Living to create an earthly legacy is a short-sighted goal. You weren't put here to be remembered, you were put here to do God's will and to prepare for eternity. If you're wise you'll keep that in mind!

SHOW SOME GRATITUDE!

Let us continually...praise...God...giving thanks.

HEBREWS 13:15 NKJV

At a *Women of Faith* conference they were short of space for 150 people, so the staff brought in narrower chairs. Everyone had a seat, but conditions in the auditorium were cramped and nobody was happy. The director asked the guest speaker, Joni Eareckson Tada, to help calm the crowd. A childhood diving accident had left Joni quadriplegic and confined to a wheelchair. As the attendants pushed her out onto the platform she addressed the audience: "I understand some of you don't like the chair you're sitting in. Well, neither do I! But I've a thousand handicapped friends who'd gladly trade places with you." Immediately the hall went quiet and the complaining stopped.

When Paul was training Timothy he said, "Be strong in the grace that is in Christ" (2Ti 2:1 NKJV), and gratitude is an offshoot of grace. The Bible says, "Let us continually [not just when you feel like it!] offer the sacrifice of praise to God... giving thanks to His name." After the Bible expositor Matthew Henry was accosted and robbed he wrote in his diary: "Let me be thankful, *first*, that I was never robbed before, *second*, that although they took my purse they didn't take my life, *third*, that although they took everything I had, it wasn't much, *fourth*, that it was I who was robbed, and not I who did the robbing."

If you're struggling to find something to be grateful for today, here's a good reason: "Give thanks to the Lord, for he is good; his love endures forever" (Ps 118:29 NIV).

ARE YOU A WORKAHOLIC?

Put God first, and he will...
crown your efforts with success.

PROVERBS 3:6 TLB

When you experience rejection early in life, you feel like you constantly have to "prove" yourself, so you become a workaholic in order to gain people's acceptance. One woman writes, "I can still hear my father yelling, telling me I'd never be any good, never amount to anything. The more he yelled, the more determined I became to prove him wrong." Do you have voices like that in your head? It's true that you'll succeed by working hard, but to experience lasting satisfaction you must know that you're fulfilling God's will for your life. When all is said and done, what matters most is knowing you're loved and accepted by God. What can top that?

God measures with a different yardstick. He won't ask what kind of car you drove, but how many people you gave rides to. He won't ask the square footage of your home, but how you raised your children and treated your family. He won't ask about the brand names in your closet, but who you helped to clothe. He won't ask about your salary, but how much you invested into the building of His kingdom. He won't ask about your job title, but if you tried to perform with excellence and integrity. He won't ask how many friends you had, but how many people you were a friend to. He won't ask what neighborhood you lived in, but if you loved your neighbor. He won't ask about your politics or the color of your skin, but about the quality of your character. So don't just work hard, work hard for the right reasons!

INNER BEAUTY

Beauty, the...kind...God delights in.

1 PETER 3:4 TM

A lady was applying face cream when her little girl asked, "What's that you're putting on, Mom?" "Moisturizer," she replied. "The saleslady said it would make me beautiful." With an honesty only children have, she replied, "Mom, I don't think it's working." There's nothing wrong with looking good, but there's much more to you than your clothes and your hairstyle. Plus, you can go broke fixing up the outside, because "what Mother Nature giveth, Father Time taketh away!" Ralph Waldo Emerson said, "To find beauty we must carry it with us."

It's a big mistake to focus on the outside and fail to appreciate the inner qualities God's given you. Solomon said, "Beauty is...[not lasting]" (Pr 31:30 AMP). When God made you He didn't just decorate the outside, He gave you "inner beauty, the gentle, gracious kind...God delights in." However, because Peter also talked about "fancy hair, gold jewelry...fine clothes" (NCV), a few well-intentioned people have used that to create a legalistic standard by which to measure and judge others. Does the Bible teach us to dress appropriately? Absolutely. Paul writes: "I...want women to dress modestly, with decency and propriety...appropriate for women who profess to worship God" (1Ti 2:9-10 NIV). But when you focus on the wrong area you get the wrong results. "Man looks at the outward appearance, but the Lord looks at the heart" (1Sa 16:7 NIV). Don't allow what you see on TV or in the mirror to define your worth. Work instead to develop the kind of *inner* beauty God commends.

"BOOTS, OR NO BOOTS"

Let every living, breathing creature praise God!

PSALM 150:6 TM

In pre-Emancipation days it was common practice for white people to occupy the main floor of a church while African-Americans were assigned to the balcony. Every Sunday a black man called Frank would interrupt the sermon by praising God out loud from the balcony. Irritated, Frank's boss promised him a pair of new boots if he'd stay quiet. So Frank made up his mind not to utter a peep. The following Sunday the pastor spoke about all the wonderful gifts God gave us through His Son Jesus. Frank struggled to stay quiet, but inside he was shouting, "Hallelujah...Praise the Lord." Still, he kept his lip buttoned, thinking about the new boots. But eventually the Word of God connected with the Spirit of God that was within him. Unable to contain himself he jumped up and shouted, "Boots or no boots—I'm gonna praise the Lord!"

We sit in church every week with our mouths closed, maintaining a façade of respectability and decorum. Not in the New Testament times! When Jesus "came near...the whole crowd...began joyfully to praise God in loud voices for all the miracles they had seen: [saying] 'Blessed is the king who comes in the name of the Lord'...the Pharisees...said to Jesus ...'rebuke your disciples!'... he replied, 'if they keep quiet, the stones will cry out'" (Lk 19:37-40 NIV). Isaiah said, "The mountains and hills will burst into song, and the trees...will clap their hands" (Isa 55:12 NLT). Stones! Mountains! Trees! Are you getting the message? God's Word says, "Let every living, breathing creature praise God." Unless you're *dead*, that's what you should be doing!

GETTING THINGS DONE

If any of you lacks wisdom...ask God.

JAMES 1:5 NIV

L arge tasks tend to overwhelm us. And overwhelmed people seldom get things done. So ask God to help you, then apply these principles: *(1) Focus on the task.* The secret of success is making every action count—being intentional. That kind of focus helps you live without regrets because it directs you and makes the most of your talents and your opportunities. If you know you have talent, and you are energetic and active, but you don't see concrete results, then lack of focus is likely your problem. *(2) Prioritize it by importance.* When we don't prioritize what we must do according to its importance, the tasks begin to arrange themselves according to their urgency. And when the urgent drives you instead of the important, you lose your edge. Instead of activating your talent it robs you of the best opportunities to use it. *(3) Order it by sequence.* Create a timetable, give yourself deadlines, and stick with them. The biggest lie we tell ourselves is, "I'll do it later." *(4) Assign it by abilities.* When you divide a large task into smaller ones, you begin to understand what kinds of people you'll need to get the job done. The most important step in accomplishing something big, is determining who will be on your team. Jesus spent three and a half years discipling twelve men, then He delegated responsibilities to them. And the job got done! *(5) Accomplish it by teamwork.* Even if you break a task down, strategically plan it, and recruit great people, you still need one more element to succeed. Teamwork! Teamwork is the glue that can bring it all together.

"ISSUMAGIJOUJUNGNAINERMIK"

Forgive...because the Lord forgave you.

COLOSSIANS 3:13 NCV

In a comedy routine Joe complains to Jerry about the irritating habit of a mutual friend who pokes his finger into people's chests when he talks to them. Then Joe shows Jerry a little vial of highly-explosive nitroglycerin attached to a string and explains, "This is going around my neck, hanging over the spot where he sticks his finger. The next time he does it, he'll pay!" And so will Joe! Because an eye for an eye becomes a neck for a neck, a job for a job and a reputation for a reputation! Paul says, "Forgive...because the Lord forgave you." Get over it before it turns into hatred! Moravian missionaries searched for a word for *forgiveness* in the Eskimo language. That's when they discovered "issumagijoujungnainermik," a twenty-four-letter tongue-twister which literally means "not being able to think about it any more." Genuine forgiveness is about moving on, and refusing to think any more about what happened.

It's easy to forgive the one-time offender who cuts you off in traffic, but repeat offenders like Saul who *continually* pursued and threatened David, must be turned over to God. You don't have to endorse their behavior or pretend it didn't happen. Be merciful, but keep your distance. After confronting Saul, David didn't take him out to dinner. The Bible says, "Saul returned home, but David...went up to the stronghold" (1Sa 24:22 NIV). You can forgive the offender without pursuing a close relationship with him. Paul writes, "Watch out for those who cause divisions and put obstacles in your way...Keep away from them" (Ro 16:17 NIV). Forgiveness isn't foolishness; it's just seeing the offender through God's eyes.

NURTURE YOUR CHILD'S VISION!

Your young men will see visions.

JOEL 2:28 CEV

There's a scene in *Man of La Mancha* where Don Quixote and his servant are standing gazing at a dilapidated inn. When Quixote describes his vision of turrets and magnificent gates, comparing the building to the *Alcazar,* the royal palace in Seville, the servant tries hard to see his master's vision. However, all he can see are ruins. When he attempts to describe them, Quixote tells him to stop, saying, "I will not allow your facts to interfere with my vision!"

In the last days God promised to pour out His Spirit on all kinds of different people (not just the ones *we* think deserve it). He said, "Your sons and daughters will prophesy. Your old men will have dreams, and your young men will see visions." One Bible teacher writes: "When the Holy Spirit fills us, we have visions that defy facts. When I deal with young people who get a vision of doing something big for God, I can always count on their parents to throw cold water on it. The parents say they want them to be realistic. But such parents don't understand that when God takes possession of young people, He gives them dreams and visions that force them to look beyond the facts, and sometimes run counter to reason. We dare not turn them from these…they are what give meaning to our lives." Parent, don't be the last link in the chain. And don't try to pour your children into the mold of your own unfulfilled expectations. Encourage them to seek God and get a vision for their future. And when they get it, become their biggest cheerleader!

"THE PRAYER OF FAITH"

The prayer of faith shall save the sick.

JAMES 5:15

When a pastor visited a lady in a nursing home, she asked him to pray for her healing. So he did. Then she said, "Would you help me out of this wheelchair?" Startled, he complied. She took a few steps then started running and jumping till the whole building heard her. Later in his car the pastor looked up and said, "Lord, don't *ever* do that to me again!" The Bible says, "The prayer of faith shall save the sick." So why are we surprised when He does?

A visiting preacher told the congregation if anyone needed prayer to come forward, though inwardly he was thinking about his past lack of results. Thirty people responded and he prayed for them. Later that week a woman called and said, "Last Sunday you prayed for my husband. He had cancer, and he died." "Much good my prayers did," he thought. The lady continued, "When we walked into church my husband was angry. He wanted to see his grandchildren grow up, and every day he cursed God. Being around him was unbearable. But after you prayed for him he walked out a different person. His last days were the best we'd ever had; we talked, laughed, and sang hymns together. He wasn't *cured,* but he was *healed.*"

Only God knows why some are healed while others aren't. But our instructions are clear. "Is any sick among you? Let him call for the elders of the church; and let them pray over him, anointing him with oil in the name of the Lord: And the prayer of faith shall save the sick, and the Lord shall raise him up" (Jas 5:14-15).

JUST PLANT THE SEED!

The gospel...is the power of God unto salvation.

ROMANS 1:16

A pastor tells about standing at King's Cross in Sydney, Australia, when a shabby-looking man tugged his sleeve and asked him, "If you died tonight, where would you spend eternity?" The question haunted him until he finally surrendered his life to Christ. Later a lady from his church testified to a similar experience in exactly the same spot. It motivated *her* to come to Jesus also. Years later the pastor was visiting the area and went looking for the mystery man. Sure enough, as he scanned the faces around him an old man approached him. Before he could speak, the pastor said, "You're going to ask me if I died tonight where I'd spend eternity, right?" Amazed, the man asked how he knew. The pastor proceeded to tell him about all the people who'd come to know Christ because of the question he'd asked them. Deeply moved, the old man said, 'I was a drunk before I came to Jesus. I'm uneducated, I don't speak well, and all I could think of was to go round asking people that question. I've been asking it now for eight years and today's the first time I'd any idea I was making a difference."

Some people come to Christ on the first call, but the hard-headed among us usually take the long route home. Your job is not to change people. Just share the life-giving Word and let God change them. Jesus said, "I, when I am lifted up...will draw all men to myself" (Jn 12:32 NIV). Just plant the seed and let the Lord of the harvest do the rest!

THE 212-DEGREE ATTITUDE

Fervent in spirit.

ROMANS 12:11

When a motivational products company interviewed Tim Dumler by phone for a sales job, he told them his goal was to become their number one employee. After meeting him in person they were shocked to discover he was legally blind. But he promised he'd buy a machine that magnifies letters. So despite serious misgivings, they hired him. And it's a good thing they did. He came in early, worked late, and within six years became their top producer. His clients loved him, because when you're blind you become a great listener. And his associates loved him because of his caring, positive attitude. He said, "It's unfortunate that I'm visually impaired, but adversity made me a better person. I *have* a lot more than I *don't* have." Tim has the 212-degree attitude!

What's the 212-degree attitude? Motivational speaker Mack Anderson explains: "At 211 degrees water is hot. At 212 degrees it boils. With boiling water comes steam. And steam can power a locomotive. One extra degree makes all the difference in business and in life; it separates the good from the great."

Here's some straight talk for slackers, those with no ambition, and those who see no purpose or value in this life: "Serve wholeheartedly, as if you were serving the Lord, not men, because you know that the Lord will reward everyone for whatever good he does" (Eph 6:7-8 NIV). The Bible tells us to be "fervent in spirit." This word *fervent* means "bubbling or boiling." In other words, having the 212-degree attitude! By the way, when God promises to reward such an attitude, you don't have to wait until you get to heaven to enjoy it.

IN HARNESS WITH JESUS

You will find rest for your souls.

MATTHEW 11:29 NIV

One of the greatest promises Jesus ever gave us was: "Come to me, all you who are weary and burdened, and I will give you rest. Take my yoke upon you and learn from me, for I am gentle and humble in heart, and you will find rest for your souls" (Mt 11:28-29 NIV). How could Jesus talk about being yoked in a harness, which suggests hard work, and about rest in the same breath? To most of us, rest means kicking back in the recliner. That's not the kind of rest Jesus was thinking about.

A yoke is a harness that goes around the necks of two oxen so they can pull a load. Accepting Jesus' yoke is a picture of *submission*. It's also a picture of *help*, because you're not pulling the load alone. In each team of oxen one is the leader and the other follows. Jesus will take the lead, but you must be yoked to Him to get the benefit. So to enjoy intimacy with Christ, you have to bow before Him and accept His will. Jesus promises that His yoke won't choke you, it won't be wearisome or confining; you won't chafe under it. In fact, the irony is, if you want to be truly free you must allow yourself to be yoked to Jesus by submitting your will to His.

Now it's possible to accept Christ's yoke, then start pulling against it when life doesn't go the way you want it to. Peace and rest come only when you relax in the yoke, and let Christ lead the way.

COURAGE (1)

Act with courage.

2 CHRONICLES 19:11 NIV

The English word for courage comes from the French word *coeur,* which means "heart." That's why we say, "Don't lose heart." The truth is: *(1) It takes courage to face the truth about yourself.* Jesus said, "You shall know the truth, and the truth shall make you free" (Jn 8:32 NKJV). But before the truth sets us free it usually puts us through the wringer, because the truth about ourselves is not something we like hearing. *(2) It takes courage to change when staying as you are feels more comfortable.* If you're willing to leave your security zone, step out in faith and follow God, you'll be tested. But you'll also reach heights you thought were beyond you. And you'll go further than others who possess greater talent than you do. *(3) It takes courage to stand for your convictions when you know they'll be challenged.* Any time you're willing to stand for something, or try something, somebody will take a shot at you. Ralph Waldo Emerson wrote: "Whatever you do, you need courage. Whatever course you decide upon there's always someone to tell you you're wrong. There are always difficulties arising which tempt you to believe that your critics are right. To map out a course of action and follow it to the end, requires the same courage a soldier needs. Peace has its victories, but it takes brave men to win them." When Nehemiah's enemies threatened him he said, "Should a man like me run away?… I will not" (Ne 6:11 NIV). As a result he rebuilt the walls of Jerusalem in a record fifty-two days, and got a book in the Bible named after him. How's *that* for courage?

COURAGE (2)

Act with courage.

2 CHRONICLES 19:11 NIV

When it comes to acting with courage you'll notice: *(1) Courage usually involves getting it wrong before you get it right.* It's easy to be brave where you're strong; it's much more difficult where you're weak. That's when you need courage most. General Omar Bradley remarked, "Bravery is the capacity to perform properly, even when scared half to death." We mistakenly believe that learning is passive, that we learn by reading a book or listening to a speaker. No, the learning process is summarized in these five steps: 1. Observe. 2. Act. 3. Evaluate. 4. Readjust. 5. Go back to step two. *(2) Courage always takes the "high road."* Jesus said, "If someone strikes you on the right cheek, turn to him the other also" (Mt 5:39 NIV). Dr. James B. Mooneyham writes: "When we keep score of wrongs committed against us, we reveal a lack of maturity. Theodore Roosevelt once said, 'The most important single ingredient in the formula of success, is knowing how to get along with people.' Those who do not forgive are persons who have not yet learned this truth, and they are usually unsuccessful people. If you wish to improve this area of your life, here are some things that should help. First, practice forgiving. Second, think good thoughts of those persons; it's difficult to have hostile feelings toward one in whom you see good. Finally, let people know through your actions that you can forgive and forget. This will gain respect for you. Remember this: committing an injury puts you below your enemy; taking revenge makes you even with him; forgiving him sets you above."

COURAGE (3)

Act with courage.

2 CHRONICLES 19:11 NIV

Paul writes: "Every detail works to your advantage…So we're not giving up. How could we! Even though on the outside it often looks like things are falling apart on us, on the inside, where God is making new life, not a day goes by without his unfolding grace" (2Co 4:15-17 TM). Note the words, "we're not giving up." Any time we want to move forward, obstacles are going to get in the way. And God's Word teaches us that we should expect nothing less. H.G. Wells asked, "What on earth would a man do with himself if something didn't stand in his way?" Why would he make such a comment? Because adversity is our friend, even though it doesn't feel that way. Each obstacle we overcome teaches us about our strengths and weaknesses. It shapes us, makes us wiser and more confident. The greatest people in history were those who faced the most difficult challenges with courage, and rose to the occasion.

That was certainly true of Winston Churchill. In his book *American Scandal,* Pat Williams writes about Churchill's last months. He says in 1964, President Eisenhower went to visit the former Prime Minister. Eisenhower sat by the bold-spirited leader's bed for a long period of time, neither speaking. After ten minutes, Churchill slowly raised his hand and painstakingly made the "V" for victory sign which he had so often flashed to the British people during the war. Eisenhower, fighting back tears, pulled his chair back, stood up, saluted him and left the room. To his aide out in the hallway, Eisenhower said, "I just said goodbye to Winston, but you never say farewell to courage."

WALKING BY FAITH

The just shall live by faith.

HEBREWS 10:38

Walking by faith is not easy. When you make up your mind to trust God the odds are usually stacked against you. Remember Noah? When he built the ark there had never been *rain!* And the outcome isn't always what you expect. Walking by faith doesn't mean your problems suddenly evaporate. Sometimes faith doesn't change your circumstances, it changes *you* by giving you the tenacity to hang in there when the check doesn't come in the mail, the doctor says, "It's malignant," your spouse asks for a divorce, the kids are running amok, or the place you've worked for thirty years closes its doors. Faith gives you the fortitude to endure these things, confident that God is working on your behalf. "Faith is being sure of what we hope for and certain of what we do not see. This is what the ancients were commended for" (Heb 11:1-2 NIV). So walking by faith means: (1) trusting in the faithfulness of God; (2) following in the footsteps of ordinary people who did extraordinary things; (3) using your faith, because it's the currency of heaven. When the Bible says, "The just shall live by faith," it doesn't mean little sporadic bursts. No, it's talking about a lifestyle! Anybody can go the first few rounds in the ring; it's when you're knocked down in the ninth that you need the faith to get back up and keep fighting. When the plane you're flying on encounters turbulence you don't throw away your ticket or bail out, you sit still and trust the pilot. *So discount your circumstances, dethrone your doubts, and start walking by faith!*

TO LIVE IN GOD'S BLESSINGS

Blessed is the man who…

PSALM 112:1 NIV

Psalm 112 is a description of what it means to live in God's blessings. The first verse is the door through which you must walk in order to receive them. "Blessed is the man who fears [trusts in, honors and obeys] the Lord, who finds great delight in his commands [takes pleasure in what God says, then does it]." Now, when you see what God offers to such people you'll want to rush into the next verses. But you can't, you must qualify! This verse is the price tag; check it carefully. You can't do anything to earn God's love, but you must obey Him to live in His blessings. But when you qualify, here's the payoff:

"His children will be mighty in the land; the generation of the upright will be blessed. Wealth and riches are in his house, and his righteousness endures forever. Even in darkness light dawns for the upright, for the gracious and compassionate and righteous man. Good will come to him who is generous and lends freely, who conducts his affairs with justice. Surely he will never be shaken; a righteous man will be remembered forever. He will have no fear of bad news; his heart is steadfast, trusting in the Lord. His heart is secure, he will have no fear; in the end he will look in triumph on his foes. He has scattered abroad his gifts to the poor, his righteousness endures forever; his horn [name] will be lifted high in honor" (Ps 112: 2-9 NIV). *That's* what it means to live in God's blessings.

RESTORE WITH THE RIGHT ATTITUDE (1)

If a man is overtaken in any trespass...
restore such a one in a spirit of gentleness.

GALATIANS 6:1 NKJV

When somebody messes up, God says; "Restore such a one in a spirit of gentleness." But what if they've disgraced themselves and provided fodder for the skeptics who already think all Christians are hypocrites? Why bother with somebody like that?

First: Because the Bible says, "If a man is overtaken [caught by surprise]...[consider] yourself lest you also be tempted." If it happened to you you'd want somebody to help you, right? And if you're thinking you would never embezzle money, have an affair, or slap a child in anger, think again. When you're under financial pressure, sleep deprived, lonely and depressed, or your marriage is on shaky ground, you might be surprised what you'd do. Paul says, "We are just as capable of messing it up as they were. Don't be so...self-confident...You could fall flat on your face as easily as anyone else" (1Co 10:12 TM).

Second: Because Jesus is your example. While He had no time for Pharisees who hid their sins under a religious façade, not once did He condemn anybody who was "overtaken" by temptation and failure. When they repented He forgave and restored them. Theologian Victor Shepherd writes: "When we're face-to-face with someone who's been surprised because trespass overtook them, do we deflect their shame back into their face, or do we own it as ours? Do we rub their nose in it, or do we absorb it, put an arm around them and affirm our solidarity-in-sinnership? Do we regard ourselves as superior, or do we say, 'Take my hand...I know the way to the cross?'"

RESTORE WITH THE RIGHT ATTITUDE (2)

If a man is overtaken in any trespass...
restore such a one in a spirit of gentleness.

GALATIANS 6:1 NKJV

The word *trespass* comes from the word "misstep," which means to take a step in the wrong direction or to make an error in judgment or conduct. When you lose your footing or you slip on an icy sidewalk, you didn't intend to fall, but now it's happened and you need help to get back up again. That's the kind of trespass the Bible talks about when it says, "Restore such a one in a spirit of gentleness." In Greek the word *restore* has two shades of meaning:

(1) Resetting a broken bone. Paul says, "Christ makes us one body...connected to each other" (Ro 12:5 GWT). When you think about it, your spiritual family is even more important than your physical family, because it will last forever. By reinstating a brother or sister who has been overtaken by sin, you help to heal their pain and enable them to become a vital, functioning part of Christ's body again.

(2) Removing a tumor. Malignant tumors are life-threatening, and spiritual tumors are soul-threatening. By removing one you not only help save somebody, you obey the Scripture, "Bear one another's burdens, and...fulfill the law of Christ" (Gal 6:2 NKJV). And make no mistake, sharing their shame and humiliation *is* a burden. Nevertheless, "We should do it ...[giving] special attention to those who are in the family of believers" (Gal 6:10 NCV). In God's army we are not supposed to shoot our wounded. Indeed, if the wounded can't find mercy in the ranks of the redeemed, where are they going to find it?

IMPORTANT LEADERSHIP PRINCIPLES

I have chosen you.

HAGGAI 2:23 NIV

Over the years leadership coach Angie Ward has enlisted dozens of ministry volunteers. She says that most of the time she hears the same excuses: "I'm not a leader...I don't know anything about teens...I'm not an extrovert" (or as Moses told God, "Send Aaron"). Instead of trying to convince them otherwise, Ward tells them they have only two major responsibilities:

(1) To love people. Face it, ministry would be easy if we didn't have to deal with people. But people matter to God and they should matter to us! Like being part of a family and knowing what's best for your own children, you need to spend time getting to know the people who depend on you and look to you for direction. Consider their needs, not just your own. And look for ways to serve them instead of seeing them as distractions from your "real" work. Jesus spent most of His time with people, not offering pious platitudes, but loving and ministering to them. And He said, "Love each other as I...loved you" (Jn 13:34 NCV). It's always easier to ask people to do something, when you're modeling the same kind of behavior in your own life.

(2) To try to think like a leader. One mega-church pastor says that before he makes any important decision, he asks himself what the other leaders he respects would do in the same situation. That's wise! Asking somebody to be a leader can be intimidating and overwhelming, whereas, asking them to *think* like one takes the pressure off, allows them to be less-than-perfect, and encourages them to grow into the job!

BEFORE YOU TAKE THE PLUNGE

Marriage isn't for everyone.

MATTHEW 19:11 TM

A third-grade teacher received this hilarious essay on Ben Franklin: "Benjamin Franklin was born in Boston, but he didn't like it there so he traveled to Philadelphia. When he got off the boat he walked up the street and bought a loaf of bread. *Then he met a lady, and discovered electricity!*" We smile, but as one marriage counselor observes, "Society has made romance the basis for marriage. Now there's nothing wrong with romance; it's a potent force in driving people into matrimony. But it's become the primary factor. Romance is highly conditional on physical appearance. Romantic love excites and entices, which means there's often shallowness about romantic relationships. Because emotions are so overpowering people don't realize what they're getting into till it's too late. One morning you look across the bed and she's not awake yet. Her mouth's open and her hair's hanging over her face. Or worse, she wakes first, looks across the bed, and in your case there's *no* hair hanging down! That's when romance takes a nose dive!"

A marriage is what you create *after* the wedding. It doesn't just happen. You have to build it with courtesy, patience, support, and a "love marked by giving, not getting" (Eph 5:21-28 TM). That's why Jesus said, "Not everyone is mature enough to live a married life. It requires a certain aptitude and grace. Marriage isn't for everyone…if you're capable of growing into the largeness of marriage, do it." On the other hand, a husband and wife who put Christ at the center of their relationship, can grow it into something that makes society's definition of romance look lightweight by comparison.

PEACE—IT'S YOUR INHERITANCE!

My...peace I...bequeath to you.

JOHN 14:27 AMP

Paul said, "Let the peace that comes from Christ rule in your hearts" (Col 3:15 NLT). Peace is your birthright. Jesus said, "My...peace I...bequeath to you." The word *bequeath* is used in the execution of a will. When somebody dies they bequeath their most valuable possessions to the people they love; they don't leave them junk. However, just because Jesus left His peace to us doesn't mean it automatically operates in our lives. It's a reserve we must draw from every day. And the enemy will do everything he can to deplete it. He knows when you're in turmoil you do and say things you later regret, plus, when you've lost your peace it's harder to hear from God.

Anxiety is often our first reaction to conflict or problems. In those moments getting peaceful may seem disloyal or apathetic. Subconsciously we think, "If I care, I'll worry. If this is important, I must stay upset." It's a misguided belief that the outcome will be positively affected by the amount of time we spend worrying. No, your best problem-solving resource is peace. Solutions arise more easily and naturally out of a peaceful state, whereas, fear and anxiety block solutions. Anxiety empowers the problem; it doesn't help to harbor turmoil. God's peace is available if you choose it. So, refuse to let negative emotions run amok in your life. The Bible says, "When the Holy Spirit *controls* our lives he will produce...in us...peace" (Gal 5:22 TLB). Jesus said, "Do not *let* your hearts be troubled" (Jn 14:1 NIV). That means you have the option of choosing between peace and inner conflict. So choose peace—it's your inheritance!

KEEP YOUR EYES ON JESUS!

Consider him who endured such opposition...
so that you will not...lose heart.

HEBREWS 12:3 NIV

A re you feeling misunderstood? You're not alone! The most misunderstood individual who ever lived was Jesus. Critics joked about His birth, disputed His divine origin, scorned His purposes, reviled His teachings, were suspicious of His motives, critical of His methods, and angered by His message. Ultimately they put Him to death on a cross! That explains what the Apostle John meant when he wrote, "The Light shines in the darkness, and the darkness did not comprehend it...He came to His own, and those who were His own did not receive Him" (Jn 1:5-11 NAS). Wherever He went, Jesus met with misunderstanding and rejection. Yet in spite of it, He endured. And by His grace you can too!

The Bible says: "Let us throw off everything that hinders and the sin that so easily entangles, and let us run with perseverance the race marked out for us. Let us fix our eyes on Jesus, the author and perfecter of our faith, who for the joy set before him endured the cross, scorning its shame, and sat down at the right hand of the throne of God. Consider him who endured such opposition from sinful men, so that you will not grow weary and lose heart" (Heb 12:1-3 NIV). So, as you run your race today: (a) Recognize the things that slow you down. (b) Recognize the things that trip you up. (c) Recognize that obstacles and opposition are par for the course, and don't get discouraged. How do you do this? By keeping your eyes on Jesus and drawing strength from Him each day.

SEEING JESUS IN THE UNDERDOG

You did it to Me.

MATTHEW 25:40 NAS

A minister on Chestnut Street in Philadelphia noticed a homeless man coming towards him. He was filthy and his beard was caked with rotten food. He was holding a cup of coffee and the lip of the cup was dirty. Staggering up to him the hobo exclaimed, "Hey, mister. You want some of my coffee?" The pastor really didn't, but he thought it was the right thing to do, so he said, "Sure, I'll take a sip." When he handed the cup back he remarked, "You're generous giving away your coffee." Looking at him the derelict replied, "Well, it was particularly delicious today, and I think if God gives you something *that* good you should share it!"

The pastor continued: "I figured I was being set up and it would cost me five bucks. So I asked him, 'Is there something I can do for you in return?' The man answered, 'Yeah, you can give me a hug!' (To tell the truth, I was hoping for the five dollar option!) He put his arms around me, and I suddenly realized he wasn't going to let me go! People were passing by and staring at me. There I was, dressed in my establishment garb, hugging this filthy bum! I was embarrassed. Then little by little my embarrassment changed to awe. I heard a voice echoing down the corridors of time saying, 'I was hungry; did you feed Me? I was naked; did you clothe Me? I was sick; did you care for Me? *I was the bum you met on Chestnut Street*...did you hug me? For if you did...you did it to Me.'"

ONE DAY AT A TIME

Don't get worked up about...tomorrow.

MATTHEW 6:34 TM

Max Lucado says, "Worry is to joy, what a vacuum cleaner is to dirt; you might as well attach your heart to a happiness-sucker and flip the switch." Jesus said, "Don't get worked up about...tomorrow. God will help you deal with whatever hard things come up when the time comes." When it looks like things are falling apart, Paul reminds us, "Every detail in our lives...is worked into something good" (Ro 8:28 TM). When it seems like the world's gone mad, don't forget God "existed before anything else, and he holds all creation together" (Col 1:17 NLT). When worry whispers, "God doesn't know what you need," remember God promised to "take care of everything you need" (Ph 4:19 TM).

Jesus taught us to pray, "Give us *this* day our daily bread." You won't get the wisdom or resources to handle tomorrow's problems till you need them. When we "go confidently to the throne...[we'll] find kindness, which will help us *at the right time*" (Heb 4:16 GWT).

Over a century ago Charles Spurgeon said: "Enough for today is all we can enjoy. We cannot eat, drink, or wear more than today's supply of food and clothing. The surplus gives us the care of storing it and the anxiety that someone might steal it. One staff aids a traveler; a bunch of staves is a heavy burden. Enough is as good as a feast, and more than gluttony can enjoy. Enough is all we should expect, a craving for more is ungratefulness. When our Father doesn't give you more, be content with your daily allowance."

TAKE CHARGE OF YOUR LIFE!

Don't let the world...squeeze you into its own mould.

ROMANS 12:2 PHP

Do you feel like you no longer control your own life? Like life's running you instead of you running it? That's because you're in the passenger's seat, conforming to people, events and circumstances. They're in the driver's seat, not you. No wonder your frustration level is high and your contentment level is low. "Don't let the world...squeeze you into its own mould." If you're feeling "squeezed," you've two options.

(a) Remain a conformer, or become a transformer. Either choose to stay in the passenger seat, or get behind the wheel. The Bible says, "Do not be conformed to this world" (Ro 12:2 NKJV). Instead be transformed into the proactive, faith-driven person God meant you to be. *(b) Take charge of your life by "renewing your mind."* Instead of struggling to change the people and circumstances around you, change how you think and what you tell yourself. The Greek word for renewing means "to align your thoughts with God's." Abandon those self-defeating thoughts that tell you "you're not, you can't, and you'll never be able to." God says: "You are, you can, and you certainly will be able to," because of His indwelling power! John writes, "This is the victory that conquers the world—our faith" (1Jn 5:4 NCV). Go to God's Word! Discover what He says about the things that intimidate and control you, then pull the plug on them. The Word for you today is: "Don't be afraid ...I am your God. I will make you strong...I will support you" (Isa 41:10 NCV). Align your thoughts with God's thoughts. Get into the driver's seat and take charge of your life!

TRY PRAYING ABOUT IT!

In the night his song shall be with me.

PSALM 42:8

Nothing fuels prayer like real need. In a crisis, even those who say they don't believe in God, pray secretly. It's an admission that there are certain things we can't resolve. David said, "In the night his song shall be with me, and my prayer unto the God of my life." Some prayers are midnight cries for help, intended for God's ears only; the fear is too deep and the feelings too private; we don't want others around when those inner feelings surface. In prayer you "Cast all your anxiety on him because he cares for you" (1Pe 5:7 NIV), and because you know He will handle it for you.

A mother watched her son run into the house clutching his bloody hand. "Let me see!" she said. Backing away he cried, "No, you'll hurt me." When he finally opened his hand, instead of a major injury she saw a tiny scrape that bled a lot. As she marveled at his theatrics, she realized she'd done the same to God. When her husband left her she was so hurt, she refused to pray. God kept saying, "Let me help you," as she clenched her fists and said, "No, you'll hurt me." Once she realized this she gave it to God and her healing began. Catherine Marshall called this "the prayer of relinquishment," which means giving the situation to God, taking your hands off it completely, refusing to discuss it any further, and trusting the One who makes "all things work together for good" (Ro 8:28). That's why prayer makes it possible for you to stop struggling with the situation and have peace about it!

LOOKING FORWARD TO V-DAY!

*Shielded by God's power
until the coming of the salvation.*

1 PETER 1:5 NIV

In World War II, if you'd asked the brave souls in the French Resistance how they ever hoped to prevail against the forces of evil when they were ill-equipped and outnumbered, they'd have told you: "While we're struggling on this side of the Channel, an invasion force is assembling on the other side. Nobody knows exactly when, but soon a signal will be given, a fleet of ships will come, we'll join them and they'll carry us on to victory."

Every war has pivotal battles that shape the outcome, like Waterloo and Gettysburg. The Battle of Normandy determined the outcome of World War II, but it didn't immediately end it. In fact, things got worse before they got better. The *battle* was fought and won on D-day, but it wasn't until V-day that the *war* officially ended and victory was declared. On earth we're in a life-or-death fight against the forces of evil. We live waiting for the trumpet that heralds Christ's return to lead us to victory. Jesus said, "No one knows...that day or hour" (Mt 24:36 NIV). In the meantime He tells us to "Occupy till I come" (Lk 19:13). He also gives us, "A living hope through the resurrection...into an inheritance that can never perish...for you, who through faith are shielded by God's power until the coming of the salvation...to be revealed in the last time" (1Pe 1:3-5 NIV). Christ's resurrection removes all our doubts about the final result. We won't limp out battered and broken, we'll march out triumphant, "a radiant church...holy and blameless" (Eph 5:27 NIV). So live your life in the light of God's V-day!

ANTS

The ants are a people not strong,
yet they prepare their meat in summer.

PROVERBS 30:25

The message of the ant is "prepare yourself!" He prepares for winter while he is still in summer. That's because: *(1) His eyes are on the future.* You can't undo the past, but if you let it, it can undo you. The summer of your opportunities is passing quickly. Winter will come whether you're ready or not. Remember Christ's parable about the five foolish virgins who had no oil in their lamps and were excluded from the wedding? If you're not ready when your time comes, you'll miss out. *(2) He has the ability to delay gratification.* If you don't have the patience to wait, you'll miss, or mess up, what God has in mind for you. The ant takes the resources he has in summer, and moves it towards his winter. Will somebody else show up and do this for him? No. Are there predators looking for a chance to steal what he's got? Yes. But he's so focused on where he's going, he doesn't have time to worry about where he is. *(3) He has a cause bigger than himself.* Ever watch an ant work? He sinks his teeth into a piece of bread three times bigger than himself and drags it to where he's trying to go. Are you saying, "This is too big for me, I can't carry it by myself?" You don't have to. Read this: "Glory be to God who by his mighty power at work within us is able to do far more than we could ever dare to ask or even dream of" (Eph 3:20 TLB).

CONIES

The conies are but a feeble folk,
yet make they their houses in the rocks.

PROVERBS 30:26

A coney looks like a rabbit but he can't run like one. He resembles a mole but he can't dig deep like one. So he moves to higher ground and positions himself in rocks, in a place of strength. What's the message of the coney? Reposition yourself! How? *(1) By realizing who you are in Christ.* When you accepted Jesus as your Savior, your status in God's eyes changed completely. You're no longer an outsider, but a fully accepted member of God's redeemed family, with direct access to your heavenly Father and all the rights and privileges that go with it. Knowing that allows you to operate from a place of strength and not weakness, faith and not fear. When that happens you begin to pray for more, believe God for more, and enjoy more of His blessings. *(2) By recognizing that your limitations don't limit God.* Who does God use? "Feeble folk." How? By putting them in positions of strength. Sometimes that means putting extra support around them. When you have a bad leg, you don't put the brace on your good leg, you put it on the feeble one. And if He has to, God will put braces on you and get you there ahead of the folks who sit around complacent and complaining. "Feeble folk" praise God differently! Others praise Him because they have a feeling of entitlement, but not conies; they remember where they were when God found them and what He brought them through, and they say, "If it had not been the Lord who was on our side" (Ps 124:1).

LOCUSTS (1)

The locusts have no king,
yet go they forth all of them by bands.

PROVERBS 30:27

In Bible days people feared a cloud of locusts more than all the armies of their enemies combined. They could literally black out the light of the sun, devour everything in sight, and bring down a kingdom. They were unstoppable! What's the message of the locust? *(1) Don't quit, your victory is assured!* The locust is not big, but he's bold! If he can't get through the door, he'll come in through the window. If he can't get in through the window, he'll climb down the gutter and come up under the porch. But he never gives up. So keep praying, keep believing, keep fighting; your victory is assured. "If God be for us, who can be against us?" (Ro 8:31). Pastor, a hundred locusts will do more to win your community to Christ than a thousand bench warmers. *(2) Alone you can't, but together we can!* The locusts operate in "bands." Some of us have issues when it comes to letting people into our life. Because of fear, insecurity or pride, we don't want to talk to anybody, or open up and admit to anybody that we need anything. To reach your destiny you must surround yourself with the right people. You can't run with weak, satisfied, laid-back, mediocre people. No, you need people with an appetite for life and a hunger for God. In God's kingdom the mathematics are different: "One can face a thousand, but two can chase ten thousand" (See Dt 32:30). "If two of you on earth agree about anything you ask for, it will be done for you by my Father in heaven" (Mt 18:19 NIV).

LOCUSTS (2)

The locusts have no king,
yet go they forth all of them by bands.

PROVERBS 30:27

Locusts can't really fly; their wings are too narrow. But they can jump two hundred times their own height. And timing is everything! The locust waits till the wind blows, then he jumps, and the wind carries him to his destination. What's the message of the locust? *(1) When God moves, be sure you move!* A locust cannot navigate where he goes, or fly against the wind, or chart his own course, or change direction. No, he's totally dependent on the wind. Thank God for self-help books and leadership seminars, etc. But there comes a moment when you have to trust God, recognize His timing, take a leap of faith and let the wind of His Spirit take you where you need to go. All your flapping around and wearing yourself out won't get the job done. *(2) Stay sensitive to the wind.* God, not you, determines your life's purpose. He's the One who schedules your seasons of opportunity. But spiritual lethargy can dull your senses and cause you to miss your time. "Though by this time you ought to be teachers, you need someone to teach you the elementary truths of God's word all over again" (Heb 5:12 NIV). Perhaps instead of flying, your life is falling apart because you let the fire of God in your heart go out. Well, it's not too late! The wind will blow again. So start praying, "Lord, I may have missed my time before, but not this time. I don't want to end up wishing I'd done something I didn't get to do, not because You weren't ready but because I wasn't."

LOCUSTS (3)

The locusts have no king,
yet go they forth all of them by bands.

PROVERBS 30:27

The locusts have one more important lesson to teach us: *Instead of following, lead the way!* If you keep hoping someone will take you by the hand and tell you how it's all going to work out, you'll never get anywhere. "The locusts have no king [leader], yet they go forth." Note the word "go." Has it occurred to you that God may have called *you* to blaze the trail and set the pace? You've sat in church for years and heard all the sermons, now "it's time to cross the Jordan and take possession of the land the Lord your God is giving you" (See Jos 1:11).

But you say, "Nobody in my family has ever done anything like this before." Good, then you'll be the first! Who are you going to listen to? The voices of your dysfunctional past or the God who is saying to you, "Be strong and courageous ...for the Lord your God will be with you wherever you go" (Jos 1:9 NIV). Having folks think your ideas are crazy, is just part of every success story. When God moves, He doesn't commission a focus group or call for a vote. No, He looks for somebody like Isaiah to say, "Here am I. Send me!" (Isa 6:8 NIV). Then He underwrites them, equips them and sends them out to be "The head, and not the tail...above only, and...not... beneath" (Dt 28:13).

And the people God uses are people He can trust with success; people who say, "My wings were too small to travel this far. It wasn't my flapping around that got me here, it was God."

SPIDERS (1)

The spider taketh hold with her hands,
and is in kings' palaces.

PROVERBS 30:28

Everything a spider needs to survive and succeed in life, God put within it. Swipe it with a broom and before it hits the ground, its fall is broken. It just reaches inside, releases another protein-filled silk-like thread, slides down, finds a safe place, then comes back stronger than ever and builds a new web. What's the message of the spider? *Everything you need, God has placed within you!* The Bible says, "His divine power has given us everything we need for life and godliness...he has given us his very great and precious promises, so that through them you may participate in the divine nature" (2Pe 1:3-4 NIV). What has God given us? "Everything we need." What has God made us participants in? "His divine nature." Wow! Your future is not determined by who you know and who you don't, who likes you and who doesn't. The power to fulfill your destiny is within you! The warfare over your life and the struggle you're in, is about what you were born, called and gifted to do. So, "Stir up...the...gift of God...that is in you" (2Ti 1:6 AMP). In other words—start producing!

Life may have knocked you down, but it hasn't knocked you out. What's at work within you will triumph over what's at work around you. Stand on God's Word, draw on your faith, hold on, and when the smoke clears, rise up and announce, "By the grace of God, I'm back!" You say, "But I've lost so much." As long as you still have what God put within you, you can make it!

SPIDERS (2)

*The spider taketh hold with her hands,
and is in kings' palaces.*

PROVERBS 30:28

When it's time to lay eggs the spider produces a particular type of silk thread and spins it into a protective sac, then deposits them. When an enemy comes to steal the spider's offspring, it gets trapped on the sticky fluids that line the silk. Then the spider wraps the enemy in another kind of thread, and turns it into food. What's the message of the spider? *The battle is over your future!* Don't let the enemy have your children. Don't let him rob you of your potential. Don't let him steal your destiny. When those with weak wills, weak knees and weak faith saw the giants in the Promised Land they wanted to go back to Egypt. But not Caleb. He said, "Neither fear ye the people of the land; for they are bread for us" (Nu 14:9). When you understand what the battle in your life is about, you actually begin to feed off the stuff the enemy throws at you and say, "Bring it on, what does not destroy me will only make me stronger."

Be like Shammah. "When the Philistines banded together at a place where there was a field full of lentils, Israel's troops fled...But Shammah took his stand in the middle of the field. He defended it and struck the Philistines down, and the Lord brought about a great victory" (2Sa 23:11-12 NIV). Shammah knew what he was fighting for. That lentil patch put food on his table. It represented his family's future. It was his legacy. And when Shammah stood up to the enemy, "The Lord brought about a great victory." And He'll do the same for you!

SPIDERS (3)

*The spider taketh hold with her hands,
and is in kings' palaces.*

PROVERBS 30:28

The spider has eight eyes, yet it can barely see. What makes it an avid hunter is that the hair follicles on its legs are full of sensitivity and it can discern everything that's going on around it. What's the message of the spider? *Use your God-given sense of discernment!* You can discern more with your spirit than you can see with your eyes. "Ye have an unction from the Holy One, and ye know all things" (1Jn 2:20). God will let you know things you can neither prove nor explain. Jesus said that He would show us "things to come" (See Jn 16:13). But He won't do it so that we can ego trip, or run around acting flakey. No, "He shall glorify me: he shall receive of mine, and shall [show] it unto you" (Jn 16:14). God gives "inside information" to those who seek to glorify Him. So stop living beneath your spiritual privilege. The old country church folks used to sing, "The Holy Ghost done told me, everything's gonna be all right." That may not be good grammar, but it's sound Bible truth. Can't you remember a time when your eyes told you, "You're not gonna make it," but your spirit kept telling you, "Everything's gonna be all right"? A time when you met somebody who looked good, too good, and your spirit warned you that something was wrong with them? "His anointing teaches you about all things ...that anointing is real, not counterfeit—just as it has taught you, remain in him" (1Jn 2:27 NIV). The way to walk in discernment is to stay close to God.

SPIDERS (4)

The spider taketh hold with her hands,
and is in kings' palaces.

PROVERBS 30:28

How come a spider can walk across the sticky threads of its web and not get stuck, yet those same threads will trap every predator that enters? The secret is—oil! Its tiny suction cup shaped feet exude fresh oil with every step, so it glides through stuff others can't survive, or get bogged down in. What's the message of the spider? *You need to be continually anointed with the oil of God's Spirit!* Looking back, you realize that's what kept you sane when you thought you were going to lose your mind. It's why you made it when others didn't. And it's why you need to stay filled with God's Spirit every day. The Psalmist said, "I shall be anointed with fresh oil! (Ps 92:10).

But there are four truths in Exodus, chapter 30, concerning the anointing oil, that we need to keep in mind if we're going to live an anointed life: *(1) Without it, our ministry is ineffective.* "Thou shalt anoint Aaron and his sons...that they may minister unto me" (Ex 30:30). *(2) Our children need to experience it.* "This shall be a holy anointing oil unto me throughout your generations" (Ex 30:31). *(3) God won't anoint our fleshly efforts and agendas.* "Upon man's flesh shall it not be poured, neither shall ye make any other like it" (Ex 30:32). *(4) We are in danger when we try to substitute it with other things.* "Whoever makes any like it...must be cut off" (Ex 30:38 NIV). Before you leave home every morning get down on your knees and pray, "Lord, anoint me with fresh oil!"

SPIDERS (5)

*The spider taketh hold with her hands,
and is in kings' palaces.*

PROVERBS 30:28

Some spiders have so much venom in them that they can kill anything they come in contact with, simply by releasing what's in their mouth. What's the message of the spider? *Check what's coming out of your mouth!* Paul writes, "Faith cometh by hearing, and hearing by the word of God" (Ro 10:17). What are you taking in? What are you giving out? Faith or fear, hope or discouragement, joy or sadness, truth or error, love or bitterness? The Bible says, "Death and life are in the power of the tongue: and they that love it shall eat the fruit thereof" (Pr 18:21). Notice two things in this Scripture: (1) This is a life and death issue. (2) Your words are like seeds; they always produce fruit. You can't believe God for His best, then go around expecting and expressing the worst. When what you say consistently, contradicts what God's Word says, you're sabotaging yourself. The words you speak have power—and consequences. So begin to correct yourself. Instead of saying, "I can't change," or, "I'll never get out of this mess," start saying what God's Word says. Do what Jesus did in the wilderness: open your mouth and declare, "It is written." Jesus knew the Scriptures so well that He was able to tell Satan, "It's written that I don't have to bow to you. It's written that I don't have to come to you for what I need." And what was the result? "The Devil left him, and angels came and attended him" (Mt 4:11 NIV). When you're under attack open your mouth, declare God's Word, and the forces of heaven will come to your aid!

SPIDERS (6)

The spider taketh hold with her hands,
and is in kings' palaces.

PROVERBS 30:28

We learn from the spider that: (a) your size doesn't deter-mine your potential, your spirit does; (b) no matter where you start, you can end up in the king's palace. What's the message of the spider? *As long as you live, keep producing!* You might not produce as much as somebody else, but you've got to keep producing. You might not be able to produce what you used to, but keep producing. Jesus taught that some of us pro-duce thirtyfold, others sixtyfold, and some a hundredfold (See Mt 13:8). We don't all produce at the same level, but we must all produce at some level. Don't get intimidated because the other guy is producing a hundredfold and you're only producing sixtyfold. You're only accountable for what God gives you!

The Bible says, "They shall bring forth fruit in old age" (Ps 92:14). Look out; retirement can be dangerous to your health! Keep your mind alert, your dreams alive, and your body moving. You might be old and feeble, but you have to have a reason to get out of bed every morning, because if you don't, after a while you won't be able to get out of bed. Get up and get dressed, even if you're not going anywhere. If you can't fly, get in the car. If you can't get in the car, run. If you can't run, walk. If you can't walk, stand up. If you're lying down, sit up. If you can't sit up, wiggle your toes, but let the Devil know you're still in the game. By the grace of God, keep producing!

ABIDE

He who abides in Me...bears much fruit.

JOHN 15:5 NAS

Jesus said, "I am the vine, you are the branches; he who abides in Me...bears much fruit, for apart from Me you can do nothing." As branches we *bear* fruit, but the life-giving substance required to do it, *flows* to us from the vine. Any time we try to produce our own fruit, it's going to be wax fruit.

When someone says, "I don't love my wife or my husband," that's not the issue. The issue is, can Christ love your wife or husband through you? The answer is yes, because love is a fruit that's produced in you by the Holy Spirit (See Gal 5:22). So, the question is, are you willing to allow Christ's love to flow through you?

Abiding in Christ is just another name for intimacy with Christ. He wants to express His life through you, which comes through your attachment to Him. If your prayer life is just a matter of shooting up an occasional SOS as emergencies arise, you're missing this intimacy. If you just have your devotions in the morning so you can "get them out of the way and get on with your day," you don't understand abiding.

After years of smoking, one lady decided to kick the habit. She tried every stop-smoking product on the market but nothing worked. Finally she decided that instead of focusing on all the things she was doing to quit, she would just focus on being in God's presence and coming to really know Him. Within thirty days she had quit smoking—because of the power of the vine. So the word for you today is "abide."

THE "CHURCH OF ADULLAM" (1)

Adullam...where...
all who were down on their luck came.

1 SAMUEL 22:1-2 TM

David didn't choose wilderness living, he had nowhere else to go when Saul isolated him from his family, ended his military career and banned him from the palace. The wilderness experience starts out with feelings of disconnection and isolation, and usually gets worse before it gets better. Hoping to form an alliance with the Philistines in Goliath's hometown, David went to Gath. After all, when Saul's your mutual enemy you naturally become friends, right? Wrong! The Philistines wanted nothing to do with David. So with yet another door closed, he escaped to the cave of Adullam where he turned back to God. There he became a magnet for "those who were in distress or in debt or discontented" (1Sa 22:2 NIV). The Bible says, "They came to David...to help him, until it was a great army, like the army of God" (1Ch 12:22 NKJV). Not exactly a model congregation! Do you know what the name Adullam means? A place of refuge! Jesus said, "It is not the healthy who need a doctor, but the sick. I have not come to call the righteous, but sinners to repentance" (Lk 5:31-32 NIV). Strong churches are built from people who were "in distress or in debt or discontented." Do *you* remember being there? Paul said: "Take a good look...at who you were when you got called... I don't see many of 'the brightest and the best'...not many influential, not many from high-society families....God deliberately chose men and women...the culture overlooks... exploits and abuses, chose these 'nobodies' to expose the hollow pretensions of the 'somebodies'" (1Co 1:26-28 TM). Welcome to the "Church of Adullam."

THE "CHURCH OF ADULLAM" (2)

Adullam...where...
all who were down on their luck came.

1 SAMUEL 22:1-2 TM

Although he was raised in a good home, Whit Criswell got hooked on gambling and ended up embezzling from the bank where he worked. When the auditors found out, he decided to end his life. He wrote a suicide note, drove to the outskirts of town, parked his car and put a gun to his head, saying, "Go ahead, you no-good slob, it's what you deserve." But he couldn't do it. So at dawn he returned home where police arrested him. He felt humiliated being handcuffed in front of his friends and family. But he was also liberated, because he no longer had to live a lie. Criswell's prison cell became his "cave of Adullam," the place where he turned back to God. When he was released he joined a church doing odd jobs, and eventually became a staff member. In 1998 another church asked him to be their senior pastor, and today it's one of Kentucky's fastest growing congregations. Another cave dweller "ransomed, healed, restored, forgiven," by the amazing grace of God!

The introduction to Psalm 57 describes it as "A song of David when he fled from Saul into the cave." In the first verse he says, "Be merciful to me, O God...my soul trusts in You; And in the shadow of Your wings I will make my refuge, until these calamities have passed by" (NKJV). Are you feeling down on your luck today? Do you see yourself as damaged goods? Instead of wandering alone in the wilderness, come and find what you need in God's presence; come, find purpose and direction among His people in the "Church of Adullam."

BE A WEED-KILLER!

You must not give sin a vote.

ROMANS 6:12 TM

When it comes to dealing with sin in our lives, the Bible doesn't mince words: "Our old way of life was nailed to the Cross with Christ, a decisive end to that sin-miserable life —no longer at sin's every beck and call! What we believe is this: If we get included in Christ's sin-conquering death, we also get included in his life-saving resurrection. We know that when Jesus was raised from the dead it was a signal of the end of death-as-the-end. Never again will death have the last word. When Jesus died, He took sin down with Him, but alive He brings God down to us. From now on, think of it this way: Sin speaks a dead language that means nothing to you; God speaks your mother tongue, and you hang on every word. You are dead to sin and alive to God…That means you must not give sin a vote in the way you conduct your lives. Don't give it the time of day. Don't even run little errands that are connected with that old way of life. Throw yourselves wholeheartedly and full-time—remember, you've been raised from the dead!—into God's way of doing things. Sin can't tell you how to live. After all, you're not living under that old tyranny any longer. You're living in the freedom of God" (Ro 6:6-14 TM).

Sin is like weeds. To love roses you must hate weeds, declare war on them and uproot them before they spring up. Why? Because left unchecked, they'll take over your garden and destroy every good thing that grows. So the word for you today is—be a weed-killer!

UNDER PRESSURE!

We are pressed...but not...broken.

2 CORINTHIANS 4:8 TLB

Do you feel like you're in a tunnel with no way out? Rejoice, you're positioned for a miracle! Paul said: "We are pressed on every side by troubles, but not crushed and broken. We are perplexed...but we don't give up and quit. We are hunted down, but God never abandons us. We get knocked down, but we get up again and keep going." A certain amount of pressure is necessary to release our faith, and God knows exactly how much to apply. He allows us to get to where: (a) we've exhausted our own resources; (b) we're tired of Satan stealing what God says is ours; (c) the opinions of others no longer control us. It's the place Hannah found herself in when she prayed in the temple, "In distress of soul...and weeping bitterly" (1Sa 1:10 AMP). She was under such pressure because of her childless state that when she began to unburden herself before God, the church hierarchy thought she was drunk. But when you're desperate, you're not overly concerned about blowing the minds of religious onlookers; your only concern is touching the heart of God.

With God there are no hopeless situations, just people who've grown hopeless about them. Real faith comes into its own when push collides with shove. After all, you don't need God to part the Red Sea when there are bridges all around, right? It's when there's nothing you can do to avoid the inevitable, that you start trusting God to do the impossible! So the crisis you're experiencing today could be a blessing in disguise—an opportunity to experience a greater degree of His power at work in your life.

GETTING PAST YOUR PAST (1)

Do not dwell on the past.
See, I am doing a new thing!

ISAIAH 43:18-19 NIV

When God determines your future, He doesn't consult your past. Mary Magdalene was a known prostitute. But after Christ redeemed her she became one of the last people to leave the cross (See Mt 27:55-61) and one of the first to discover and announce His resurrection (See Mt 28:7). Because she embraced Christ and the future He offers all of us, she's been mentioned with honor by every ensuing generation. Peter was a fisherman with a hair-trigger temper and some anti-social tendencies. Yet God filled him with so much spiritual power that when he preached, multitudes came to Christ (See Ac 2:40-41). Jacob lived up to his name "deceiver." But God gave him an extreme makeover and changed his name to Israel, which means, "A Prince with God" (See Ge 32:24-30). Ruth was a Moabite who grew up worshipping idols—not a promising start. But after turning to serve the true God, she became part of the ancestry of King David and our Lord Jesus (See Mt 1:5). Zacchaeus, a well known embezzler, hosted Jesus overnight in his home and ended up becoming a philanthropist. And how about Paul? Killing Christians didn't put him off limits to God. As an apostle he wrote over half of the New Testament by divine revelation, was taken into heaven where he saw incredible things (See 2Co 12:1-4), and when aprons and handkerchiefs taken from his body were placed on the sick they were healed (See Ac 19:11-12). Now, if God could do all that for "people with a past," He can give you a new beginning too!

GETTING PAST YOUR PAST (2)

Do not dwell on the past.
See, I am doing a new thing!

ISAIAH 43:18-19 NIV

Did you know that Abraham Lincoln lost several elections before finally becoming one of America's greatest presidents? In fact, he failed so often it was amazing he kept trying. Did you know that the material used to make Kleenex tissues was invented as a gas mask filter during World War I, and it failed? Then when inventors tried to make it into cold cream it flopped again. Finally they repackaged it as disposable handkerchiefs, and guess what, people buy 200 billion of them annually. Not bad for a product that bombed twice!

You can't seize your future while you're obsessing over your past. So learn from it and let it go. Heed the advice of author Susan Scott: "My dog and cat have taught me a great lesson in life—learn to shed a lot!"

Nobody starts out being good at everything. Tackling new ventures usually means learning by trial and error. When Charles Darrow got married he promised his wife they'd become millionaires. But the Great Depression came and they ended up hitting rock bottom. Darrow was ready to give up his dream but his wife encouraged him to keep going. Then one day he devised the idea of using "play money" to buy "pretend properties," and he turned his vision into a board game with little houses and hotels. It's called *Monopoly,* and Parker Brothers bought it from Darrow for—you've guessed it—a million dollars! Remember, when you're on the right track and you refuse to give up, God can do something great through you. So keep going and don't look back.

HOW'S YOUR DISPOSITION?

A cheerful disposition is good for your health.

PROVERBS 17:22 TM

Born before the telephone or the Eiffel Tower, Jeanne Calmont died at 122 after outliving twenty-seven French presidents, and entered the *Guinness Book of World Records* as the world's oldest woman. Asked the secret of her longevity she replied, "Laughter!" Medical science proves that laughter strengthens your immune system, lowers your blood pressure and counteracts the inertia caused by depression. The Bible is right: "A cheerful disposition is good for your health."

In Scripture, wine represents joy. And Christ's first miracle was turning water into wine; the best they'd ever had. Jesus is a joy-giver! So how come we don't show more of it? Jesus said, "These things have I spoken unto you, that my joy might remain in you, and that your joy might be full" (Jn 15:11). How can you say your sins are forgiven, God guides and protects you and when you die you're going to heaven, yet walk around looking like sour grapes? Paul had so much joy, his jailors were won to Christ and a church sprang up in the "household of Caesar" (See Php 4:22). People are more impacted by your attitude than your theology. When they see you rejoicing in hard times, they wonder what your secret is. They think, "Whatever you've got, I need it" and they become more receptive to the truth. The happiness this world offers is only a reaction to circumstances, but joy is a choice that lifts you above them. The Bible says, "The joy of the Lord is your strength" (Ne 8:10). Joy is the fuel you run on, and the Lord is the source of it. So, how's your disposition?

WORK IT OUT

Streams of living water will flow from within him.

JOHN 7:38 NIV

One of the dangers in seeking to be filled with the Holy Spirit, is that we can reduce it to an "experience" rather than releasing it to accomplish great things for God. If there's an infilling, there must be an outflowing! Every time someone in the New Testament was filled with the Holy Spirit, things happened. Amazing healings took place. They had book burnings in the town square. Idol makers and pornographers went out of business. They didn't just celebrate in church, they took it to the streets. There must be an outflow!

The first picture we have of God in the Bible is of Him in His creative role. He makes us in His image, breathes life into us, then says, "Go out and become productive" (See Ge 1:28).

Are you hoping your life will "just change for the better?" Are you praying for somebody with all the answers to come along and improve your circumstances? No, what's inside you will change what's outside you, if you put it to work! This is not some glib, "can do" self-help sentiment. "It is God who works in you" (Php 2:13 NIV). The struggle in your life right now may be over what God wants to do through you! What's within you is greater than the trouble you've been through, the situation you're in, or the obstacles that lie in your path. When everything around you is saying "no," but something deep within you is saying "yes," that's your God-given destiny. Acknowledge it, anchor your life to it and begin to work it out. If you do, God will work with you.

DON'T TRY TO GET EVEN!

God has put your enemy in your grasp.

1 SAMUEL 26:8 TM

When David had a chance for revenge after Saul tried to kill him, all he did was cut off a corner of Saul's robe. Later while Saul slept, one of David's men said, "God has put your enemy in your grasp." Again David refused. Later he told Saul, "God put your life in my hands today, but I wasn't willing to lift a finger against God's anointed" (v. 23 TM). David didn't see Saul the enemy, he saw Saul the *anointed*—God's property. Max Lucado writes: "A Rottweiler attacked our puppy at a kennel, leaving her with gashes and a dangling ear. I wrote to the dog's owner urging him to put the dog to sleep. But when I showed the letter to the kennel owner she begged me to reconsider. 'What that dog did was horrible, but I'm still training him and I'm not finished with him yet.'" God would say the same about the person who attacked you. "What he did was inexcusable, but I'm not finished with him yet."

Are you keeping track of old scores? Don't do it! God said, "Don't insist on getting even; that's not for you...I'll take care of it" (Ro 12:19 TM). By seeking revenge you're saying, "God, you're not handling things properly, not punishing them sufficiently, not moving fast enough." Dick Innes said: "To be hurt without forgiving, crushed without becoming more caring, suffer without growing more sensitive, makes suffering senseless, futile, a tragic loss, the greatest waste of all." Make Jesus your example: "When he suffered, he didn't make...threats but left everything to the one who judges fairly" (1Pe 2:23 GWT).

THE POWER OF PERSEVERANCE

Blessed is the man who perseveres.

JAMES 1:12 NIV

Ever seen one of those inflatable clowns with a round base? When you knock him down he bounces back up wearing a big, cheesy grin! Perseverance: it's a powerful tool! The Bible says, "Blessed is the man who perseveres." Paul was flogged, shipwrecked, persecuted, and imprisoned in establishments without weight rooms, HDTV, and time off for good behavior! He could have thrown in the towel, but instead he said, "I have no regrets. I couldn't be more sure of my ground—the One I've trusted in can take care of...me...to the end" (2Ti 1:12 TM). Can *you* say that?

God isn't impressed by human ability, dynamic personalities, titles, and designer clothes. He respects people who, when they get knocked down, bounce back with their faith intact, more determined than ever to live for Him. It's Satan's job to attack you—it's your job to fight back. If you are passive he will demolish you! Paul writes: "Resist the enemy...[and] after the battle you will still be standing" (Eph 6:13 NLT). Perseverance means staying in the fight and refusing to give up. It empowers you so you stop feeling like a victim of circumstances. It builds your confidence and becomes a tool you automatically use.

Somebody said the nose of the bulldog is slanted backward so he can keep breathing without letting go! Plus, your reward in heaven is determined by your level of perseverance here on earth. "To him who overcomes I will grant to sit with Me on My throne" (Rev 3:21 NKJV). So keep persevering.

DON'T GET SIDETRACKED

Everyone is looking for you!

MARK 1:37 NIV

Former U.S. Secretary of State Henry Kissinger once quipped, "There can't be another crisis. My schedule's already full!" That can happen when other people determine your agenda. Jesus refused to live that way. During His early ministry when word spread about His miracles, "The whole town gathered… and Jesus healed many" (Mk 1:33-34 NIV). The next morning another crowd of needy people was waiting on His doorstep. But how Jesus responded this time might surprise you. "While it was still dark, Jesus…left the house and went off to a solitary place, where he prayed…his companions went to look for him, and when they found him they exclaimed: 'Everyone is looking for you!' Jesus replied, 'Let us go somewhere else…so I can preach there also. That is why I have come'" (vv. 35-38). What was He thinking! There were headlines to be made, people to be healed, and fans waiting to pat him on the back! Could *you* resist the lure of all that? Jesus did, because He followed God's agenda, not man's.

Jesus loved people so much that one day He would die for them. But that didn't stop Him from saying no when He needed to. Appeasing people in order to win their approval is never a good idea; it puts somebody other than God in the driver's seat. Instead of getting sidetracked, Jesus: (a) made prayer and uninterrupted time with His Father a top priority; (b) recognized that doing God's will was more important than "being all things to all people;" (c) refused to let other people's definition of what was urgent, distract Him from fulfilling His life's purpose. So, don't get sidetracked.

"THIS IS THE DAY"

This is the day the Lord has made;
we will rejoice and be glad in it.

PSALM 118:24 NKJV

Some days the road seems too long and the climb too steep. Max Lucado describes them as days when "Hope is Hindenberged by crisis. You never leave the hospital bed or wheelchair. You wake up in the same prison cell, the cemetery dirt is still fresh, the pink slip still folded in your pocket, the other side of the bed still empty. *'This is the day'* includes divorce days, final-exam days, surgery days, tax days, sending-your-firstborn-off-to-college days. God made this day. He knows the details of each wrenching moment. He isn't on holiday. He still holds the conductor's baton, sits in the cockpit, and occupies the universe's only throne. *'We will rejoice and be glad in it!'* Oops, there's another word we'd like to edit: *in*. Perhaps we could swap it for *after?* Or *through*, or *over*. 'I'll rejoice when this day ends!' Paul rejoiced *in* prison. David wrote psalms *in* the wilderness; Paul and Silas sang *in* jail; the Hebrew children remained resolute *in* the fiery furnace; John saw heaven *in* his exile, and Jesus prayed *in* the garden of pain. You no longer have yesterday. It slipped away as you slept. You don't yet have tomorrow. You can't spend its money, celebrate its achievements or resolve its riddles. Days are bite-sized portions of life: 84,000 heartbeats, 1,440 minutes, a rotation of the earth, a sunrise and sunset, a gift of twenty-four unlived, unexplored hours. And if you can stack one good day on another, you'll link together a good life. *'This is the day,'* live in it."

FEELINGS CAN BE MISLEADING

Be careful what you think.

PROVERBS 4:23 NCV

A Christian writer says: "For many years I lived according to my feelings. It was like riding a roller coaster; one day laughing and feeling good, the next crying and feeling sorry for myself. I was being tormented and controlled. I needed emotional maturity, but I needed God's help to attain it. It's easy to fall into the trap of believing your fickle feelings more than what God says in His Word. And it will take a constant act of your will to *choose* to do things His way rather than your own. But when you do, you'll discover that life is more enjoyable when you're living according to God's plan."

Just as you don't let everybody who knocks on your door come in and make themselves at home, don't let every emotion that surfaces dictate the direction of your day or decide your responses. The Bible says: "Be careful what you think, because your thoughts run your life" (Pr 4:23 NCV); "Capture every thought and make it give up and obey Christ" (2Co 10:5 NCV); if it doesn't line up with God's Word—don't think it. Paul says, "We walk by faith, not by sight" (2Co 5:7), because (and this may come as a surprise) you won't always *feel* God's presence. After the crucifixion two disciples were walking along the Emmaus Road when Jesus came up and walked along with them. But they didn't recognize who He was. They didn't know the leader they'd followed for three years because "he appeared …in a different form" (Mk 16:12 TM). God is a God of faith and He works in ways that faith, not feelings, can discern.

SEEING GOD IN OUR SITUATION

Because of this I rejoice.

PHILIPPIANS 1:18 NIV

When Paul wrote, "What has happened to me has really served to advance the gospel" (Php 1:12 NIV), he was in prison using his situation to tell people about Jesus. He goes on to say, "It has become clear throughout the whole palace guard …that I am in chains for Christ" (Php 1:13 NIV). Then he points out that through his imprisonment "most of the brothers in the Lord have been encouraged to speak the word of God more courageously and fearlessly" (Php 1:14 NIV). Even when Paul found out some people were preaching the Gospel to make trouble for him, he said, "What does it matter? The important thing is…whether from false motives or true, Christ is preached. And because of this I rejoice" (Php 1:18 NIV). Arrested unjustly, treated unkindly, his future uncertain, Paul looked for God's hand in every situation. Therefore he could say in all things "because of this I rejoice." What perspective! What an attitude!

A century ago, following a coal mining accident, the Bishop of Durham told mourners, "It's difficult to understand why God let such a disaster happen, but we know and trust Him and all will be right. At home I have an old silk bookmark given to me by my mother. When I examine the *wrong* side I see nothing but a tangle of threads…it looks like a big mistake. One would think someone had done it who didn't know what they were doing. But when I turn it over and look at the *right* side I see beautifully embroidered, the words *GOD IS LOVE*. We are looking at this today from the wrong side. Someday we shall see it from another standpoint and we shall understand." When we begin to see God in our situation, we can say "because of this I rejoice."

WHEN GOD MAKES UP HIS MIND

For I am the Lord.
I speak, and the word which I speak will come to pass.

EZEKIEL 12:25 NKJV

There are two possible explanations for what happened in Swan Quarter, North Carolina, in 1876. It was either the most astounding coincidence, or an act of God—literally. The Methodist Episcopal Church South needed a new building, so when somebody donated a lot on Oyster Creek Road they accepted. It was low-lying land so they constructed a sturdy little white-frame church and put it up on brick pilings. Days later a storm lashed the town and those within sight of Oyster Creek Road witnessed something amazing. The church building —still intact—was afloat! The flood had lifted it off its pilings and sent it down the road. They tried to moor it with ropes but the church moved on. At the town center, as dozens of people watched helplessly, it made a sharp, inexplicable right turn and continued on. Finally, in the same decisive manner it veered off the road, it headed straight for a vacant lot and stopped dead in the center! The flood waters eventually receded but the building is still there. In fact, 130 years have passed since the church, now called Providence Methodist Church, floated itself to the most desirable property in town. What's amazing is this: The lot where it settled had *originally* been the congregation's first choice for their building, but landowner Sam Sadler turned them down. The morning after the flood, he presented the pastor with the deed.

"For I am the Lord. I speak, and the word which I speak will come to pass." No doubt about it; when God makes up His mind, *nothing* gets in His way!

PREPARED, PLANTED, PLACED, PRUNED, PROSPERED (1)

God planted a garden...
there He put the man whom He had formed.

GENESIS 2:8 NKJV

Before God put Adam into the garden, He "formed" him. There's a process of preparation God takes us through in order to make us what we need to be. But preparation takes time. God must deal with our inconsistencies, personality defects, areas of distrust, unresolved childhood issues, scars, flaws, etc. How long does it take? Only God knows. Admit it; even at your age don't you still recognize some childish ways in yourself? Anybody else would have given up on you, but God has a plan and He's committed to it. We should all wear a sign that says: "Work in progress. If you hire me, you need to know that. If you marry me, you need to know that."

The Bible says the Lord "formed man out of the dust of the ground" (Ge 2:7 NKJV). What's God working with? Dirt! And the tools He uses to form you are the experiences you go through in life. They shape and alter you. And the more you keep trying to have it your way, the longer the process takes. It may take you five years to learn to quit people-pleasing, or ten years to stop feeling sorry for yourself, or twenty years to stop going back and reliving your childhood. All the while God is telling you, "Stop it," and you're saying, "Yeah, I know. I'm gonna do better." Then finally a crisis happens and the truth hits you. At that point you say, "You know what? I'm going to forget those things which are behind and start reaching for those things which are before" (See Php 3:13).

PREPARED, PLANTED, PLACED, PRUNED, PROSPERED (2)

God planted a garden…
there He put the man whom He had formed.

GENESIS 2:8 NKJV

What does it mean to *plant?* To bury seeds beyond human view so that they germinate and eventually produce fruit. In God's plan for your life, He's planted blessings you experience over time. Just because you walk out into a field and don't see a crop, doesn't mean the seeds aren't there; God has planted things in your life that will come to fruition at different times.

It's amazing that God would plant. Why would He go to such trouble when He could just speak a word and create it? Think of the love, the personal involvement of the Creator of the universe, as He stoops down and plants blessings to come up at different seasons in your life. Everything God has for you hasn't come up yet, so you can't give up, or walk away and say, "That's all there is." No, God's got some stuff planted that you haven't seen or experienced. You're still becoming what He planted. Knowing that reinforces your faith that it *will* happen. It also means *God* believes in you—even when you don't believe in yourself.

There are talents in you that haven't been discovered and dreams that haven't been fulfilled. That's what the battle is about! The Devil is fighting you over your destiny. He knows what's been planted in you and he's trying to kill the seed. Don't let him. You're not the person you'll be six months or six years from now, because there's a time factor; everything doesn't come to harvest at the same time. You have to have *faith* and *patience,* otherwise you'll miss what God has for you.

PREPARED, PLANTED, PLACED, PRUNED, PROSPERED (3)

God planted a garden…
there He put the man whom He had formed.

GENESIS 2:8 NKJV

Notice, God *placed* the man in the garden, "eastward in Eden" (Ge 2:8 NKJV). It's not enough to be in the garden, you've got to be in the right location. You must pray, "Lord, place me in *my* garden."

You learn a lot by raising children. You're older and wiser, saying, "Don't do that. Don't go there." But you can't cut through the process. They have to stumble, because that's how they learn to walk and find their way. Maybe you yourself worked at several jobs before figuring out what you were supposed to do. That's because you weren't "placed" yet. At some point, if you're wise, you begin to pray, "Lord, don't let me spend my life trying stuff, place me!"

You can be in the right place and not know it—because the place has been planted, not created! Dave Thomas, the founder of Wendy's, was the child of an unwed mother. He recalls being ashamed of not having a decent pair of shoes to wear. Imagine: a school dropout, wearing shoes that don't fit, working as a busboy waiting tables—but he has a six-billion-dollar business inside him. It doesn't matter where you start, it just matters where you finish. You need to look in the mirror and announce, "There's something in me that hasn't come out yet. God, help me to be steadfast until You pull out of me what You planted in me." Don't let anyone convince you that you're a failure because you don't wear the right shoes, or have it all together right now. God has a *place* in mind for you. Just walk with Him and He'll get you there.

PREPARED, PLANTED, PLACED, PRUNED, PROSPERED (4)

God planted a garden...
there He put the man whom He had formed.

GENESIS 2:8 NKJV

The Bible says: "God took the man and put him in the Garden of Eden to work it and take care of it" (Ge 2:15 NIV). Today God may be saying to you, "I've prepared you, placed you where you need to be, planted blessings in your life that are scheduled to come up at different times, but now you've got to work it." Stop looking for gardens that are already pruned; you have to prune your own garden. You have to go through your own struggles and shed your own tears, or in the case of Dave Thomas, founder of Wendy's, wait on tables and work your way up. When people give you stuff they can take it from you. When God gives it to you, it's yours! But you've got to take care of it. You have to prune your own children; they're not going to turn out right if you neglect them (See Pr 22:6). You have to prune your own relationships; "Blessed is the man who walks not in the counsel of the ungodly" (Ps 1:1 NKJV). You have to prune your own business. That means honoring God as your partner, allowing Him to use your business to promote His business.

When you walk with God He'll protect and prosper you, even in hard times. But you've still got to "work it." Ask any farmer; wheat left unattended will eventually seed itself to death. It must be cultivated. There's nothing wrong with your life—except that you're expecting *God* to do things He's expecting *you* to do. Come on, get some shears and start pruning!

LEARN TO MAKE BETTER DECISIONS

A prudent man gives thought to his steps.

PROVERBS 14:15 NIV

If you're still making the same mistakes at fifty that you were at twenty, you need to ask God for wisdom. "The heart of the discerning acquires knowledge; the ears of the wise seek it out" (Pr 18:15 NIV). What you are in the present, was determined by the decisions you made in the past. If you want to change your future, learn to make better decisions. Be wise; let these principles guide you: (1) Never make permanent decisions based on temporary circumstances. If you do, you'll regret it. (2) Don't let your emotions blind you to reason. Pray, weigh things carefully and base your decisions on mature judgment. (3) Surround yourself with sharp people and draw on their gifts, without being intimidated by their expertise. (4) Take the time to consider all options. What looks good to you today, may not look so good tomorrow. (5) You can't fight successfully on every front, so choose your battles carefully. Simply stated: some things are not worth fighting for. (6) Take time to get all the facts; conjecture leads to crisis. (7) Consider the consequences of each action. Ask yourself, "Am I ready to handle this right now?" (8) Make sure your expectations don't exceed your potential and your resources. Be realistic. If you can't count, don't apply for a job in the finance office. If you can't sing, don't cut an album. Focus on what God gifted you to do. That's where you'll succeed. (9) Time is your most limited and valuable resource. Don't waste it. (10) Allow yourself a 10% risk of being wrong, a 50% likelihood of betrayal, and a 100% commitment to trust God, go forward and survive it all.

GET UP AND RUN!

For though a righteous man falls...he rises again.

PROVERBS 24:16 NIV

Carole Mayhall writes: "The other night Jack and I watched a television drama called 'See How She Runs.' In it a forty-year-old, divorced schoolteacher decided to become a jogger and eventually entered the twenty-six-mile Boston Marathon. It's a grueling test of heart, mind and body. To finish the race became her goal, and in spite of being jeered at and assaulted she didn't lose sight of it. When the day of the race came she faced her ultimate test. As she ran huge blisters developed on her feet. She was hit and injured by a bicycle. Several miles short of the finish line found her utterly exhausted, yet she kept going. Then within a few hundred yards of her goal, late at night when most other runners had finished or dropped out, she fell and lay flat on her face too tired to get up. But her friends put a crude tape across the finish line and began to cheer her on. She lifted her head, saw the tape and realized her goal was within sight. With supreme effort she got back up, and with a burst of energy dredged up from deep within her, ran the last few yards."

Victory belongs to those who keep looking not at the going, but the goal; not the process, but the prize; not the trial, but the treasure that's promised to those who persevere. A twofold theme of Christianity is, *rising again* and *running the race*. But you can't win if you don't run and risk falling. And no matter what caused you to fall, the word for you today is, "Take God's hand, get up, and run!"

DON'T JUST PRAY, LISTEN!

As I hear, I judge.

JOHN 5:30 NKJV

Ever wonder why Jesus never made a single misstep? He tells us: "The Son can do nothing of Himself, but what He sees the Father do; for whatever He does, the Son also does in like manner. For the Father loves the Son, and shows Him all things that He Himself does…I can of Myself do nothing. As I hear, I judge; and My judgment is righteous, because I do not seek My own will but the will of the Father who sent Me" (Jn 5:19-20, 30 NKJV).

Jesus often prayed all night, yet few of His prayers are recorded. Why? Because He didn't just *talk* to His Father, He took time to *listen* and get instructions. Jesus prayed on mountaintops and in gardens. He even prayed on the street outside the house where He slept last night. No doubt if He'd had a car, He'd have prayed driving to work. Prayer and listening to God were as natural to Him as breathing; it was the spiritual oxygen He thrived on. When the Bible says, "Pray without ceasing" (1Th 5:17), it means we are to stay in touch with God at all times, to be spiritually sensitive and attuned to the still small voice of His Spirit within us. That calls for having an uncluttered mind and heart.

Thank God for the understanding of who we are in Christ, and our authority as believers. But there's more to prayer than coming "boldly unto the throne" (Heb 4:16). That kind of prayer is usually about what *we* want. This kind of prayer is about what *God* wants! Now, since God designed the plan for your life, don't you think it's wise to get quiet before Him so that He can tell you about it?

CLEANSING

The blood...cleanses us from all sin.

1 JOHN 1:7 NKJV

John writes: "If we walk in the light as He is in the light, we have fellowship with one another, and the blood of Jesus Christ His Son cleanses us from all sin." This Scripture gives us three ways to stay clean in a spiritually polluted world:

(1) By walking in the light. That means striving to be so honest before God and man, you wouldn't be ashamed to have anyone read in tomorrow morning's newspaper, what you did today. *(2) By being accountable.* To grow strong in an area of weakness, sometimes you need someone mature enough to deserve your confidence, gracious enough to put up with your inconsistencies, and honest enough to confront you. Above all, they should be committed to you in love. *(3) By dealing with your sin right away.* The moment that brings the consciousness of sin, should lead to the confession of sin. At that point you must believe that "the blood of Jesus Christ His Son cleanses us from all sin," then get up and go on with God; don't wallow in self-condemnation.

If there's something rotten in your refrigerator you know it every time you open the door. You may not know exactly where it's located, but the smell tells you it's in there. Our lives are like that. If there's something wrong within us, those we come into contact with are going to sense it, whether or not they know what it is or why it's there. It gives off an odor that's detectable. That's why we must continually open ourselves to God and allow the Holy Spirit to come in, cleanse our hearts, and remove whatever's hindering us in our walk with Him.

SERVE, DON'T STRIVE!

Jesus...made Himself of no reputation.

PHILIPPIANS 2:5-7 NKJV

The story is told of an ambitious student at a very competitive college. Just before entering his senior year he met an Eastern mystic who said, "Can't you see you're polluting your soul with this success-oriented way of living? Your idea of happiness is to work around the clock, to study so you can get a better grade than the next guy. That's not how you are supposed to live. Come join us in a special place where we all share together and love one another." Thinking it was a great idea, he called his parents and told them he was dropping out of school to live in a commune. Six months later they received a letter from him: "Dear Mom and Dad, I know you were upset about my decision. But I want to tell you how it has changed my life. For the first time, I'm at peace. Here there's no competing, no trying to get ahead of anyone. This way of life is so in harmony with my inner self, that in only six months I've become the number two disciple in the entire commune. And I think I can be number one by June." Hello!

When competition leads to *excellence* it's a good thing, but not when it leads to *striving!* One day Christ's disciples started arguing about who would be the greatest in His kingdom. Jesus listened, then He picked up a towel and a basin of water and began to wash their feet. When He finished they were speechless, their hearts exposed, their attitudes corrected. "Let this mind be in you which was also in Christ Jesus, who...made Himself of no reputation." Bottom line: serve, don't strive!

MAKE THAT YOUR ATTITUDE, TOO!

Think on these things.

PHILIPPIANS 4:8

Your ability to succeed in life often comes down to a single choice: how you react to what has been done to you in the past, or is being done to you right now. Dr. Viktor Frankl endured the Holocaust by this principle. The Nazis killed his family, placed him in a concentration camp, starved and beat him. When the war ended Frankl was neither broken, bowed nor bitter. When asked how he endured such treatment with a positive outlook he said, "Everything can be taken from a man but one thing: the last of human freedoms, to choose one's attitude in any given set of circumstances, to choose one's own way."

Ground Zero is a massive canyon where the Twin Towers once stood. Three thousand people died there. And how did New Yorkers choose to respond? A sign at the edge of Ground Zero proclaims, "The human spirit is not measured by the size of the act, but by the size of the heart." That's an attitude terrorists will never conquer. And it's the attitude God's Word calls us to adopt: "Whatsoever things are *true,* whatsoever things are *honest,* whatsoever things are *just,* whatsoever things are *pure,* whatsoever things are *lovely,* whatsoever things are of *good report*...think on these things."

Every day you choose the clothes you wear, the food you eat, and the attitude you adopt. And there are only two kinds of attitudes—good ones and bad ones. A good attitude is the one the Psalmist adopted when he woke up each morning: "This is the day the Lord has made; we will rejoice and be glad in it" (Ps 118:24 NKJV). Make that your attitude too!

RANSOMED, REDEEMED, RESTORED!

He provided redemption for his people.

PSALM 111:9 NIV

Ever been to a pawnshop? You'll find them in most major cities. The idea is simple; if you need money, you take a valuable item like jewelry or a musical instrument to the shop where the pawnbroker appraises it and gives you cash. But if you don't return within the specified time to redeem it, you forfeit ownership. Although it was yours originally, you no longer have legal possession till you pay the price to get it back. And if you wait too long, it can be lost forever.

Have you ever thought of *yourself* as somebody who needs to be redeemed, so you can be returned to your rightful owner? The Bible says God created us to enjoy fellowship with Him. But sin caused us to fall into "the snare of the devil...held captive...to do his will" (2Ti 2:26 NAS). Restoration to God, your rightful owner, could only come through redemption. And that's exactly what God did! "God so loved the world, that he gave his only begotten Son, that whosoever believeth in him should not perish, but have everlasting life" (Jn 3:16). Christ's death on the cross was the price of your redemption; *that's* how much God values you! But redemption only becomes a reality when you realize that you're a sinner, and trust in Christ as your Savior. The moment you do, He reunites you with your heavenly Father—ransomed, redeemed, restored to your original owner. So the question is: have you taken God up on His offer of salvation, the one that makes you a member of His family? *If you're able to read this, it's not too late. You can do it right now wherever you are.*

CARING FOR THE CAREGIVER (1)

Bear one another's burdens.

GALATIANS 6:2 NKJV

Millions of caregivers are at risk because of self-neglect. Suzanne Mintz of the National Family Caregivers Association has been taking care of her husband, who has multiple sclerosis, for years. Her breaking point came the day he fell. "All I could do was drag him across the floor," she said. "I'm five feet one; he's five feet eight. It took forty-five minutes... that's when I knew this wasn't a one-person job." The Bible says: "We who are strong ought to bear the weaknesses of those without strength" (Ro 15:1 NAS). Experts in care giving offer this helpful advice:

Compromise: If you're a relative, avoid family disputes. Don't let old issues divide you; it's time to stick together. *Coordinate:* If you're good with insurance and legal documents, offer your services. Help prepare a game plan for when an illness advances; adult children often avoid that conversation. *Encourage:* Help the caregiver to find professional support. If they're uncomfortable with in-person support groups, many organizations have on-line resources. *Facilitate:* Ask somebody objective, a pastor or social worker, to negotiate in stressful situations where the caregiver is struggling with the patient, family members, or medical providers. *Investigate:* Locating books and websites and contacting organizations that help the caregiver learn more about a patient's illness, can save them time. *Listen:* Asking the caregiver to tell you their story, can provide a much-needed release and help you understand their needs. *Socialize:* Organize events with family, community and church, and if possible include the patient. Remember, by carrying somebody else's burdens even for a little while, you're fulfilling "the law of Christ" (Gal 6:2).

CARING FOR THE CAREGIVER (2)

When my spirit was overwhelmed.

PSALM 142:3 NAS

Following her parents' deaths five weeks apart, in a nursing home 1,200 miles away, Beth Witrogen McLeod succumbed to clinical depression. She writes: "By ignoring my physical and mental health...I set myself up for a breakdown it would take two years to recover from...Despite its rewards...care-giving can be overwhelming." The Psalmist said, "When my spirit was overwhelmed...You knew my path." God understands. He also expects you to exercise wisdom. As gerontologist D. Helen Susik says: "A burned-out caregiver can't provide quality care." So: *Protect your time, especially with family:* It's easy to schedule every waking minute with nothing left over for yourself. Find something that feeds you—read your Bible, pray, exercise, enjoy some solitude—and schedule it. *Ask for help:* If your siblings aren't pulling their weight, call a family meeting and delegate. It's tempting to try to do it all yourself, but don't deny others the blessing that comes from "encouraging the faint-hearted and helping the weak" (See 1Th 5:14 NAS). *Stay connected:* "It is not good for man to be alone" (Ge 2:18). Invite two friends over who've volunteered to help. One can cook and look after your loved one, while you and the other friend take a walk and savor your freedom. *Be aware of destructive coping patterns,* like misusing medication, overeating, and drinking to take the edge off. *Set boundaries:* Protect your time and energy by saying no where before you routinely said yes. Remember, there's nothing selfish about taking care of yourself, so you can give the best possible care to someone else.

ALLOW GOD TO SHAPE YOU

We are the clay, and You our potter.

ISAIAH 64:8 NKJV

Imagine a beautiful china teacup saying: "I wasn't always like this. There was a time when I was just a cold, hard, colorless lump of clay. One day the potter picked me up and said, 'I could do something with this.' Then he started to put pressure on me and change my shape. I said, 'What are you doing? That hurts. Stop!' But he said, 'Not yet.' Then he put me on a wheel and began to spin me around and around until I shouted, 'Let me off.' He replied, 'Not yet.' Then he shaped me into a cup and put me in a hot oven. I cried, 'Let me out of here, I'm suffocating.' But he looked at me and said, 'Not yet.' When he took me out, I thought his work on me was over, but then he started to paint me. I couldn't believe what he did next. He put me back into the oven, and I said, 'I can't stand this, please let me out!' But he said, 'Not yet.' Finally he took me out of the oven and set me on a shelf where I thought he had forgotten me. Then one day he took me off the shelf and held me up before a mirror. I couldn't believe my eyes. I had become a beautiful teacup that everyone wants to buy."

There are things going on in your life today that you don't understand. When you finally get to the place God wants you to be, you'll realize that He has been making you into a vessel He can use, bless, and use to bless others. So, allow God to shape you!

GOD'S INDWELLING SPIRIT
INTERPRETS FOR US

*We do not know what we should pray for…
but the spirit…makes intercession for us.*

ROMANS 8:26 NKJV

When you go to a foreign country you can feel uncomfortable and a bit lost, because you don't speak the language. Everything is different from what you're accustomed to.

The language of the spiritual world is prayer. And since the spiritual world is the source of our power, victory, peace, joy, and everything else we need, it's essential that we learn to speak it. The good news is, we have the perfect teacher and interpreter —the Holy Spirit Himself. One of His jobs is to teach us the language of prayer and guide us when it comes to addressing God. And He's good at this job! The Bible says the Holy Spirit can interpret our prayers to God even when we don't know what to say. "If we don't know how or what to pray, it doesn't matter. He does our praying in and for us, making prayer out of our wordless sighs, our aching groans" (Ro 8:26 TM). Isn't that wonderful?

Prayer is the link between the physical and the spiritual world—and since the spiritual world controls the physical, getting connected to the world above affects our functioning in the world below. And because prayer is relational, the Holy Spirit will communicate God's heart back to us by connecting with our human spirit so that we'll hear God talk to us in the deepest part of our being. That's why prayer cannot be *rushed.* It's also why taking time to *meditate* and be *still* before God is so important. It allows the Holy Spirit to share God's thoughts with us, so that we begin thinking His way. How valuable is that?

A LOVE LETTER FROM JESUS (1)

You...are a letter from Christ.

2 CORINTHIANS 3:3 NIV

John 3:16 is the greatest message ever sent to man. "For God so loved the world, that he gave his only begotten Son." God sent Jesus to demonstrate His love—and He sends us to declare it! "You...are a letter from Christ...written not with ink but with the Spirit of the living God," to a lost, stressed-out world searching for answers.

Now, when a letter arrives certain questions arise: *(1) Who is it addressed to?* This letter is addressed to "whoever believes." For every person you meet, you have something they need, something more important than a tax cut, a salary increase, a solution for global warming or a cancer cure. Friends, enemies, relatives, neighbors, workmates and strangers need the message you have and the hope you bring. *(2) Who is it from?* The author's identity determines the reader's interest level. You are a letter from Christ, about Christ. "For we do not preach ourselves, but Jesus Christ as Lord" (2Co 4:5 NIV). Our message is not about us; it's about Jesus. "I am the way, the truth, and the life. No one comes to the Father except through Me" (Jn 14:6 NKJV). Religious folks advertise their religion. We advocate Christ. "But are people really interested in Jesus?" you ask. Yes! In His lifetime He drew multitudes. Since His death and resurrection He draws countless millions of both sexes, all strata of society and every nation on earth. "But I, when I am lifted up...will draw all men to myself" (Jn 12:32 NIV). Today nothing is more needed than a living portrait of Jesus Christ, so deliver your love letter to "whoever" crosses your path!

A LOVE LETTER FROM JESUS (2)

You...are a letter from Christ.

2 CORINTHIANS 3:3 NIV

The Bible says your life is a love letter from Jesus, "known and read by everybody." But a letter is only effective, if it is easily read and understood. An older friend said of his deteriorating handwriting, "I can still read writin', but I can't write readin'!" Incomprehensible writing distorts the message and discourages the reader. The purpose, to convey the writer's thoughts, is lost, and the reader either stops reading or fails to get the message.

To ensure that your love letter from Jesus gets through to the people He's sending it to, here are some common distortions to avoid: (a) Dishonesty, like padding your expense account, stealing company time or taking home items you think won't be missed. (b) A begrudging, resentful attitude when a friend, fellow worker or boss asks you to go the extra mile and help at an inconvenient time. (c) Shoddy workmanship, reflected in a substandard product or service. (d) Undependability and inconsistency, such as when you can't be counted on to be where you're supposed to be, or to fulfill your obligations. (e) Being a killjoy. Christians who lack a sense of humor and resiliency, who act like they're "joy-impaired," hurt the cause of Christ. (f) Touchiness, like when you wear your feelings on your sleeve, are easily upset and overreact to unintended offenses. (g) Temper tantrums, where you're crabby and grumpy because things don't go your way. (h) "Holy Joe-itis" that makes you speak in self-righteous, supercilious tones. Since you are being "known and read by everybody," guard against these behaviors that distort the life-giving message God wants to send to others through you.

A LOVE LETTER FROM JESUS (3)

You...are a letter from Christ.

2 CORINTHIANS 3:3 NIV

Once you know a letter is addressed to you, the question becomes—what does it say? Certain key words in 2 Corinthians stand out: "transformed," "renounced," and "made new!" "We ...are being transformed into his likeness" (2Co 3:18 NIV). "We have renounced secret and shameful ways" (2Co 4:2 NIV). "If anyone is in Christ, he is a new creation; the old has gone, the new has come!" (2Co 5:17 NIV). The message in our letter should make it clear that we're not the people we used to be, because:

(a) Christ has changed us *mentally*. Being "transformed by the renewing of [our] mind" (Ro 12:2) we now look at life, ourselves, others, our challenges and options in light of God's thoughts, not ours. We see opportunities where we saw only obstacles, and possibilities where we saw only problems. Minds that were frazzled with worry, are now filled with confidence and peace. (b) Christ has changed us *morally*. The list of wrongdoers mentioned in 1Co 6:9-10 was a lifestyle all too familiar to us. It includes the immoral, thieves, greedy, drunkards, slanderers, swindlers, etc. Then comes glorious verse 11: "And that is what some of you were. But you were washed...sanctified ...justified in the name of the Lord Jesus Christ" (NIV). He has transformed our character. (c) Christ has changed us *spiritually*. Once we were unable to enjoy His Word, His worship and His ways. Now, alive by His indwelling Spirit, we revel in these things (See 1Co 2:14)! Your letter should read: "Jesus changed my life, and if you let Him, He will change yours too!" So today, deliver your love letter to everyone you meet.

LET GOD HEAL YOUR WOUNDS!

I will...heal your wounds.

JEREMIAH 30:17 NIV

Addressing the student body at Virginia Tech after a shooting rampage that left thirty of them dead and dozens more wounded, Philip Yancey said: "Peter said to Jesus...'Lord, to whom can we go? You have the words of eternal life.' You've heard, 'Things will get better, you'll get past this.' Those who offer such comfort mean well, and what you feel now you *won't* always feel. Yet you're a different person because of that day. When three of my friends died I came across these lines: 'Grief melts away like snow in May,' as if there were no such thing as cold. I clung to that, even as grief smothered me like an avalanche. It did melt away, but like snow it came back in fierce, unexpected ways, triggered by a sound, a smell, a fragment of memory."

Yancey continued: "Pain is a sign of life and love. I'm wearing a neck brace because I broke my neck in an accident. Initially medical workers refused to give me medication because they needed my response. The doctor kept asking, 'Does this hurt? Can you feel that?' The answer he desperately wanted was, 'Yes, it hurts, I can feel it,' proof that my spinal cord hadn't been severed. Pain offers proof of life, of connection. In deep wounds two kinds of tissue must heal: *connective* tissue, plus the outer *protective* tissue. If the outer protective tissue heals too quickly the inner connective tissue won't heal properly, leading to complications later." Don't attempt healing alone; real healing takes time; it takes place where God's presence, God's peace, and God's people are. Are you hurting today? Turn to God. His promise to you is "I will...heal your wounds."

SEE YOU IN CHURCH ON SUNDAY!

Let us go into the house of the Lord.

PSALM 122:1

What's your reason for not going to church? Before you answer, read *Ten Reasons Why I Never Wash!* (1) I was forced to wash as a child. (2) People who wash are all hypocrites; they think they are cleaner than everyone else. (3) There are so many different kinds of soap; I just can't decide which one is best for me. (4) I used to wash, but I got bored and stopped doing it. (5) I only wash on special occasions like Christmas and Easter. (6) None of my friends wash. (7) I'll start washing when I get older and dirtier. (8) I don't have time to wash. (9) The bathroom is never warm enough in winter or cool enough in summer. (10) The people who make soap are only after your money! Sound familiar?

Speaking of the church, Paul writes: "There should be no division...its parts should have equal concern for each other ...each one of you is a part of it" (1Co 12:25-27 NIV). You are part of Christ's body, the church, so you need to be there! Watchman Nee says: "Alone I cannot serve the Lord effectively, and he will spare no pains to teach me this. He will bring things to an end, allowing doors to close and leaving me effectively knocking my head against a wall until I realize that I need the help of the body, as well as of the Lord." There are truths taught in God's house that you won't hear anywhere else. There you'll find a spiritual *family* to belong to, a *faith* to live by, and a *focus* that gets your eyes where they should be—on Christ! So, see you in church on Sunday!

THE ULTIMATE SELF-ESTEEM!

Perfect love casts out fear.

1 JOHN 4:18 NKJV

Since God's love is the only "perfect" love, it removes our fears. What are you afraid of? That you won't get something you *need,* or that you'll lose something you've *got?* "His perfect love for us eliminates all dread...If we are afraid, it... shows that we are not fully convinced that he really loves us" (1Jn 4:18 TLB). Today, ask God to give you a fresh understanding of how much He loves you, for what He loves He prizes, protects, and provides for.

We are drawn to people who love us, so why is it so difficult for us to go to God in prayer? It's because we need a fresh understanding of His love for us! Paul writes: "[I pray]... that...you'll be able to take in...the extravagant dimensions of Christ's love" (Eph 3:18 TM). Extravagant love! God couldn't love you any more than He does right now! You say, "What does God's love look like?" Look at the cross. If you had been the only person who ever lived, Jesus would have died just for you. "What does God's love cost me?" you ask. It comes with no strings attached. You didn't do anything to deserve it, so when you fail you don't forfeit it. He never stops loving you! The Bible says: "Absolutely *nothing* can get between us and God's love" (Ro 8:39 TM).

Once you're secure in God's love you can begin to acknowledge your weaknesses, seek His help, grow strong, and use the gifts He's given you. When you know God loves you based on who you are, not the color of your skin or your life's accomplishments, you have the ultimate self-esteem—born of God's esteem for you.

THOUGHTS ABOUT AARON'S ROD

The rod of Aaron...sprouted and...produced blossoms.

NUMBERS 17:8 NKJV

New leadership was urgently needed in Israel. So God ordered an elder from each of the twelve tribes to bring a wooden staff with his name on it, and leave it overnight in the tabernacle. He said, "It shall be that the rod of the man whom I choose will blossom" (Nu 17:5 NKJV). Next morning Aaron's rod "sprouted and...produced blossoms."

Please notice: *(1) Whose* rod blossomed—Aaron's! Obviously God doesn't pick His leaders because they're perfect. Aaron's résumé included making a golden calf for Israel to worship, then defending himself by saying, "That cow just walked out of the fire all by itself." Would *you* pick somebody like that? God did. That's because He hears the cry of our hearts, and sees in us qualities He can use to fulfill His purposes. Keep that in mind, next time a leader disappoints you. And remember it, should God call you to lead. *(2) Where* it blossomed—in the presence of the Lord. Certain things only happen in God's presence. In Aaron's case a walking stick came to life in "the tabernacle of meeting...where I meet with you" (Nu 17:4 NKJV). Hey, rearrange your priorities. Schedule a set time to meet with God each day, and keep it. If you don't, you won't make it! *(3) When* it blossomed—during the darkness. In Genesis we read: "So the evening and the morning were the first day" (Ge 1:5 NKJV). Observe, God starts your day with a nighttime experience. In order for your faith to blossom, it must first be incubated in the dark. Real faith only germinates in adversity, so if you try to escape, you lose the opportunity to move into higher realms of faith.

GO "A LITTLE FARTHER"

He went a little farther...and prayed.

MARK 14:35 NKJV

Dutch Sheets says: "Through intercessory prayer we meet the powers of darkness, enforcing the victory Christ accomplished when He met them in His work of intercession." *Intercession* means "mediating between parties with a view to reconciling those who differ or contend." It happens every day in the court system when lawyers intervene on behalf of their clients. Throughout history God has looked for men and women to pray and intercede on behalf of a lost world. More often than not, He's been disappointed. "I sought for a man... who would...stand in the gap before Me on behalf of the land, that I should not destroy it; but I found no one" (Eze 22:30 NKJV). That Scripture is God's "help wanted" ad.

The disciples were willing to go with Jesus into the garden of Gethsemane. Yet in spite of knowing the urgency of the hour, they still fell asleep. Even Peter, James and John, the guys in the inner circle, didn't "get it," so in the end Jesus prayed alone. Interceding is a lonely business. It demands open-ended commitment. You can go for months and years before seeing the fruits of your labor. On the other hand, when you go deeper with God, you get to share things that the angels alone were privy to that night in the garden.

When Pastor Jim Cymbala took a broken-down church in a bad neighborhood, there were fewer than twenty-five members. Now, twenty-five years later, over 6,000 people attend Brooklyn Tabernacle. He says, "It didn't happen because of programs, it happened because of intercessory prayer." How about it, is God calling *you* to go "a little farther?"

TAKING PERSONAL RESPONSIBILITY (1)

If you are wise, your wisdom will reward you.

PROVERBS 9:12 NIV

To display the kind of responsibility that makes you successful in life: *(1) Recognize that gaining success means practicing self-discipline.* Every time you stop yourself from doing what you shouldn't and start doing what you should, you're increasing your capacity for responsibility and the rewards it brings. *(2) What you start, finish.* There are two kinds of people: those who will and those who might. Responsible people follow through. And that's how others evaluate them. *(3) Don't expect others to do it for you.* Paul writes: "Each one should carry his own load" (Gal 6:5 NIV). Addressing students at the University of South Carolina, Chief Judge Alexander M. Saunders said: "As responsibility is passed to your hands it will not do to assume that someone else will bear the major burdens, that someone else will demonstrate the key convictions, that someone else will run for office, take care of the poor, visit the sick, protect civil rights, enforce the law, transmit value, and defend freedom. What you do not value will not be valued, what you do not remember will not be remembered, what you do not change will not be changed, what you do not do will not be done. You can, if you will, craft a society whose leaders…are less obsessed with the need for money. It's not a question of what to do, but simply the will to do it."

Sometimes we don't take responsibility because we believe others are more qualified. No, those who make a difference in life, don't do so because they're the best qualified, but simply because they decided to try. Plus: *God doesn't call the qualified, He qualifies the called!*

TAKING PERSONAL RESPONSIBILITY (2)

*Each one should use whatever gift
he has received to serve others.*

1 PETER 4:10 NIV

Each time you make a responsible decision, you become a more responsible person. Successful people don't blame others, they take responsibility for their actions and attitudes. They show response-ability—the ability to choose a correct response no matter what situation they face. Responsibility is always a choice, and only you can make it. If being responsible hasn't been one of your strengths, then start small. You can't start from any place other than where you are right now.

Which areas of responsibility are the toughest for you? *(1) Following through—taking responsibility to finish what you start?* If you've a tendency to quit, give yourself relatively small goals that require you to stretch. Start in areas you care about deeply, then with a few wins under your belt, begin tackling other areas. *(2) Taking care of the small stuff?* How often do you forget small things—that are big things to others? Like forgetting anniversaries and birthdays, not picking up the dry cleaning or taking out the trash, missing your child's game or recital. "Let your light shine...that they may see your good works and glorify your father" (Mt 5:16). *(3) Stepping forward —not expecting someone else to do it for you?* Most of us have a tough decision that's waiting to be made, and we keep putting it off. What's yours? Why aren't you taking action? Write down the reasons, so you understand clearly what they are. Now write down the advantages of making the decision. Once you know in your heart what you should do, ask God for strength, do it, and stand by it. That's taking personal responsibility!

MAKING JESUS LORD OF YOUR LIFE

I am crucified with Christ.

GALATIANS 2:20

Paul writes: "I am crucified with Christ." Those words are about as appealing as a root canal, to our carnal minds. Yet God's kingdom can only come and His will be done in us, when self is "crucified." In what areas of your life are you hearing the hammering of the nails? Those are the *un-surrendered* areas; they're the ones that give you the most trouble, right?

Paul addresses the struggle between the flesh and the spirit that we all face daily: "Among those who belong to Christ, everything connected with getting our own way and mindlessly responding to what everyone else calls necessities is killed off for good—crucified. Since this is the kind of life we have chosen, the life of the Spirit, let us make sure that we do not just hold it as an idea in our heads or a sentiment in our hearts, but work out its implications in *every* detail of our lives" (Gal 5:24-25 TM). What does it mean to be "crucified with Christ?" In *Tell Me Again, Lord, I Forget,* Ruth Calkin writes: "At first, Lord, I asked you to take sides with me. With the Psalmist I prayed, 'The Lord is for me…maintain my rights, O Lord.' But with all my pleading I lay drenched in darkness, until in total surrender I cried, 'Don't take sides, Lord, just take over,' and suddenly it was morning." It's said that one day Martin Luther answered a knock at his door. "Does Dr. Martin Luther live here?" a man asked. "No," Luther answered, "He died; Christ lives here." Your rights, your ego and your comfort levels, no longer matter. You say, "What does?" Dying to self, and making Jesus Lord of your life!

DOUBLE UP.
BRING IN REINFORCEMENTS!

If two of you...agree about anything.

MATTHEW 18:19 NIV

Sometimes you need somebody to agree with you in prayer—somebody who knows how to stand on God's Word and intercede with Him for *your* finances, *your* children, *your* marriage, etc.

James had just been executed and Herod was planning to kill Peter in the morning. Now, you'd think Peter would have been up all night praying, but he wasn't. The Bible says he was sleeping (See Ac 12:6). Where did he get *that* kind of faith? The Bible says: "The church was earnestly praying to God for him" (Ac 12:5 NIV). Any time you can sleep in the face of danger and experience grace in the midst of chaos, it's one of two things: (1) You know God well, you're standing on His promises and you've handed the situation over to Him. (2) Somebody is praying for you, somebody with "clout" in the heavenly realm. Notice, the church didn't say, "If Peter was in God's will, he wouldn't be in this mess right now," or "Since Peter's in jail, who's going to preach for us next Sunday?" No, while they were praying in faith for a breakthrough, God was at work on the other side of the city dispatching an angel to set Peter free. That's how prayer works. John Wesley said, "We can do great things *when* we pray; but we can do nothing great *until* we pray!" Do you feel like your prayers aren't getting the job done? Double up. Bring in reinforcements! Find somebody who'll agree with you, for Jesus said, "If two of you...agree about anything...it will be done for you."

YOUR FAITH GETS GOD'S ATTENTION

Your faith has healed you.

LUKE 8:48 NIV

The Bible says: "A woman was there who had been subject to bleeding for twelve years, but no one could heal her. She came up behind him and touched the edge of his cloak, and immediately her bleeding stopped. 'Who touched me?' Jesus asked. When they all denied it, Peter said, 'Master, the people are crowding and pressing against you.' But Jesus said, 'Someone touched me; I know that power has gone out from me.' Then the woman, seeing that she could not go unnoticed, came trembling and…told why she had touched him and how she had been instantly healed. Then he said to her, 'Daughter, your faith has healed you. Go in peace'" (Lk 8:43-48 NIV).

Notice three important things in this story: *(1) She did something she'd never done before.* She decided to try Jesus. Wise move! Faith means stepping into the unknown and the untried, finding God's grace at work in unexpected ways. *(2) She recognized her moment.* She knew that Jesus was visiting her town, and might not be back. There are "God-moments" in life when you've got to overcome your fear and move out in faith. If you don't, you'll miss them. *(3) She opened the door for others.* Up until this time, no one in Scripture had been healed by touching Jesus' garment. So her act of faith opened the door for others. "People brought all their sick to him and begged him to let the sick just touch the edge of his cloak, and all who touched him were healed" (Mt 14:35-36 NIV). God's looking for people who are willing to break with tradition. When He finds them, He uses them to open doors and new dimensions of His power, so that others might be blessed and made whole.

CONSULT GOD!

We make plans...but the Lord decides.

PROVERBS 16:9 CEV

George dreamed of joining the Navy, but his mother, who was a widow raising her children alone, didn't like the idea. Nevertheless she put on a brave face and agreed to let him go. The day he was due to sail he hugged her good-bye. In an uncharacteristic show of emotion she started to cry. After enduring so much heartbreak she refused to endure any more. George must *not* board that ship; instead he must stay and be strong for the rest of the family. The boy in the midshipman's uniform wanted a Navy career, but not if it meant adding to his mother's grief. So reluctantly he returned his uniform and ordered his belongings ashore. Of all the young men who might have left home in search of adventure and didn't, he was just one more. Yet his decision had profound influence on the Revolutionary War. A mother's eleventh-hour anxiety prevented her fifteen-year-old from ascending the ranks of the British Navy and embarking on an adventure very different from the one for which he eventually became famous. That's because the boy's name was *George Washington*, first president of the United States of America.

"We make...plans, but the Lord decides where we will go." "The...steps we take come from God; otherwise how would we know where we're going?" (Pr 20:24 TM). Henry Blackaby writes: "We can be deceived into believing we are on the right path, yet be heading the opposite direction from God's will. Apart from the guidance of the Holy Spirit, we'll do what makes sense based on our own wisdom. So seek [God's] direction, He knows the full ramifications of your choices."

FAITH IS (1)

Now faith is the substance of things hoped for.

HEBREWS 11:1 NKJV

Notice two important things about faith: *(1) Faith is a substance.* In the U.S., people trade in dollars; in Europe they trade in Euros. But in God's Kingdom, faith is "the coin of the realm!" It's what's required to do business with God (See Heb 11:6). And it grows only by feeding on His Word (See Ro 10:17). *(2) Faith must be connected to hope.* If you're not hoping for anything, you don't need faith. But your hope must be based on what God's Word says. When God promised to make Abraham the father of many nations, Abraham spent the next twenty years looking for a son, even though the situation seemed impossible. How did he do it?

(a) "He believed—God, who...calls those things which do not exist as though they did" (Ro 4:17 NKJV). God "sees" it, then He reveals it to you. And His willingness to bless you with it, rests on your willingness to believe Him for it. (b) "Who, contrary to hope...believed...according to what was spoken" (Ro 4:18 NKJV). What has God said? *That's* what your hope should be built on. (c) "He did not consider his own body, already dead (since he was about a hundred years old)" (Ro 4:19 NKJV). You say, "But considering the circumstances...!" No, believe God; He's bigger than the circumstances! (d) "He did not waver...through unbelief, but was strengthened in faith, giving glory to God, and being fully convinced that what He had promised He was also able to perform" (Ro 4:20-21 NKJV). So, strengthen your faith through the Scriptures. Keep giving glory to God for what He's promised you. Be resolute. Such faith honors God, and God honors such faith!

FAITH IS (2)

Now faith is the substance of things hoped for.

HEBREWS 11:1 NKJV

Before Israel went into battle, the prophets would ask God if He had given them the city. That's because God honors faith when it's connected to what He's promised. What you should fight for—is what *God* has promised you. Don't say God failed you, if He didn't promise it to you in the first place! And don't get angry, because misguided desire made you reach for what He gave to somebody else. The old timers used to sing, "Every promise in the book is mine, every chapter every verse every line." That's so, in the sense that God loves us all equally. But there are certain promises He wants to fulfill in *your* life, because your calling is different from that of others. And you must seek Him for clarity and guidance.

"He who has an ear, let him hear what the Spirit says to the churches" (Rev 2:29 NKJV). Don't just listen to the preacher, try to hear what God is saying to *you* through the preacher. You can hear something entirely different from the next guy, because God is "personalizing" it to you. The Bible is called the "Living Word," because certain Scriptures suddenly come to life and take root within you. *You* can hear what nobody else hears, or even miss several of the pastor's points, and go home with the answer you need. When you say, "I get it. It's mine," the faith that comes by "hearing" is doing its special work within you.

FAITH IS (3)

Now faith is the substance of things hoped for.

HEBREWS 11:1 NKJV

Notice the words, "Now faith." Thank God for the faith of our fathers, and the faith experiences of our own past. But to do what God's calling you to do for Him today, you need "now faith." Jesus said, "If you have faith as a mustard seed, you will say to this mountain, 'Move'...and it will move" (Mt 17:20 NKJV). Your grandmother's faith may have moved her mountain, but it's going to take *your* faith to move "this mountain." We all have a "this mountain" in our life, and God is willing to move it. So what's the problem? Unbelief. Even though Christ had given His disciples authority to heal the sick, they'd just been rendered powerless by a demon-possessed boy. So they asked Jesus, "Why could we not cast the spirits out of him?" (See Mt 17:19). Notice what He taught them that day:

(1) Start small, or you won't start at all. Mustard-seed-sized faith, like all seeds, will grow into something bigger. Just start where you are; believe God for ordinary, everyday things. And when He honors your faith, acknowledge it, thank Him for it and build on it. *(2) Guard your mouth!* "If you have faith ...you will say to this mountain, 'Move'...and it will move." Your words release the life-giving force that's in your faith, so correct and control what's coming out of your mouth. Make sure it lines up with Scripture. *(3) Sometimes you need a little extra.* Some mountains need a little extra prayer, or in the case of this boy, the power that comes through fasting. But if you're willing to meet God's conditions, you'll see mountains moved in your life.

TRY GOD'S WAY!

Trust in the Lord...
lean not on your own understanding.

PROVERBS 3:5 NIV

Ever watch someone learning to get around on crutches? What a struggle! Sometimes you find them trying to balance on one leg, or resting a hundred feet down the street, their hands raw and sore. Leaning on crutches can be exhausting. So can leaning on your *own* understanding.

If you want things to go badly for you—exclude God. Try working things out using only your own best judgment. When you hit a brick wall, try something else. When that gets you nowhere, resort to logic, then panic. The truth is, some of us act like we're addicted to anxiety. We've been living this way so long, we're not capable of seeing it or acknowledging it. When one worry is gone we put another one in its place. We have a line of them at our door, because the sign reads "All welcome!" It's like we enjoy entertaining them. But Jesus said they're a waste of life and energy. They keep you so focused on what you *need*, or what you're afraid of *losing*, that you don't have time to enjoy what you *have* (See Mt 6:25). That's no way to live!

Instead of worrying, begin living by this Scripture: (a) "Do not worry about anything." (b) "Pray and ask God for every-thing you need." (c) "Always giving thanks." (d) "God's peace ...will keep your hearts and minds" (Php 4:6-7 NCV). Go ahead—try God's way!

ARE YOU TEACHABLE?

A wise man listens to advice.

PROVERBS 12:15 NIV

Everything we know we learned from someone else, including the stuff we claim credit for! It may be new to us, but it's not new.

The Governor of North Carolina once complimented Thomas Edison on his creative genius. "I am not a great inventor," countered Edison. "But you have over a thousand patents to your credit," the Governor stated. "Yes, but about the only invention I can claim is absolutely original, is the phonograph," Edison replied. "I'm afraid I don't understand," the Governor remarked. "Well," explained Edison, "I'm an awfully good sponge. I absorb ideas wherever I can and put them to practical use. Then I improve them until they become of some value. My ideas are mostly the ideas of other people who didn't develop them themselves." Edison was a lifelong learner. He stayed open, hungry for knowledge, and teachable. And to succeed, you must too. To know whether you're teachable, ask yourself:

(1) Am I open to other people's thoughts and ideas? (2) Do I listen more than I talk? (3) Am I willing to change my opinion based on new information? (4) Do I readily admit when I am wrong? (5) Do I think and observe before acting on a situation? (6) Do I ask questions? (7) Am I willing to ask a question that will expose my ignorance? (8) Am I open to doing things in a way I haven't done them before? (9) Am I willing to ask for directions? (10) Do I act defensively when criticized, or do I listen openly for the truth? The Bible says: "The way of a fool seems right to him, but a wise man listens to advice."

HINDRANCES TO ANSWERED PRAYER (1)

He shall call upon Me, and I will answer.

PSALM 91:15 NKJV

When a nightclub opened on Main Street, a church which was only a few blocks away organized a twenty-four-hour prayer vigil. They asked God to burn the club down. Within a week lightning struck and it burned to the ground. The owner sued the church, which denied responsibility. After hearing arguments from both sides the judge said, "It seems that wherever the guilt may lie, the nightclub owner believes in prayer, while the church doesn't."

The first hindrance to answered prayer is—prayerlessness. Sounds simple, but our prayers are not answered when we don't pray. Saying we *believe* in prayer is not the same as *praying*. James writes: "You do not have because you do not ask" (Jas 4:3 NKJV). We must take the time to ask God for what we want and need. Sometimes we process situations in our minds, or talk about them with our friends, or wish, or hope, but we don't pray. Thinking, wishing, hoping, and talking with others is not prayer; only *prayer* is prayer! When we have a need or a situation that concerns us, we're only praying when we talk to God about it.

God is *waiting* for us to make requests of Him in prayer. He never gets tired of us coming to Him! He is able, willing, and ready to act on our behalf, but only if we pray. Jesus said: "Ask, and it will be given to you; seek, and you will find; knock, and it will be opened to you. For everyone who asks receives, and he who seeks finds, and to him who knocks it will be opened" (Mt 7:7-8 NKJV).

HINDRANCES TO ANSWERED PRAYER (2)

*Let us then approach
the throne of grace with confidence.*

HEBREWS 4:16 NIV

The second hindrance to answered prayer is—lack of confidence! When we understand that as God's redeemed children we have the right to approach Him at any time, we are able to overcome the enemy's attempts to make us feel condemned. As a result we become confident in approaching Him. We no longer say to ourselves, "I know God can do it, but I find it hard to believe He will do it for *me.*" We think such thoughts because we don't think we're *worthy.* Jesus has made us worthy! When we come to God, we can count on Him to be merciful to us. "Let us then approach the throne of grace with confidence, so that we may receive mercy and find grace to help us in our time of need." Grace means God will give us what we don't deserve—if we're confident enough to ask for it. We ask in Jesus' name, not in our own name. We're presenting to the Father all that Jesus is, not all that *we* are. We're nothing without Jesus! God is willing to do more than we could ask or think (See Eph 3:20). So we need to exercise faith, and avail ourselves of all He can do by asking confidently.

Helen Poole writes: "My four-year-old daughter would always pray before she went to sleep. One night she prayed and prayed—her voice getting softer, until only her lips were moving. Then she said, 'Amen.' I said, 'Honey, I didn't hear a word you said.' She replied, 'Momma, I wasn't talking to *you.*'" When you understand that you have the right to talk to God, and that He listens to every word, you pray with confidence.

HINDRANCES TO ANSWERED PRAYER (3)

If I regard iniquity in my heart,
the Lord will not hear me.

PSALM 66:18

The third hindrance to answered prayer is—sin! Lillian Pearsall says: "When I was a telephone operator, a customer talked overtime on a long-distance call from a pay phone. Even with my friendly reminders, he refused to deposit his overtime coins. Instead he slammed down the phone, irate and verbally abusive. A few seconds later he was back on the line— somewhat calmer. 'Operator, please let me out of the phone booth— I'll pay, just let me out!' Apparently he had locked himself in and mistakenly thought that I had control over the phone booth's doors. He gladly paid the overtime charge, and with my advice, gave the door a hefty kick and set himself free."

Unconfessed sin locks us in and shuts God out. If we have hidden sin in our hearts, we cannot pray with confidence that God will answer. However, if we ask Him to reveal our sin, He will. When He does, we must deal with it if we want to keep the lines of communication open. If God reminds us of a situation in which we didn't do the right thing, we can't just sweep it under the rug; we have to acknowledge it and receive His forgiveness.

What we call "little things," grow into sinful habits and lifelong patterns. So when God reveals our sin we need to repent and stop what we are doing. We need to take Him seriously— immediately! This means doing everything within our power to make sure our relationship with Him is unobstructed. That way our prayers will be heard and answered.

HINDRANCES TO ANSWERED PRAYER (4)

If we ask anything according to His will, He hears us.

1 JOHN 5:14 NKJV

The fourth hindrance to answered prayer is—praying outside of God's will. The Bible says: "Now this is the confidence that we have in Him, that if we ask anything according to His will, He hears us and…we know…that we have the petitions that we have asked of Him." One of the best ways to make sure we are praying according to God's will, is to pray according to His Word. Use a verse, a passage or a principle from Scripture to back up what you're praying, for God says, "I am ready to perform My word" (Jer 1:12 NKJV).

Sometimes there are things we want to pray for, but we aren't sure whether those things are God's will for us according to Scripture. In this case we simply need to ask God to give it, if it's His will to do so—and to help us to be satisfied with His decision. St. Augustine said, "O, Lord, grant that I may do thy will as if it were mine; so that thou mayest do my will as if it were thine." D.L. Moody said, "Spread out your petition before God, and then say, 'Thy will, not mine, be done.' The sweetest lesson I have learned in God's school, is to let the Lord choose for me."

When we pray in harmony with God, we *will* have what we ask for. We may have to wait, because God's timing is part of His will, but it will come. We can say, "I may not see it yet, but God has promised it to me, so it's on the way." And if God doesn't give us what we ask for, He will give us something *better,* if we walk in faith and keep a good attitude.

HINDRANCES TO ANSWERED PRAYER (5)

You do not receive,
because you ask with wrong motives.

JAMES 4:3 NIV

The fifth hindrance to answered prayer is—wrong motives! At a birthday party, it came time to serve the cake. A little boy named Brian blurted out, "I want the biggest piece!" His mother scolded him: "Brian, it's not right to ask for the biggest piece." The little guy looked at her in confusion and said, "Well then, how *do* I get it?" If you have the wrong motives, your prayers won't be answered. A motive is the *why* behind the *what.* In prayer, the *reason* we pray is much more important than the *words* we say. Having a pure heart that loves God and loves people, is always an acceptable motive to the Lord. Selfishness is unacceptable; revenge is unacceptable; manipulation and control are unacceptable; jealousy is unacceptable; pride is unacceptable. In fact, anything that is selfish is an unacceptable motive. A.W. Tozer writes: "The labor of self-love is a heavy one indeed. Think for yourself whether much of your sorrow has not arisen from someone speaking ill of you. As long as you set yourself up as a little god to whom you must be loyal, there will always be those who will delight in insulting your idol. How then can you hope to have inward peace? The heart's fierce effort to protect itself from every slight, will never let the mind rest."

To pray effectively we must purify our hearts on a regular basis, especially when we find ourselves wanting "the biggest piece." We need to examine our motives. Taking a look at them will be painful, but it must be done if we desire to see our prayers answered.

HINDRANCES TO ANSWERED PRAYER (6)

Without faith it is impossible to please God.

HEBREWS 11:6 NIV

God longs to be believed! The Bible says: "Without faith it is impossible to please God, because anyone who comes to him must believe that he...rewards those who earnestly seek him." Faith is a powerful spiritual force. It's the thing God responds to.

But we must expect our faith to be challenged. Satan will cloud our mind with doubts and fears. When he does, we need to examine our heart and see what it says. We can believe God's Word in our *heart,* even when our *mind* questions it. So we need to stand on what's in our heart, not on what's in our head. We must not believe our doubts; we must challenge our doubts and believe God!

Sometimes doubt begins with distraction. When we're distracted from God's promises, we start to doubt. As we think more and more about our problems, our faith begins to waver. We must focus like a laser on God's promises, His power and His willingness to work on our behalf—and merely glance at our problems. We don't deny their existence, but we refuse to pay too much attention to them. James writes: "But let him ask in faith, with no doubting, for he who doubts is like a wave of the sea driven and tossed by the wind. For let not that man suppose that he will receive anything from the Lord; he is a double-minded man, unstable in all his ways" (Jas 1:6-8 NKJV). We must be anchored to what God says, and not drift all over the place when our circumstances begin to change.

A TITLE OR A TESTIMONY

The memory of the righteous is blessed.

PROVERBS 10:7 NKJV

The Bible calls Barnabas "a good man…full of…faith" (Ac 11:24) although, unlike Paul, he never did the kinds of things that made him stand out. He's mentioned only three times in the book of Acts: (1) Selling his land to help finance God's work. (2) Vouching for Paul's character. (3) Giving John Mark a second chance. Barnabas didn't earn many titles, but he earned a pile of testimonies! The Bible says: "The memory of the righteous is blessed" because in God's eyes it's not what society considers important that counts.

During recognition day for college graduates a pastor stood up and said: "You don't think it now, but eventually you're going to die. When they lay you in the grave, are people going to stand around reciting the titles you earned, or talking about what a blessing you were? Will you leave an obituary about how 'important' you were, or about people grieving the loss of the best friend they ever had? Titles are good, but if it comes down to a choice between a title and a testimony—go for the testimony! Pharaoh had the title, Moses had the testimony. Nebuchadnezzar had the title, Daniel had the testimony. Jezebel had the title, Elijah had the testimony. Pilate had the title, but Jesus had the testimony. It's easy to think write-ups in *Who's Who* are the most important thing, but it's the loving acts you do that'll be remembered." The song goes "only one life, 'twill soon be past…only what's done for Christ will last!"

LET'S REVERSE THE GENERATIONAL SLIDE

*Another generation arose after them
who did not know the Lord.*

JUDGES 2:10 NKJV

Approaching the end of his life, Joshua calls the nation's leaders together and says, "You yourselves have seen everything the Lord your God has done" (Jos 23:3 NIV). His listeners could remember being supernaturally fed for forty years, seeing the Red Sea divide and the walls of Jericho fall. Then Joshua nails it squarely: "Choose...whom you will serve" (Jos 24:15 NIV). What did they do? "Israel served the Lord all the days of Joshua" (Jos 24:31 NKJV). So far, so good! But take a closer look. They served God *partly,* and only when it *suited* them. The one military action remaining to be taken after Joshua's death, was to clean out the last pockets of pagan worship. But Israel "did not drive out the inhabitants" (Jdg 1:27 NKJV).

While Joshua had been fully committed to God, the elders were only partly committed. And the result? Their sons and daughters began marrying their neighbors and adopting their sinful lifestyles. "Another generation arose after them who did not know the Lord...they provoked the Lord to anger...They did not cease from their own doings nor from their stubborn way" (Jdg 2:10-12,19 NKJV). What shaped the spiritual values of these children? The compromise of their parents! It's called *the generational slide.* It helps us to understand how our parents shaped us, and predicts how our commitments, or the lack of them, will shape our children. Parent, you get the first crack at it. Give your children deep spiritual roots as early as possible. That way if they rebel, they'll have the *memories* and *values* to return to. Don't just tell them about God, model a godly lifestyle before them every day!

OUT WITH THE OLD...IN WITH THE NEW

No one pours new wine into old wineskins.

MARK 2:22 NIV

Jon Walker writes: "A few miles from my house there's a convenience store that went through a make-over. However, the employees may have missed the make-over memo. The kid behind the counter wore a new uniform...but he also wore the same sullen look I'd seen before. It made me think about how we try to put new wine into old wineskins. Jesus says we're bound to fail because 'the wine will burst the skins and both ...will be ruined.' But don't we [do the same] when it comes to our Christian walk? The new wine of honesty-at-work, poured into the old wineskin of cutting corners. The new wine of unconditional love, poured into the old wineskin of hatred for the family two doors down. The new wine of worship, poured into the old wineskin of idolizing money, power, music or the latest video game. The new wine of Bible study, poured into the old wineskin of 'gotta-go-pop-tart-for-breakfast' busyness. The new wine of humility, poured into the old wineskin of conceit. The new wine of forgiveness, poured into the old wineskin of bitterness. The new wine of others first, poured into the old wineskin of selfish ambition. The new wine of joy, poured into the old wineskin of jealousy and factions. The new wine of peace, poured into the old wineskin of discord."

Any of these ring a bell? If they do, it's time you asked God to help you abandon the old wineskins of carnality and make you a strong, new, clean vessel. As a new creation, you're no longer defined by old behaviors; you're defined by your relationship with Christ.

CHOOSE TO LIVE!

Do you want to be made well?

JOHN 5:6 NKJV

He can't walk, the pool isn't easily accessible, and there are no motorized lifts. Then Jesus comes along and asks this man who'd been incapacitated for thirty-eight years, "Do you want to be made well?" What a question! Now, Jesus didn't ask it because He didn't know the answer; He did it to direct his (and our) thinking along the right lines. He could just as easily have asked:

"Are you ready to assume responsibility for your life? Do you really want that promotion, or is it easier to just gripe about money? Are you ready for marriage, for somebody who'll share your life and make you reconsider your self-centered ways?" Answers to our prayers often come with a price. For example, the family of an addict sometimes spends years praying for change, then when it happens they experience their own crises. Because their lives have centered around drama and dysfunction, they've never learned how to live any other way. At that point they have a choice to make: to keep blaming their problems on somebody else, or to accept that they have their own issues to work on. "Do you want to be made well?"

Like it or not, asking God for solutions often means new challenges. A child might solve his need for pocket money by bagging groceries, but when he grows up, hopefully he'll be solving bigger ones, like how to provide for his family. But the good news is, solving bigger problems brings bigger rewards. So ask God to stretch you today by helping you "take up your bed and walk" (Jn 5:8 NKJV), burn your bridges of dependency and "learned helplessness," and move on to greater things. In other words, "choose to live!"

RECOVERING FROM DIVORCE

When you walk through the fire,
you will not be burned.

ISAIAH 43:2 NIV

Divorce is like amputation; you survive, but it feels like there's less of you. And it's worse if you didn't want the divorce, or feel abandoned by a church that does nothing to help. So, how can you "walk through this fire" without being burned? By doing four things:

(1) Forgive yourself. "I…am he who blots out your transgressions, for my own sake, and remembers your sins no more" (Isa 43:25 NIV). God forgives and forgets, and He will give you the grace to forgive yourself, too. *(2) Forgive those who've hurt you.* Forgiveness is the one power you always have over anybody who hurts you. So keep on forgiving, until the past no longer controls you. Make forgiveness your fixed attitude! Only by forgiving and forgetting can you set it down and move on. *(3) Take your time.* Don't make any big changes right now. You're on an emotional roller coaster, vacillating between wanting them back and wanting them to suffer. You're vulnerable to other people's comments and easily drawn toward anybody who pays you attention. Slow down! Healthy people make healthy choices, so spend time reading God's Word, praying, seeking counsel, and allowing yourself to be made whole. *(4) Start giving back.* "Your God is gracious and compassionate. He will not turn his face from you if you return to him" (2Ch 30:9 NIV). Realizing God hasn't turned His back on you, is what enables you to "Comfort those in any trouble with the comfort [you] have received from God" (2Co 1:4 NIV). When that happens you're becoming whole, your future's bright and your possibilities unlimited.

THAT'S GRACE!

Grace was given me.

EPHESIANS 3:8 NIV

The word "grace," is so important that Paul mentions it three times more than any other writer. Remembering the violent life he lived, he writes, "Although I am less than the least of all God's people, this grace was given me: to preach... the unsearchable riches of Christ." The word grace comes from the Greek word *charis,* meaning "pure joy." Although you didn't deserve it, God considered saving you a "pure joy." How about that?

In John, chapter 8, a woman is caught in the act of adultery. The law is unmistakable about her punishment. The Pharisees are ready to stone her. She knows that Jesus, being righteous, must agree. She has no lawyer to defend her, not even a character witness! Suddenly Jesus stoops and begins to write in the sand. Some scholars have suggested that perhaps He wrote down *their* sins, times, places, etc. Ouch! When He looks up, her accusers are gone. He says, "Neither do I condemn you ...Go now and leave your life of sin" (Jn 8:11 NIV). Jesus lifted her from a position of undeniable guilt to one of unconditional pardon. She didn't deserve it, and didn't know it was possible. And that's *your* story too, isn't it?

One day Abraham Lincoln watched a plantation owner bidding for a slave girl. Figuring he was going to buy her and abuse her, Lincoln paid the price to set her free. "Does this mean I can say whatever I want to say?" she asked. Lincoln replied, "Yes." Again she asked, "Does this mean I can go wherever I want to go?" Again Lincoln responded, "Yes, you're free!" With tears streaming down her face she replied, "Then, sir, I will go with you." That's grace!

REFUSE TO ROLE PLAY

Love the Lord your God with all your heart.

DEUTERONOMY 6:5 NIV

Modern life is custom made for role playing. We live in a neighborhood all our lives yet we hardly know the family next door. We commute to a church miles away, walking in and out, never getting known, never getting involved or serving. We work with one crowd and play with another. The opportunities for undercover activity are almost limitless. Since no one knows us in any other context, we can reinvent ourselves in each one. Someone has said that our life is like a chest of drawers: a separate one for each interest, value or pastime—one for work, one for play and one for church. For each we have a separate set of values and a different language. With each new situation we add another drawer to ensure complete appropriateness and safety. Rather than having a oneness and integrity of character, we role play.

But God doesn't see us as a chest of drawers or a collection of separate performances, He sees us as a whole person. Who we are when no one is looking, is just the same to Him as who we are when we're standing in plain view. God asks for integrity in our lives. That's because life doesn't work any other way! God made us with one will, one mind, one heart, and one spirit. It's Satan's lie that we can "have it both ways," which leaves us mentally and emotionally fragmented, and worse—distant from God! "What is the answer?" you ask. The Bible says: "Love the Lord your God with all your heart and all your soul and all your strength." In other words, refuse to role play!

GIVE GOD A TITHE OF YOUR INCOME

Bring...(the whole tenth of your income).

MALACHI 3:10 AMP

Whether you believe tithing to be an Old Testament law or a New Testament truth, one thing is certain, giving God the first tenth of your income demonstrates that He's *first* in your life. To those who practice tithing, God promises two things:

(1) His blessing. God said He will "Open for you the windows of heaven and pour out for you such a blessing that there will not be room enough to receive it" (Mal 3:10 NKJV). A farmer, who was a faithful tither, was prospering while others around him were barely getting by. When one of his neighbors asked, "What's your secret?" he replied, "No secret, I just shovel it into God's bin and He shovels it back into mine—but God's got a bigger shovel!" By tithing, you partner with God. Think what God's blessing could mean to your business, your family, your ministry or your future—your possibilities are out of sight!

(2) His protection. "I will rebuke the devourer...he shall not destroy" (Mal 3:11). "What's the devourer?" you ask. Anything that devours your blessings. The dishwasher breaks down for the third time in a month. The kids are ill and have to be taken to the doctor all the time. The day after the warranty runs out on your car, the transmission goes. One of the Hebrew words for tithe is *charam*, which means "marked for destruction." Your tithe literally becomes a force in the hand of God to destroy the works of the enemy. It puts a hedge of protection around you. "Is God after my *money?*" you ask. No, He's after your *lack!* He wants you to be blessed and protected every day of your life.

TAKING OFF AND PUTTING ON

You have taken off your old self…
and have put on the new self.

COLOSSIANS 3:9-10 NIV

Some of us are perfectionists when it comes to our physical appearance, yet we think nothing of running around spiritually threadbare. We're more concerned with how we look to others, than how we look to God. What's the answer? *Spend more time in front of the mirror!* James writes: "Anyone who listens to the word but does not do what it says is like a man who looks at his face in a mirror and, after looking at himself, goes away and immediately forgets what he looks like. But the man who looks intently into the perfect law that gives freedom, and continues to do this, not forgetting what he has heard, but doing it—he will be blessed in what he does" (Jas 1:23-25 NIV).

Your old carnal clothes must be discarded, not hung in the closet for the next time you want to wear them. Your focus each day must be to "Clothe [yourselves] with the Lord Jesus Christ, and do not think about how to gratify the desires of the sinful nature" (Ro 13:14 NIV). Chuck Swindol says: "The number one enemy of change is the hard-core, self-sustained sin nature within you. Like a spoiled child it's been gratified and indulged for years, so it won't give up without a temper tantrum. The flesh dies a slow, bitter, bloody death—kicking and struggling all the way. Lasting change takes place in first gear, not overdrive. So expect occasional setbacks, and don't let them derail you. When you feel like throwing in the towel, get down on your knees and ask God to help you get back on track. He'll do it."

ACCEPTING YOURSELF

Love others as much as you love yourself.

MATTHEW 22:39 CEV

Only by loving yourself in a healthy way, can you love others the way God intended. When you don't love yourself you live with insecurity, and you keep looking to others for approval. When you don't get it, your self-worth shrivels. As a result, you live far beneath your potential. *You* are the only person you can't get away from, so unless you learn to accept yourself, you'll be miserable. Stop and think about the last time you were around somebody you didn't enjoy being with—how did it feel?

Whether good or bad, you project onto others the thoughts and feelings you have about yourself. So if you want people to think well of you, have a good opinion of yourself—one that's based on God's Word and nurtured by the right relationships. No question, the Bible cautions us about having an overinflated opinion of ourselves. But don't go to the other extreme! Living with continual self-rejection is an open invitation to Satan, who is always "sneaking around to find someone to attack" (1Pe 5:8 CEV). Don't play into his hands!

Paul writes: "Nothing good lives in me, that is, in my sinful nature" (Ro 7:18 NIV). That means the good qualities you do possess, are *evidence* that God is at work in your life. So be sure to acknowledge them. The Bible says, "We have this treasure in earthen vessels, that the excellency of the power may be of God, and not of us" (2Co 4:7). Instead of focusing on your flaws and feeling bad about yourself, recognize the "treasure" of God's presence, power, and potential that lives within you, and build on it.

WHAT ARE YOU TALKING ABOUT? (1)

He who invokes a blessing on himself...
shall do so by saying, May the God of truth...bless me.

ISAIAH 65:16 AMP

Did you know you can bless yourself by what you *say?* The Bible says: "He who invokes a blessing on himself...shall do so by saying, May the God of truth...bless me...because the former troubles are forgotten." Two important truths are taught in this Scripture: (1) Your own words have more power to affect you than anybody else's. Ultimately it's not what others say that counts; it's what *you* say to yourself after they get through talking! You always have the last word. (2) You'll never enjoy what God has for you in the future while you're still living in the past. To enter the Promised Land, you must first leave the wilderness. So come into agreement with God; begin to say what *He* says about you. This is no small matter. What you say from the time you get up in the morning until you go to bed at night not only influences your day, it influences the entire outlook and direction of your life. If you've been praying and asking God for specific answers, you can affect the outcome by making sure what *you* say lines up with what *He* says. In other words—get in harmony with God.

Your body is God's temple, so be careful what you allow to come out of your mouth (See 1Co 3:16). Faultfinding and negativity destroy and tear down, but scripturally-based, faith-filled words open the door to God's blessings. That's why Paul writes: "Let no...worthless talk [ever] come out of your mouth, but only such...as is...beneficial" (Eph 4:29 AMP). So before you sound off, ask yourself—is this beneficial?

WHAT ARE YOU TALKING ABOUT? (2)

*Those who are careful
about what they say protect their lives.*

PROVERBS 13:3 NCV

After failing in business, Paul Gavin attended an auction of his own company. He was "down" but he wasn't "out!" With his last $750 he bought back the department which later became—*Motorola!* How's that for a comeback story? The Bible says, "In...prosperity be joyful, but in...adversity consider [examine it and see what you can learn]...God has appointed the one as well as the other" (Ecc 7:14 NKJV). Whenever we face new challenges like changing careers, going back to school or starting a new relationship, our old programming kicks in and tells us we're not equal to the task. Look out! The Bible says, "Those who are careful about what they say protect their lives...whoever speaks without thinking will be ruined" (Pr 13:3 NCV).

The wonderful thing about being the person God created you to be, is that He pre-programmed you to handle new situations, to change and to grow. Don't build a case against yourself by listening to old voices without or within, or speaking words that undermine your confidence. Doing something you've never done before usually involves an anxiety-induced learning curve that follows along these lines: "There's no way I can do this...I suppose I can try...I'm doing it, but not very well ...I'm still doing it but I'm scared...I'm doing better...Oops, I made a mistake, guess I *can't* do this after all...Maybe I'll try again...I'm not doing much better this time...I'll give it one more shot...Hey, I'm doing pretty good...I *can* do this!" The Bible says you'll "be rewarded for...how [you] speak" (Pr 18:20 NCV), so turn all those "I can'ts" into "I cans" and get your self-talk in sync with the Scriptures.

SEVENTY-SEVEN TIMES!

How many times shall I forgive?

MATTHEW 18:21 NIV

Lamech was a descendent of Cain, one of Adam's sons. Now when Cain killed his brother Abel, God put a mark on him, saying that if anyone killed Cain they'd pay for it seven times over. One day somebody hurt Lamech, so he gave in to resentment, killed the offender, and said, "I have killed a man for wounding me...If Cain is avenged seven times, then Lamech seventy-seven times" (Ge 4:23-24 NIV). In Lamech's mind he was absolutely justified. The guy who did him wrong, had it coming. The philosophy of Lamech is: if you hurt me, I'll hurt you. And not just once, but seventy-seven times over. The spirit of revenge is never satisfied. Simply stated: "It doesn't work!"

Like Lamech, Peter had been hurt by someone close to him, and it happened more than once. So he went to Jesus and asked, "How many times do I have to forgive this man? Seven times?" Peter thought he was being extremely generous and expected Jesus to pat him on the back. So he probably wasn't too pleased when Jesus deflated his ego by saying he must forgive the offender, "not seven times, but seventy-seven times." Where did Jesus get that number? From the Old Testament. Jesus knew the Scriptures well, so He chose it deliberately. He was doing away with the philosophy of Lamech! "Peter, you can follow in the footsteps of Lamech and retaliate, or you can follow Me and *keep* extending forgiveness—but you can't do both!"

HOW TO FIGHT SO EVERYBODY WINS (1)

Watch out or you will be destroyed by each other.

GALATIANS 5:15 NIV

Healthy relationships aren't conflict free; they're conflict resolving. The problem is: we fight for victories instead of fighting for solutions. The result is: one wins, one loses, and the relationship suffers! Here are some practical insights for fighting so that the relationship wins:
(1) Differences are inevitable, normal, and potentially beneficial. They're inevitable, because relationships bring together very different people. They're normal, because all relationships, including great ones, experience them. They're potentially beneficial, because handled effectively, relationships grow through them. *(2) Here are three conflicting handling styles:* (a) The avoid style. These are the "don't want to rock the boat" and "let sleeping dogs lie" people. They fear confrontation, so they bury their feelings, not realizing they're buried alive and will rise again down the road. They go from clam-up, to build-up, to blow-up, inviting physical and emotional illness. Meanwhile offenses accumulate, unaddressed issues multiply, and unfinished business erodes the relationship. (b) The attack style. These are the "get them before they get you" people; ruthless fighters who refuse to give in, they inflict terminal wounds on each other. The Bible says, "If you keep on biting and devouring each other, watch out or you will be destroyed by each other." Attack begets counterattack, both sides "dig in" and nothing gets resolved. (c) The approach-assert style. These are the "no price is too high for a good relationship" people. They're sensitive to the feelings of others, yet insist on dealing directly with important issues. They avoid blaming, confront the issue, not the individual, and invite others to partner with them in solving the problem and saving the relationship!

HOW TO FIGHT SO EVERYBODY WINS (2)

Speaking the truth in love, we will...grow up.

EPHESIANS 4:15 NIV

There are two ways to tell the truth. The "give them a piece of your mind" style, which only drives the wedge deeper. Or the Bible way: "Speaking the truth in love," which resolves conflict and strengthens relationships. Suppose a couple is fighting because he's habitually late. How can she speak "the truth in love" and get her message heard? Here's a five-step process that's effective in marriage, friendship or work. She could say to him: *(1) "I feel frustrated."* No blame, no attack; just an honest expression of her own emotion. *(2) "When you are late."* No judging, name-calling or labeling; just a concrete description of his action. *(3) "It seems to say to me that my time is not really important to you."* No moralizing; just honestly sharing her feelings. *(4) "Please try to be on time, or call and let me know when you'll be here."* Instead of focusing on past actions he can't change, she's telling him what she'd like him to do differently next time. *(5) "Would you be willing to do that for me?"* No demanding or taking for granted; just asking for consideration and cooperation. When he agrees, they have a "contract." She thanks him sincerely and rewards every effort he makes to keep his word. She has effectively realigned the couple by making him her ally, not her enemy, and redefined the focus as a shared one, not something she "does to him!" The Bible says we can "walk together" when we have "agreed" to do so (See Am 3:3 NIV).

HOW TO FIGHT SO EVERYBODY WINS (3)

Do all things without complaining.

PHILIPPIANS 2:14 NKJV

He comes home flustered. "Honey, I'm late for a meeting and all my shirts are dirty!" Now, he believes he asked reasonably for a clean shirt. But she, hearing herself criticized, fires back, "If you'd fixed the washing machine like you promised, you'd have a closet full of clean shirts!" "I only *asked* for a shirt," he says. "You didn't ask, you complained!" she replies. Did he?

We complain, imagining we're asking reasonably that our partner change something we're upset about, then we're frustrated when it backfires. Why not adopt the biblical principle, "You do not have because you do not ask" (Jas 4:3 NKJV). You'll be amazed how much you'll get once you learn to ask, instead of assuming, demanding or complaining.

Therapist and author Bill O'Hanlon calls this "turning your complaints into action requests." Instead of telling your husband or wife what you don't like about their actions, ask graciously and clearly for what you'd like them to *do*. Be solution focused, action oriented, concrete and specific. Instead of, "John, we've got guests in thirty minutes and you're still watching TV!" try, "John, they'll be here soon. Would you mind bathing the kids while I finish cooking?" No complaint, just a request. Instead of, "Nobody lifts a finger around here but me," try, "Sweetheart, I'm really exhausted, would you help me clear up the dishes?" Accept responsibility for turning your complaints into action requests, then make them concrete and specific. Saying "I need you to be considerate" is much too vague. Ask yourself, "If he or she were being considerate, what would they be *doing?*" Then kindly request that behavior—and always show gratitude when you get it!

"SOMETHING ELSE!"

That in the coming ages he might show...
his grace, expressed...to us.

EPHESIANS 2:7 NIV

What you're going through right now is important, because God is weighing it in the light of your *future*. God doesn't measure us in terms of our present condition or comfort level. No, He has a far greater plan in mind. "God knew [us] before he made the world, and he chose [us] to be like his Son" (Ro 8:29 NCV). Imagine that! One day we will be just like Jesus; doesn't that blow your mind? "In the coming ages" God is going to put us on display and say, "Look at My workmanship. Can you believe that I made these glorified creatures from clay? When I first scooped them off the ground they wouldn't hold water. But I worked with them, molded them and raised them up until they held relationships, and ministries, and concepts, and jobs. What you heard about them was true. They *were* a disgrace and a disaster, but My grace was sufficient. Now they will sit with Me, ruling and reigning for ever!"

When it comes to performing the impossible, Houdini and P.T. Barnum were amateurs. Could *they* have parted the Red Sea, put the sun on hold for twenty-four hours, turned water into wine, resurrected the dead, and done it all with such style? Well, guess what? That same God is at work in your life. That's because He plans to show you off some day. Incredible as it may sound, when God gets through with you, you'll be "something else."

NO SHORTCUTS—
YOU'VE GOT TO WORK FOR IT!

Lazy hands make a man poor,
but diligent hands bring wealth.

PROVERBS 10:4 NIV

When questioned about his incredible success, Bill Gates, founder of Microsoft, offered these ten insights to anyone starting out. They are worth considering: (1) Life isn't fair—get used to it. (2) The world doesn't care about your self-esteem; it expects you to accomplish something before feeling good about yourself. (3) You won't make $60K a year right out of school, or be a vice president with a cell phone. You have to earn it. (4) Do you think your teacher is tough? Wait till you have a boss—he's not tenured. (5) Flipping burgers isn't beneath you; your grandparents called it opportunity. (6) Your parents weren't always boring; it came from feeding you, cleaning your clothes and paying your bills. So before you rush out to save the rain forest from the "parasites" of your parents' generation, try delousing your own closet. (7) Some schools may have abolished winners and losers, but life hasn't. They may have eradicated "failing grades" and given you as long as you want to get the right answer. This bears no resemblance to reality. (8) Life isn't divided into semesters. You don't get summers off. Employers aren't interested in helping you "find yourself;" you do that on your own time. (9) Unlike television, real people actually have to leave the coffee shop and go to work. (10) Be nice to nerds; chances are, you'll end up working for one someday!

The Bible says: "Lazy hands make a man poor, but diligent hands bring wealth." "The sluggard craves and gets nothing, but the desires of the diligent are fully satisfied" (Pr 13:4 NIV). No shortcuts—you've got to work for it!

IN THE FIRE

*Then the king promoted
Shadrach, Meshach and Abednego.*

DANIEL 3:30 NIV

The story of the three Hebrew children in the fiery furnace makes us realize four things: *(1) Obeying God doesn't exempt you from trouble.* Don't expect the world to always understand or appreciate you. Look at Christ: "In him was life, and that life was the light of men. The light shines in the darkness, but the darkness has not understood it" (Jn 1:4-5 NIV). *(2) You're not alone, God is with you in your trouble.* When King Nebuchadnezzar looked into the fiery furnace he said, "I see four men loose, walking in the midst of the fire, and they have no hurt; and the form of the fourth is like the Son of God" (Da 3:25). Instead of destroying them, the fire burned the ropes that bound them and set them free. So be encouraged. It may feel like you're "bound by circumstances," limited and locked in, but God is with you; He's going to vindicate you and bring you out of this victorious. *(3) Your trouble will become your testimony.* Others are watching. What they're trusting in doesn't work, and they're wondering if what you're trusting in does. Your faithfulness to God and His intervention on your behalf, will touch their lives in ways your theology never will. Everybody in Babylon knew what the three Hebrew children believed, but they wanted to know, "Does it work when you're in the fire?" It does! *(4) On the other side of your trouble, there's great blessing.* "Then the king promoted Shadrach, Meshach and Abednego in the province of Babylon." It's a Scriptural principle: when you are faithful in a hard place, God can trust you in a high place.

SERVING GOD WITH ONE EYEBROW

*The strong spirit of a man will sustain him
in bodily pain or trouble.*

PROVERBS 18:14 AMP

David Rabin was a professor of medicine at Vanderbilt University. When he was forty-six he was diagnosed with Lou Gehrig's Disease. He knew what would happen: Stiffness in the legs, then weakness; paralysis of the lower limbs and then the upper. Eventually his body would no longer obey his commands. He could form words only with the greatest difficulty, and eventually not at all. He lost his ability to treat patients and could no longer go to the hospital to work. He would have had a brilliant academic career; now he couldn't even turn the pages of a book. But there was one thing he would not surrender: his spirit! One day he heard from a fellow physician who also had Lou Gehrig's Disease, about a computer that could be operated by a single switch. That switch could be operated by anyone, however physically challenged, who retained the function of just one muscle group. David Rabin still had enough strength in one part of his body—his eyebrow. So for the next four years he used it to speak to his family, tell jokes, write papers and review manuscripts. He carried on a medical consulting practice. He taught med students. He published a comprehensive textbook on endocrinology and achieved a prestigious award for his work. And he did it with the only thing he could control, a single eyebrow.

The Bible says: "The strong spirit of a man will sustain him in bodily pain or trouble." David Rabin proved that's true. With a spirit that refused to give up, and one eyebrow, he served God and blessed the world around him!

THE JOY OF GIVING (1)

Every man shall give as he is able.

DEUTERONOMY 16:17

There are over 2,000 Scriptures in the Bible on money and giving. Here are two: (a) "Every man shall give as he is able, according to the blessing of the Lord thy God which he hath given thee." (b) "Let each one give as he purposes in his heart, not grudgingly...for God loves a cheerful giver" (2Co 9:7 NKJV). Here are two stories on the joy of giving, worth thinking about:

(1) Oseola McCarty, eighty-seven, did one thing all her life: laundry. Now she's famous for it. For decades, she earned fifty cents per load doing laundry for well-to-do families in Hattiesburg, Mississippi, preferring a washboard over a washing machine. Every week she put a little bit in a savings account. When she finally retired she asked her banker how much money she had. "$250,000," he replied. She was in shock. "I had more than I could use," she explained. So this shy, never-married laundry woman gave $150,000 to the University of Southern Mississippi to help African American young people attend college. "It's more blessed to give than to receive," she told reporters. "I've tried it."

(2) Don McCullough, President of San Francisco Seminary, says: "Scottish Presbyterians established churches in Ghana over 100 years ago. Their worship services still resemble a formal Scottish Presbyterian service. But recently they've allowed traditional African expressions into the worship service. Now the people dance at offering time. The music plays, and each individual joyfully dances down the aisle to the offering plate. According to the missionary who told me this, the offering is the only time in the service when people smile. *No doubt, God also smiles!*"

THE JOY OF GIVING (2)

Every man shall give as he is able.

DEUTERONOMY 16:17

The Academy Award-winning movie *Schindler's List* is the story of one man's efforts to make the most of a desperate opportunity. As the director of a munitions factory in Germany, Schindler decides to use his position to save lives. By employing them in his factory, Schindler is able to rescue condemned Jews from the gas chambers. But keeping them on is costly. Little by little, he liquidates his personal possessions in order to keep the business afloat. At the end of the story the Nazis are defeated. The full weight of Schindler's efforts is finally revealed as the dead are counted and the living stagger back to freedom. In one scene, kneeling by the railroad tracks that had carried thousands of Jews to their death, Oskar Schindler has a startling realization: he could have saved a few more. Overwhelmed with regret, he laments the few goods still remaining in his possession. If only he'd known when the war would end, he would have done more. But now it was too late. Oskar Schindler is a hero. He's credited with saving more lives during World War II than any other single person. But interestingly, all he could think about was what he *didn't* do. He wished he had done *more*.

We can learn a powerful lesson about giving from this man. Because, in the same way, even joyful givers will look back on their lives and wish they'd done more. And as for those who never gave at all, or gave less than they could, imagine their thoughts as they stand before God in the final audit to give an account of how they used their finances—and are rewarded accordingly!

RULES OR RELATIONSHIP

Not that we are adequate in ourselves.

2 CORINTHIANS 3:5 NAS

Have you ever watched someone walking a dog on a leash, when the dog doesn't want to go where its owner is going? The owner is constantly tugging on the leash, pulling the dog from here and there, telling it to "stop that" and "come back here." That's the way a lot of us live. We are on a "law leash." Our lives consist of "Stop that; come back here; don't do that." Only it's in terms of "Read your Bible; pray; go to church; pay your tithes; witness." Now, these are certainly the things we should be doing, but God never meant us to do them at the end of a leash. What a difference when you see a dog and its owner that have a strong relationship. The dog doesn't need a leash to go for a walk. Its owner can just speak a word and the dog responds. Now we're not comparing ourselves to dogs, we're comparing performance-based Christian living to relationship-based Christian living. Big, big difference!

Paul writes: "Not that we are adequate in ourselves to consider anything as coming from ourselves, but our adequacy is from God, who also made us adequate as servants of a new covenant, not of the letter but of the Spirit; for the letter kills, but the Spirit gives life." When God redeemed you, He wrote His law in your heart and mind (See Heb 10:16). That means He wants to relate to you from the *inside*. You shouldn't need an external system of rules to "keep you in line," because you have internalized God's Word and you have a desire to obey and please Him from your heart.

WHEN JESUS COMES!

In the fourth watch...He came to them.

MATTHEW 14:25 NAS

The "fourth watch" lasts from 3:00 a.m. until 6:00 a.m. Nighttime is when God does some of His best work! When the Israelites faced the Red Sea, we read, "All that night the Lord drove back the sea" (Ex 14:21 NCV). During "the middle watch" of the night, Gideon defeated the Midianites (See Jdg 7:19-24). Jesus rose from the dead before "daybreak" (See Mt 28:1). Matthew says: "In the fourth watch of the night He came to them, walking on the sea. When the disciples saw Him ...they were terrified...immediately Jesus spoke...'Take courage, it is I; do not be afraid'" (Mt 14:25-27 NAS). Notice two important things: (1) Jesus waited until the storm was at its worst and they'd lost all hope. That's because God dictates the timetable for our deliverance, and He's never late. (2) The disciples didn't recognize Him until He revealed Himself to them. Often the answer you need is right beside you, but you don't recognize it until God reveals it to you.

On another occasion, "When...the crowd was pushing in ...[Jesus] climbed into the boat that was Simon's...put out... from the shore...[and] using the boat for a pulpit...taught the crowd" (Lk 5:1-3 TM). In that moment it would have been tempting for Peter to feel important, thinking the Master *needed* his boat. No, God doesn't need anything we have to accomplish His purposes—not our credentials, talent, or resources. So be humble. And don't panic! When Jesus came to the disciples that night He was "walking on the sea." God is on top of your situation. Be at peace; He will do whatever it takes to reach and rescue you. *Your problem is just a platform to display His power to act on your behalf!*

THE ENGRAFTED WORD (1)

Receive…the engrafted word.

JAMES 1:21

The word "engrafted" means "to attach to, and become part of." Picture a gardener grafting a branch into a tree and that branch coming to life and bearing fruit. Now picture yourself reading God's Word and a Scripture attaching itself to you, growing in you and producing change in your life. That's how God's Word works. And that's why you need to read it daily!

Sometimes you can tell the pastor what you received through his sermon and he won't know what you're talking about because he was emphasizing something different. He was just the mailman; he didn't know what was in the letter. God sent a Word just for you. He said, "Here's what I want *you* to do," or "This is what *I'm* going to do for you in this situation." It's a Word that liberates you from fear, lifts you, directs you, and enables you to fight and win. Engrafted-Word-carrying believers are potent. That's because the engrafted Word sticks to you, takes you through the storm, feeds you in famine, quenches your thirst in drought, and brings you through the worst of times.

It doesn't have to be a sermon; Jesus just gave Peter one Word, "Come," and Peter started walking on water. It works like this: God gives you a Word, and the moment you step out on it your mind says, "It doesn't make sense, you don't have the talent, you don't have the finances, you don't have the education, etc." The amazing thing is, as long as you stand on the Word God gave you, you won't go under. That one Word, "Come," stuck to Peter's heart and propelled him through the storm. And the engrafted Word will do the same for you.

THE ENGRAFTED WORD (2)

Receive...the engrafted word.

JAMES 1:21

The "engrafted Word" is self-sustaining. It doesn't require the accolades of men or the support of others to validate it. As Jesus was walking on the water towards His disciples in the boat, Peter said, "Lord, if it's you, tell me to come" (Mt 14:28 NIV). Jesus gave him one Word, "Come," and Peter started walking. Was he scared? Wouldn't *you* be? But his desire was greater than his fear. That's all you need to get started, a desire for God that's greater than your doubts and limitations. The other disciples probably didn't believe Peter could do it. Indeed, those who feared for his safety didn't want him to try, and those who were competitive with him didn't want him to succeed. The truth is, the other disciples didn't understand *who* was calling to Peter; they thought Jesus was "a ghost!" (See Mk 6:49). There's a lesson here for you:

When God gives you a Word and you step out on it, don't expect everybody to validate it. It's normal for you to want certain people to see what you see and believe what you believe. But in this verse God prepares you for disagreements between you, and those who don't understand what God has told you. If you're not careful, people's opinions will short-circuit your faith and make you doubt what God has said. God says: "I'm not going to confirm what I've told you through them. In fact, I don't even need them to agree with what I've spoken concerning you." Relax. Be confident in God. You may *want* all these external support systems, but the truth is, you don't *need* them!

THE ENGRAFTED WORD (3)

Receive…the engrafted word.

JAMES 1:21

When God gives you an "engrafted Word," it will make you hunger for more of the same. But be careful; don't go "cherry-picking" the Bible for feel-good Scriptures. To grow in your faith you must discipline yourself to spend time each day in God's Word. You don't discover an engrafted Word all by yourself, or decide that one particular Scripture is for you and another is not. "All Scripture is…profitable" (2Ti 3:16 NKJV). To make a profit in business you must know your business thoroughly, otherwise you'll soon be out of business. The way to succeed in your Christian life is to make it your business to know your Bible. Don't just seek a Word *from* God, study the entire Word *of* God.

Do you want your life to count? Saturate yourself in the Scriptures! It's the analogy of the sperm and the egg. Neither the male sperm nor the female egg is capable of reproduction. Only when the sperm impacts and is embraced by the egg, is there conception and reproduction. And it's the same with our spiritual growth. When God's Word and the receptive heart get together, something is going to happen. That's a combination that works every time!

There's nothing to beat prolonged personal exposure to the Scriptures. It's vital. Without it you won't be able to hear what God is saying to you. You'll always have to depend on somebody else. Imagine dealing with your husband or wife on that basis? How long do you think your marriage would last? The same is true with God. There's no substitute for first-hand, daily, consistent exposure to His Word.

IN THE INTENSIVE CARE WAITING ROOM

If I have a faith that can move mountains,
but have not love, I am nothing.

1 CORINTHIANS 13:2 NIV

We keep *saying* that relationships are more important to us than anything else, but our actions don't *show* it. We constantly shortchange our friends and loved ones for the sake of money, or "getting ahead." Relationships are like flowers; if you don't nurture and protect them, they die. That's why Paul writes: "Do nothing out of selfish ambition or vain conceit... look not only to your own interests, but also to the interests of others" (Php 2:3-4 NIV). Sometimes it takes heartache and crisis to remind us how irreplaceable the people in our lives are.

One author writes: "I have spent long hours in the Intensive Care waiting room watching anguished people, listening to urgent questions: 'Will my husband make it? Will my child walk again? How do you live without your companion of thirty years?' The Intensive Care waiting room is different from any other place in the world. And the people who wait are different. They can't do enough for each other. No one is rude. The distinctions of race and class melt away. The garbage man loves his wife as much as the university professor loves his, and everyone understands this. Each person pulls for everyone else. In the Intensive Care waiting room the world changes. Vanity and pretence vanish. The universe is focused on the doctor's next report. If only it will show improvement. Everyone knows that loving someone else is what life is all about. Could we learn to love like that, if we realized that every day of life, is like a day in the Intensive Care waiting room?"

GOD'S GOT TOO MUCH INVESTED IN YOU

We were...chosen.

EPHESIANS 1:11 NIV

Before you were born, God already had a plan for your life. "We were...chosen, having been predestined according to the plan of him who works out everything in conformity with ...his will." The Living Bible puts it this way: "All things happen just as he decided long ago." Notice, it says "all things." That includes the things you want to run from! When Jonah tried to run from God and go to Tarshish, God said, "No way. My plan is in place. If I let you escape I wouldn't be God. If I have to I'll send a storm, rock your boat and put your life on hold in order to accomplish My purpose." When Jonah could go no lower he prayed and God answered him, just in time to go and preach in Nineveh, his original destination. You can go the easy way or the hard way, but you'll go! The Psalmist said, "Your way...is in the sanctuary...Your way was in the sea [storm]" (Ps 77:13 & 19 NKJV). The choice is yours.

Understand this: you have been picked for a purpose; God has too much invested in you to let you get away with things. If you have to come on a stretcher when He calls you'll come. If you have to leave behind a relationship, or an addiction, or a personal agenda, you'll come. And you'll know it's God, because you'll be willing to leave behind those things which now mean *nothing,* in order to live for those things which now mean *everything.*

So, for your own good, make up your mind to walk with Him and follow His plan.

VICTORY THROUGH INTIMACY

That I may know Him.

PHILIPPIANS 3:10 NKJV

Paul writes: "That I may know Him and the power of His resurrection, and the fellowship of His sufferings." Now, we know about resurrection power. It's the power that raised Jesus from the dead. Think—what problem or need do you have that resurrection power can't handle? What's dead in your life that needs to be raised, or broken that needs to be fixed? When you make intimacy with Christ your top priority, you tap into this power.

Why is it that some Christians live as "more than conquerors," while others seem to go around defeated all the time? The answer isn't in their circumstances, because victorious Christians and defeated Christians face basically the same kind of trials. And the answer isn't in who goes to church more often, or who reads the Bible and who doesn't. The answer is, victorious Christians know Christ more intimately, therefore they experience His life-giving power!

But a lot of us would like to put a period after the words, "The power of His resurrection." No, if we're going to know Christ intimately we must also know Him in "the fellowship of His sufferings." This word "sufferings" means more than just enduring a bad allergy season or having your mother-in-law move in with you. For Paul it meant being beaten to a pulp and beheaded! But it also meant a special kind of intimacy with the Lord that can't be known any other way. If you've ever suffered deeply with another person you understand what this means. We'll never truly be intimate with somebody if we say to them, "I only want to share the good times with you, keep your suffering to yourself." Getting the idea?

USE WHAT GOD GAVE YOU (1)

Each according to his ability.

MATTHEW 25:15 NIV

In His famous parable of the talents, Jesus said three people were given something to invest, "each according to his ability." Note, God will give you only what you have the ability to handle. If you didn't get the same talents as your neighbor, don't worry, just use what He gave you. The first worker doubled his. Wouldn't you like to have *him* advising you? The second did the same. But the third caved in to fear and buried his. Now when you fail to invest what God gives you, He loses His return and you lose the rewards you would have enjoyed.

Fear is your number one enemy; it freezes your faith and cripples your creativity. Your money, time, talent, love, etc. are seeds that must be sown; so sow them into something you *believe* in, something that will *outlive* you. Everything God gives you is meant to be multiplied. By failing to do so, you eventually forfeit it. Christ's parable ends with these sobering words: "Take the talent from him and give it to the one who has the ten talents" (Mt 25:28 NIV).

Ever notice how those who pour generously into the lives of others are constantly refilled, while those who worry about parting with it, end up losing it or not enjoying it? "Whoever sows sparingly will also reap sparingly, and whoever sows generously will also reap generously" (2Co 9:6 NIV). Ask any farmer; your harvest only begins when you take your seed out of the barn and put it into the ground. That way God has something to work with. So the word for you today is—use what God gave you!

USE WHAT GOD GAVE YOU (2)

While the earth remaineth,
seedtime and harvest...shall not cease.

GENESIS 8:22

To succeed in life you must seek God's direction, prepare yourself, work hard, and invest in the right things. The Bible says God gives us the ability to make money (See De 8:18). So never apologize for that ability! But material success is only *part* of it. God's *real* objective is to make you a channel through which His blessings flow to others. He's not opposed to you owning things, as long as they don't own you! God wants your greatest joy to be in Him, the Giver, not His gifts. Money can be a tool for good or evil, and one reason God wants you to have it, is to make sure it gets to the right places and funds His purposes.

Parent, teach your children that saving and investing are essential to good stewardship. And don't just preach it, practice it. For example, if you earn $40,000 a year and spend it eating out and buying the latest clothes, you'll end up with a full stomach, an expanding waistline, a crammed closet and empty pockets! The Bible says: "While the earth remaineth, seedtime and harvest...shall not cease." Notice the sequence in this Scripture: first you plant your "seed," then you give it "time," then you reap your "harvest." Consistent sowing guarantees consistent reaping. Each seed planted, schedules a harvest. For example, four dollars a day (a cup of cappuccino) invested at 6 percent, becomes almost a million dollars in forty-six years. Isn't it worth foregoing a few luxuries now in order to be secure later, to be in a position to fulfill God's purposes, and hear Him say, "Well done, good and faithful servant" (Mt 25:21)?

BATTLING SELFISHNESS

Nobody should seek his own good,
but the good of others.

1 CORINTHIANS 10:24 NIV

As citizens of God's kingdom, we live by a different value system. "Nobody should seek his own good, but the good of others." Now let's be honest; that's hard to do and easy to forget, because selfishness is a battle we fight daily. When Jesus was hanging on the cross in intense pain, He took time for a condemned criminal hanging next to Him (See Lk 23:39-43). When Stephen was being stoned to death, he prayed for those who were killing him, asking God not to lay the sin to their charge (See Ac 7:59-60). Though Paul and Silas were beaten and wrongly imprisoned, they took the time to minister to their jailer. Even after God sent a powerful earthquake that broke their chains and opened their prison doors, they remained there just for the purpose of ministering to their captor. How tempting it must have been to run away while the opportunity was there. How easy it would have been to take care of themselves and not worry about anybody else. But their act of love moved the jailer to ask how he might be saved. As a result, he and his entire family were won to Christ (See Ac 16:25-34).

When we begin to win the war against selfishness and walk in love, others will take notice. We'll never win the world by being like them. So here's the question you need to answer: How many of your loved ones might come to know Jesus if you demonstrated that you genuinely loved them, instead of ignoring, judging or rejecting them? It's time to find out!

MAKE RIPPLES

God chose the weak things.

1 CORINTHIANS 1:27 NIV

The story's told of Elzéard Bouffier, a fifty-five-year-old widower who lived in a French village in 1910, surrounded by poverty and despair. So he did something: he collected thousands of acorns and planted them throughout the area. When they took root, he cultivated beeches. When *they* became saplings, he planted birches. One day, amidst the death and devastation of World War I, a mysterious grey mist appeared on the horizon. It was the oaks of 1910, below them the adolescent beeches, and below them the tiny birch seedlings. Bouffier kept planting, and at the end of World War II, French environmentalists announced that a "natural forest" had "mysteriously" sprung up, flourishing amidst its barren surroundings. But the story doesn't end there; his forest started a chain reaction. Water flowed in brooks that had dried up. The wind scattered seeds, and willows, rushes, meadows and gardens sprang up. New people came to live there, bringing with them hope and prosperity. Elzéard Bouffier found acorns, planted them, and God did the rest.

God can do much with little. Look what He did for David with a sling and a stone. Watch Him feed five thousand with a boy's lunch. And He will do the same for you! Your life is like a pebble: it may not look like much, but drop it into a pond and watch the ripples spread in every direction. Every day you live you have three options: (a) Think only of yourself and your own interests. (b) Since success doesn't come without the possibility of failure, take no risks and go no further. (c) Ask God to show you what you've got, then use it to make ripples.

THE ANSWER TO MICHAEL'S QUESTION

To depart and be with Christ...is far better.

PHILIPPIANS 1:23 NKJV

Things we've never experienced before tend to frighten us. A little boy wrote a letter to God, addressed it to heaven and mailed it. Letters like that usually end up in the dead letter office, but somehow this one was opened. It read, "Dear God, what's it like to die? I don't want to do it, I just want to know. Your friend, Michael." It's a question we've all pondered.

Harold Sala writes: "When I'm going to a part of the world I've never been to, I read and investigate to find out what it's like. I browse travel books, go on the Internet, talk with someone who can tell me what it's like from personal experience. No other book in the world can tell me what the Bible tells me about heaven. The only person who has been there and can tell me what it's like, is Jesus." Knowing that for the believer, death is just a transition into God's presence, Paul writes: "When our...body wears out...we have...an eternal house in heaven" (See 2Co 5:1).

At the end of his book *The Last Battle,* the characters die in a train accident, and C.S. Lewis concludes the story like this: "The things that [happened] after that were so beautiful I cannot write them. For us this is the end of all the stories, but for them it was only the beginning of the *real* story." Speaking about heaven Paul says: "If I had to choose right now, I hardly know which I'd choose...The desire to break camp here and be with Christ is powerful. Some days I can think of nothing better" (TM). And that's the *real* answer to Michael's question!

CONTROL YOUR ANGER (1)

In your anger do not sin.

EPHESIANS 4:26 NIV

In the era when commuters routinely traveled by train, a businessman en route to an important meeting asked a porter to make sure he got off the train at 5:00 a.m. Imagine how he felt when he woke at 9:00 the next morning, miles past his destination. Furiously he ripped into the porter, and he didn't mince words! "That's one angry man," remarked a passenger who overheard the tirade. "If you think *he* was angry," said the porter, "you should've seen the guy I put off the train at 5:00 this morning!" We smile, but as Dr. James Comer of Yale Medical School observes: "We have a sense the world's closing in on us, that there are too many people around, that we're getting ripped off. We feel powerless about our problems and we explode in frustration."

Paul says: "If you are angry, be sure that it is not a sinful anger...don't give the devil that sort of foothold" (Phillips). Does that mean it's always bad to get mad? No, Paul is making the point that *misdirected* anger opens the door to the enemy. In the temple, Jesus showed us there's a place for *righteous* anger over injustice and exploitation. But much of the time we're angry because we think people don't appreciate us, or take advantage of us, or don't give us what we deserve. Again Paul writes: "Get rid of all...anger...forgiving each other...as...God forgave you" (Eph 4:31-32 NIV). But even the best advice in the world is useless unless you *do* something with it. So if you're inclined to be hot-tempered, start your day by asking God to help you act in ways that honor Him.

CONTROL YOUR ANGER (2)

Refrain from anger and turn from wrath.

PSALM 37:8 NIV

A bad temper is not something to be proud of, but prayed over. When you blow your top, you just reveal your contents. And which of us hasn't done that, and regretted it? The Bible says losing your temper "leads to harm" (NLT), because God knew we'd be dealing with:

(1) Stress: By cramming too much into too little time, you set yourself up! Like violin strings that are pulled too tight, you end up snapping, then feeling guilty because you're not "spiritual" enough. "Have a sane estimate of your capabilities" (Ro 12:3-4 PHPS). In life "it's always something," so anticipate and allow time for the unexpected. *(2) Frustration:* Defined as "someone or something that upsets you all the time." A recent news story told of a guy who went hunting on his mountain bike. When it broke down he shot it to pieces. Crazy! It makes no sense, but as Robert Green Ingersoll said, "Anger is like wind that blows out the lamp of the mind." *(3) Perceived violations of our rights:* When you walk around feeling angry it clouds your judgment, because when the only tool you have is a hammer every problem looks like a nail. The bottom line is, it's *not* always about you! This is especially true in marriage. Jesus said that in order to receive, you must first learn to give (See Mk 9:35). *(4) Things that challenge your values:* Sometimes "enough is enough" and you need to speak up. When Jesus got angry in the temple it was because of dishonest practices and people being mistreated. In this case, "it is a sin to know what you ought to do and then not do it" (Jas 4:17 NLT).

DON'T COVET!

I saw...the spoils...I coveted them and took them.

JOSHUA 7:21 NKJV

Have you ever looked at a glossy home-decorating magazine and found that the home you were thankful for an hour ago, now seems junky? Or watched a slick TV ad for a new automobile, and suddenly the car in your driveway seems like a jalopy? God expects you to have goals and to provide for your family, but be careful about coveting things so much that you become obsessed with how to get them. When Israel went to war with Jericho, God said everything in the city was to be destroyed; that His anger was going to fall on the Canaanites because of their sin. But later when Israel stormed the small town of Ai, the inhabitants defeated them. Joshua asked God why they'd lost the battle, and God said it was because there was sin in the Israelite camp. When Joshua investigated, Achan, one of his soldiers, confessed, "When I saw...the spoils...I coveted them and took them." When he tried to conceal his sin by burying the stolen goods under his tent, it cost him his life and the lives of his family.

When you covet, you question God's *willingness* and His *ability* to provide for you. Instead, when you find yourself wanting something, pray about it and trust God to give it to you—if it's His will! In the meantime be grateful for the blessings He's already given you. Watchman Nee wrote, "I have never met a soul who has set out to satisfy the Lord, and has not been satisfied himself." The Bible says: "God can give you more blessings than you need. Then you will always have plenty of everything—enough to give to every good work" (2Co 9:8 NCV). So, don't covet!

LIVING YOUR FULLEST LIFE

My purpose is to give life in all its fullness.

JOHN 10:10 TLB

Living your fullest life requires three things: *(1) A good mentor.* Paul writes: "Dear brothers and sisters, pattern your lives after mine" (Php 3:17 NLT). Good mentors lead by example; they know that in order to be followed they must first be respected. They carefully tailor their instructions by understanding your strengths and weaknesses—knowing whether you are right-brained creative/ intuitive or left-brained analytical. They know whether you learn visually or verbally. They know when you need a pat on the back or a kick in the seat of the pants. If you have such a mentor you're blessed. If you don't, ask God for one. *(2) Your best effort.* Andrew Carnegie said, "There's no use in trying to help people who won't help themselves. You cannot push anyone up a ladder unless he or she is first willing to climb it." *(3) A little extra.* This is the "extra mile" principle Jesus taught (See Mt 5:41). It involves: (a) A little extra effort. Art Williams said, "You beat 50% of the people by working hard; you beat the other 40% by being a person of honesty…and the last 10% is a dog fight." If you want to win that fight, make up your mind to always do a little extra. (b) Extra time. "Though it linger, wait for it; it will certainly come" (Hab 2:3 NIV).Gutzon Borglum, the sculptor who created the memorial to the American Presidents at Mount Rushmore, was asked if he considered his work to be perfect. He supposedly replied, "Not today. The nose of President Washington is an inch too long. It's better that way though. It will erode and be exactly right in ten thousand years."

BE GRATEFUL FOR YOUR BLESSINGS

I went away full,
but the Lord has brought me back empty.

RUTH 1:21 NIV

When it comes to valuable life-lessons, the book of Ruth tops the best-seller list. (Have you read it yet?) For the next few days let's look at some of them.

When famine came to Bethlehem, Naomi, her husband and two sons moved to Moab where the economy was thriving. What they hoped would be a short stay turned into ten years. Their sons married two local girls, Ruth and Orpah. Then the unthinkable happened. Naomi's husband and sons died. As a result of her loss she became bitter. When she heard that times were good in Bethlehem she decided to go back home. After she arrived she said, "I went out full, and the Lord has brought me home again empty" (NKJV). What did she mean? She was saying that despite the famine at home in Bethlehem, at least *there* she had her husband and sons, whereas in Moab, "the land of plenty," she'd lost them.

You never miss the water till the well runs dry! The truth is, you can be blessed and not know it. Only as you look back do you realize that what you have, is much more important than all the things you don't have. When Naomi lost what she loved most, even a famine seemed insignificant by comparison. Have you been saying, "I'll be happy when…"? No, happiness doesn't come from getting what you want, it comes from appreciating what God's given you. Instead of whining and complaining about your lot in life, stop and ask yourself, "What would I take in exchange for what I have?" If you don't know the answer, begin counting your blessings and thanking God for them.

YOU GAIN THROUGH YOUR PAIN

*Naomi was left without
her two sons and her husband.*

RUTH 1:5 NIV

When their husbands died, Naomi, Ruth, and Orpah experienced a unique bonding process. Unless you've been through it, it's hard to understand. It's a fellowship not born of age, race, background or status, and it brings together the oddest people. When you're hurting, don't look for understanding and support from those who haven't walked in your shoes. People can't give you what they don't have. Often the best they have to offer is the kind of advice that's glib, and quickly becomes annoying. Furthermore, until you start to make sense of your pain and see the greater good in it, you can feel like a victim. But once you see God's grace at work, and His hand in it all, you can begin to move ahead: to marry, to have another baby, to get another job, to dream another dream, to live again.

Charles Spurgeon wrote: "Just as old soldiers compare stories and scars, when we arrive at our heavenly home we'll tell of the faithfulness of God Who brought us through. I wouldn't like to be pointed out as the only one who never experienced sorrow, or feel like a stranger in the midst of that sacred fellowship. Therefore be content to share in the battle, for soon we will wear the crown."

When life suddenly changes and you're fighting just to get through another day, remind yourself that Satan hasn't snatched the steering wheel from God. No, God is aware of what you're going through and He *still* has a plan for your life. Be encouraged. You gain through your pain. Victory is born out of struggle. Hold on to His hand; He will bring you through this!

WHO BELONGS IN YOUR LIFE?

Where you go I will go.

RUTH 1:16 NIV

Ruth told Naomi, "Where you go I will go." You can spend your life anywhere with anybody doing anything, then suddenly meet someone and sense that there is a connection between you. It's what made Elisha quit farming and follow Elijah, an eccentric prophet; it's why Timothy hung out with Paul, an old man soon to be executed. You know intuitively, "I won't reach my destiny without you in my life." Looking back you realize if you hadn't met that certain person, or taken that phone call, or read that email, you wouldn't be where you are today.

On the other hand, "Orpah kissed her mother-in-law good-bye" (Ru 1:14 NIV). Now Orpah's leaving didn't make her a bad person; it just meant her part in the story was over. Recognize when somebody's part in your story is over, otherwise you'll just keep trying to raise the dead. David pleaded with God for his newborn baby's life. "He fasted...spent the nights lying on the ground...and...would not eat" (2Sa 12:16-17 NIV). But when the child died he had to accept that there was nothing more he could do, so he "got up...washed...changed his clothes ...and he ate" (2Sa 12:20 NIV). Acknowledge when something is over. If God means you to have it, He'll give it to you. If you've tried to make it work and it hasn't, accept His will in the matter. Get up, go to the mall, buy yourself a new outfit, treat yourself to a good meal; start living again! Never beg anyone to stay with you against their will. Their leaving is no accident; it just means God has something better in store for you (and possibly them too), so trust Him and move on!

"FINDING YOURSELF"

She found herself working
in a field belonging to Boaz.

RUTH 2:3 NIV

Ruth's life was spiraling downward. Her husband died. She'd left her old home in Moab and wasn't accepted in her new one in Bethlehem. She was in survival mode, making the best of a bad deal by gleaning just enough to stay alive. Then God turned things around. The reapers began deliberately dropping handfuls of barley in her path. She started picking up undeserved blessings. Why? Because Boaz saw Ruth gleaning and told his workers, "leave them for her to pick up" (Ru 2:16 NIV). Even though Boaz had never spoken directly to Ruth, she still received the blessing. There's an important lesson here: *You don't know what God has spoken over your life, but suddenly everything changes!* Doors open, opportunities come, people you thought didn't notice you, or even like you, begin showing you favor. What's happening? Your steps are being ordered by the Lord (See Ps 37:23).When the Israelites came into the Promised Land God told them, I'm giving you "vineyards...you did not plant" (Dt 6:11 NKJV). God can put you in situations where others do the work and you get the benefit. And you don't even have to worry, or get jealous about somebody else getting what's yours, because nobody can glean it except you.

Ruth started out for one destination and "found herself" in another. When Boaz called her name, she came from the background to a place of blessing in the foreground. Instead of working in a corner of the field, she ended up owning the field. When God moves, that's how quickly it can happen. So be ready!

YOU MUST UNDERSTAND THE REASON

Let grain from the bundles fall purposely for her.

RUTH 2:16 NKJV

Can you imagine how Ruth felt? She was bereaved by loss, penniless, worried about the future, coming out of famine, then suddenly having more than she needed dropped into her lap. She didn't deserve it, didn't earn it, and couldn't even understand it. That's how God works.

But a word of caution: When you're not used to being blessed it can go to your head! The Bible says: "Remember the Lord your God, for it is He Who gives you power to [succeed in life]" (Dt 8:18 AMP). God is the One Who enables you to do what others find difficult or impossible; in some cases they are taking classes to do what you do naturally. That's because God has blessed you with ability. "Why would He do that?" you ask. Because there's a direct correlation between your blessings and your life's purpose. God doesn't bless you so you can hoard, or strut. Whether His blessings come in the form of increased finances, improved health or greater influence, God's gifts are just tools to reposition you so that you can do His will. The enemy isn't just after your provision, He's after your purpose! What good is success if you are not in the will of God? When God gives you something, He wants you to use it for His glory. So when God gives you His blessings, be sure to read the instructions that go with them—only then will you please Him and find fulfillment! And one more thing, always remember that God is the source of everything you have—and ever will have!

CULTIVATE A THANKFUL HEART!

I will bless the Lord at all times.

PSALM 34:1

David said: "I will bless the Lord at all times: his praise shall continually be in my mouth." A thankful heart should be a way of life for us. But did you know that it can *save* your life? When Jonah disobeyed God and ended up inside the whale, he told the Lord, "I will sacrifice to You with...thanksgiving" (Jo 2:9 NKJV). When he did, God made the fish spit him up on dry land. When you're in the pits and all hell is breaking loose around you, that's when you need to raise your voice in praise. Nothing demonstrates trust, like thanking God when you're in the throes of crisis. A thankful heart does two things:

(a) It builds your faith. The reason "we [can] walk by faith [and] not by sight" (2Co 5:7 NAS), is because we know that regardless of the circumstances, God's working on our behalf (See Ro 8:28). David said, "Magnify the Lord with me"(Ps 34:3). To magnify something is to enlarge it. When you focus on God instead of the problem, God becomes bigger and the problem becomes smaller. Plus, "Faith cometh by hearing...the word of God" (Ro 10:17). Hearing God's promises coming from your own lips, causes faith to rise in your heart. So start talking!

(b) It restores life. Before raising Lazarus from the dead, Jesus looked up to heaven and said, "Father...thank You that You have heard Me. And I know that You always hear Me" (Jn 11:41-42 NKJV). Something wonderful happens when you start thanking God for saving, protecting and providing for you. Your faith soars. You gain the confidence to command those things in your life that you thought were dead, to live again. So, cultivate a thankful heart!

BE GRATEFUL FOR YOUR JOB

In every thing give thanks.

1 THESSALONIANS 5:18

It's too easy to complain about your present position, whether it be as a nightshift cashier in a supermarket or the CEO of a Fortune 500 company, without appreciating how you got there. Where would we be without mothers taking in laundry so that their children could take piano lessons, or fathers working second jobs so that their children could attend college? Before you go any further, stop and give thanks for the contributions others have made in your life.

You say, "But things are not going too well for me right now." Perhaps, but when Joseph was sold into slavery by his brothers he couldn't possibly conceive that God would turn their evil intentions inside out and establish him as a leader to save the nation. The Bible records story after story where adversity leads to advancement and loss leads to gain. There's a master plan unfolding in your life. Be wise, take the lessons you've learned into the future God has in mind for you. When evil comes, be comforted in knowing that God is in control. The Devil may be stoking the fire you're in, but rest assured that God has His hand on the thermostat!

The story of Job teaches us that the Devil has to be given permission to attack us. So if God is allowing the attack, surely He's planning our victory. He wouldn't allow us to be in a battle we couldn't win! God looks for hand-picked people He can send into difficult environments, that He might be glorified. He makes all things "work together for good" (Ro 8:28) so don't be intimidated. Just keep your eyes open and see what God is up to!

HELP IN TIGHT PLACES!

God is our refuge and strength.

PSALM 46:1

We live in a troubled world. 9/11, natural disasters like Hurricane Katrina, tsunamis, wars, the sub-prime mortgage crisis and soaring gas prices have tapped the roots of our anxiety. Every night the media invades our homes bringing it all to us in real time, exposing us to a new phenomenon called "compassion fatigue." Modern-day psychiatrists identify the helplessness, stress, vulnerability and depression we feel watching and wondering, "What if we are next to be targeted by terrorists or slammed by forces of nature? Who will protect us?"

To the fearful in heart, the Bible says three things: (1) "God is our refuge and strength, a very present help in trouble." The margin of the New American Standard Bible renders this last phrase, *"Abundantly available for help in tight places."* Isn't that great! When you're in a tight spot, God is abundantly available to help you. Notice, it doesn't say that God will help you occasionally or reluctantly. No, He will do it abundantly and faithfully. What more do you need? (2) "Therefore we will not fear" (v. 2 NIV). You needn't panic, talk defeat, or give in to despair. The songwriter said, "He's as close as the mention of his name." Just breathe His name in prayer, and He'll be there for you. (3) "Let the oceans roar…Let the mountains tremble" (v. 3 NLT). When everything you once thought to be stable and dependable, is threatened and shaken to the core—you will be where you have always been—in the strong and loving arms of God; the One who is "abundantly available to help in tight places."

ARE YOU APPROACHABLE? (1)

When the Holy Spirit controls our lives he will produce...
kindness, goodness...gentleness.

GALATIANS 5:22-23 TLB

D r. John Maxwell writes: "Sooner or later, a man, if he is wise, discovers that life is a mixture of good days and bad, victory and defeat, give and take. He learns that it doesn't pay to be a too-sensitive soul, that he should let some things go over his head. He learns that he who loses his temper usually loses out, that all men occasionally have burnt toast for breakfast, and that he shouldn't take the other fellow's grouch too seriously. He learns that carrying a chip on his shoulder is the easiest way to get into trouble, that the quickest way to become unpopular is to carry tales of gossip about others, that buck-passing always turns out to be a boomerang, and that it doesn't matter who gets the credit so long as the job gets done. He learns that most others are as ambitious as he is, that they have brains as good or better, that hard work, not cleverness, is the secret of success. He learns that no one ever gets to first base alone, that it's only through co-operative effort that we move on to better things. He realizes (in short) that the 'art of getting along,' depends 98 percent on his own behavior toward others."

So, what about *you?* Jesus said, "Consider carefully how you listen" (Lk 8:18 NIV). When was the last time someone brought you news you didn't want to hear? Or strongly disagreed with you? Or confronted you? If it's been a while, you may not be a very approachable person. We can give no greater gift to others—than putting them at ease.

ARE YOU APPROACHABLE? (2)

When the Holy Spirit controls our lives he will produce...
kindness, goodness...gentleness.

GALATIANS 5:22-23 TLB

Approachable people exhibit the following characteristics: *(1) Personal warmth—they truly like people.* In an old *Peanuts* cartoon Charlie Brown says, "I love mankind, it's just people I can't stand." Hello! It's not enough to love people in theory, you have to generate personal warmth toward those you meet each day. *(2) Their moods are consistent.* Have you ever worked with someone whose moods are constantly up and down? You never know how they'll be. In contrast, approachable people are even-keeled and predictable. They're basically the same way every time you see them. *(3) Sensitivity toward people's feelings.* Although approachable people are emotionally steady, that doesn't mean they expect others to be that way. They recognize that good people have bad days; consequently they tune their moods to the feelings of others and quickly adjust how they relate to them. *(4) Understanding of human weakness, and exposure of their own.* Novelist Ed Howes said, "Express a mean opinion of yourself occasionally, it will show your friends that you know how to tell the truth." Approachable people are honest about their abilities—and shortcomings. They embrace the old proverb which says: "Blessed are they who can laugh at themselves, for they shall never cease to be amused." And because they can admit their own faults, they don't have a problem allowing other people to have faults as well. *(5) The ability to forgive, and ask for forgiveness.* Author David Augsburger wrote, "Since nothing we attempt is ever without error, and nothing we achieve, without some measure of the finitude and fallibility we call humanness, we are saved by forgiveness."

"MIND THE CHECKS"

After the fire came a gentle whisper.

1 KINGS 19:12 NIV

A respected author writes: "I was driving a safe distance behind the car in front when the driver slammed on his brakes. I stopped short, but the car behind was too close and rammed into my Jeep. There was no real damage, but as I drove off something about the incident nagged at me. Weeks later I was on a fast-moving highway. Behind me was a huge truck loaded with cars…in front were several cars…and up ahead, a school bus. Suddenly I noticed the brake lights from the cars ahead. The bus had stopped to let a child off. I pulled to a stop behind the car in front—then I remembered the lesson from the accident earlier. *Sometimes I can stop safely, but the driver behind me can't.* When I looked in my rearview mirror the truck loaded with cars was frantically trying to stop. I pulled over, giving him an extra car length, and he screeched to a stop —right behind the car ahead of me. If I hadn't listened we'd all have piled up."

A new Christian was asked the secret to her spiritual growth. Her response was, "Mind the checks." One reason we don't understand God better is because we don't heed His gentle "checks." The Bible says: "After the fire came a gentle whisper." Learn to listen for it. When you're about to speak and you feel a gentle restraint, say nothing. When you're about to go down a certain path and you sense a red light, or a different path opening up, pay attention, even when God asks you to move in the dark. Wherever His finger points, His hand will clear the way.

GET UP, GET OVER IT AND MOVE ON

You will forget the shame of your youth.

ISAIAH 54:4 NKJV

When Eve first opened her eyes on planet earth, she was already married. She never got to grow up. She just stepped into being a wife, then a mother. Did that happen to you? You were a parent before you had a chance to be a child, or know what it means to be innocent and grow up with your trust intact. If Eve's story is your story, the Word for you today is, "Do not fear, for you will not be ashamed; neither be disgraced...you will forget the shame of your youth."

You can't go back and make things different. You're not the same person and you're never going to be. You cannot relive your first marriage or your early childhood. But there are three scriptural steps you can take to get up, get over it and move on: (1) Forgive what *others* have done to you (See Eph 4:32). (2) Forgive *yourself* for what you've done (See Php 3:13). (3) Believe that *God* has truly forgiven you and act on it (See Isa 43:25).

Sometimes we hold onto the past because we believe there's something there we think we still need. We cling to certain things because we fear we'll never be able to replace them. No, God has more in store for you. If you've entrusted your future to Him you haven't seen your best days yet. There's more ahead of you than behind you. God promises: "Beauty for ashes, the oil of joy for mourning, the garment of praise for the spirit of heaviness" (Isa 61:3). So in God's strength get up, get over it and move on!

DIRECTION THROUGH PERSECUTION

*Those who were scattered
went everywhere preaching the word.*

ACTS 8:4 NKJV

The Bible says: "As for Saul, he made havoc of the church, entering every house, and dragging off men and women, committing them to prison. Therefore those who were scattered went everywhere preaching the word" (vv. 3-4). How did the New Testament church grow? Through persecution. It's the bad times, not just the good ones that cause us to grow. We receive direction through persecution. Sometimes those who attack us are agents of the Lord, without even knowing it. God uses them to get us to where we need to be, then, like Joseph, we look back years later and say, "You meant it for evil but God meant it for good" (See Ge 50:20). We cry because someone slammed a door in our face, but in retrospect we are able to say, "It was the best thing that could have happened to me."

The Psalmist wrote, "No good thing will he withhold from them that walk uprightly" (Ps 84:11). If God is allowing you to go through a tough time then it must be for your good. Or it's for the good of others and *you* are the instrument He's using to bring it about. Understanding this moves you to a deeper dimension in your walk with God. But every new dimension brings a new level of opposition. The enemy won't give up without a fight. Whether the battle is over your family, your finances, your health, your business or your ministry, expect three things: (1) The closer you get to victory the more intense the battle becomes. (2) What matters is not your comfort, but what you're called to do. (3) Your victory has been ordained by God, so keep fighting!

THE VIEW FROM THE MOUNTAIN (1)

Jesus took...Peter, James and John...
up a high mountain.

MATTHEW 17:1 NIV

Notice three things: *(1) Not everybody gets to go up the mountain.* Jesus picked the three who went. He didn't take everybody so nobody would feel slighted. And He didn't explain or apologize to the other disciples who stayed at ground level. God loves us all equally but He doesn't give us all the same assignment or experiences with Him. God makes the call, not us, so trust Him. He knows what He's doing. *(2) Those who go up the mountain aren't necessarily wiser or more spiritual.* After seeing Jesus enveloped in the glow of God's glory, Peter blurted out, "Let's build three tabernacles and stay here." Peter was sincere, but he was sincerely wrong. Resist the temptation to speak instead of waiting to hear what God has to say, or to build your ministry around an experience you've had with God that's designed to equip you personally, not become the theme and emphasis of your life. *(3) God's plan is to feature Jesus, not you.* And it's a lesson we keep having to learn over and over. "While he was still speaking, a bright cloud enveloped them, and a voice from the cloud said, 'This is my Son, whom I love; with him I am well pleased. Listen to him!'...When they looked up, they saw no one except Jesus" (Mt 17: 5-8 NIV). The greatest challenge in your life is getting to the place where you focus on "no one except Jesus." The most important relationship you have is with Him. The only plan that will work out right is the one He gives you. And the power needed to fulfill that plan comes from Him alone.

THE VIEW FROM THE MOUNTAIN (2)

If you have faith.

MATTHEW 17:20 NIV

When Christ's disciples came down from the Mount of Transfiguration, they were faced with an epileptic boy who kept falling into fire and water. His heartbroken father told Christ, "I brought him to your disciples, but they could not heal him" (v. 16 NIV). Immediately, "Jesus rebuked the devil; and he departed out of him" (Mt 17:18). Notice:

(1) Mountain-top experiences are to equip us for our next encounter with the enemy. If you don't understand that, you won't be prepared for the challenges ahead. *(2) We're called to minister to people who keep falling into situations that hurt them.* And it's going to take more than personality and religious platitudes to set them free. Christ's disciples were powerless because they were prayerless. Jesus said: "This kind goeth not out but by prayer and fasting" (Mt 17:21). If we keep doing the "same old, same old," we'll keep getting the same old results. Persistent, prevailing prayer is the price we must pay for walking in God's power. *(3) We must rise above the attitudes around us.* Jesus confronted the core problem: "O faithless... generation" (Mt 17:17). We're fighting the faithlessness of a generation molded by secular media and godless values. If we let it, it will pull us down and wear us out. But we can prevail. That day Jesus said, "If you have faith as small as a mustard seed, you can say to this mountain, 'Move'...and it will move" (Mt 17:20-21 NIV). Observe two things: (a) "If *you* have faith." Everybody around you doesn't have to have faith in order for you to see results. (b) You don't have to be a spiritual giant. Just use your tiny, mustard-seed-size faith and God will move the mountain.

THE RIGHT SIDE OF THE BOAT

Throw your net on the right side.

JOHN 21:6 NIV

When you make decisions based on doubt and unbelief, they never turn out right. After hearing Jesus promise to rise from the dead, and actually seeing Him alive, the disciples went back to what they were doing before they met Him: fishing. Now God will use our past experiences to teach us, but He always leads us forward—never back. When fear and uncertainty make us want to go back to the security of what we know, we end up like the disciples: "They went out and...got into the boat, and that night they caught nothing" (Jn 21:3 NKJV).

But there's good news: If God called you, you're *still* called. Notice how Jesus addresses them: "*Children,* have you any food?" (Jn 21:5 NKJV). In spite of your lackluster performance, you're still His child! Next He tells them: "Throw your net on the right side of the boat...When they did, they were unable to haul the net in because of the large number of fish. Then the disciple whom Jesus loved said to Peter, 'It is the Lord!'" (Jn 21:7 NIV). That morning Jesus ate breakfast with them, renewed fellowship, removed their doubts and sent them out to change the world.

What's the lesson here? When we work outside of God's will it's like fishing on the wrong side of the boat; we wear ourselves out and in the end have nothing to show for our efforts. Are you succeeding in life? No? Maybe you're fishing on the wrong side of the boat! Things aren't going to work out right until you submit to Christ, renew your fellowship with Him and allow Him to direct your steps.

"THOUGHT ATTACKS!"

Take captive every thought.

2 CORINTHIANS 10:5 NIV

Nineteen-year-old Liu Shih-Kun was an esteemed concert pianist in China till the Cultural Revolution banned all things of Western influence. Refusing to renounce his beloved music, Liu was deemed an enemy of the people, beaten and imprisoned. There he languished in a tiny cell with no books, no paper, and even worse—no piano. Six years later, for propaganda reasons, he was asked to play in Beijing with the Philadelphia Orchestra. After years without an instrument to practice on, he performed brilliantly. And eighteen months later when he was finally released, he again played flawlessly. That Liu survived is remarkable; that his hands continued to move as if they'd never stopped playing is amazing. His secret? Stripped of everything musical, for seven and a half years Liu disciplined himself to shut out negative thoughts and practice hour after hour on an *imaginary* piano.

A well respected counselor says: "We don't realize the extent to which our own thinking contributes to our mental anguish. The earlier you stop 'thought attacks' the easier it is to regroup and get back on track. Now, while the concept is simple, it's not easy to implement. Once you start paying attention you'll probably discover you have a lot more 'thought attacks' than you can possibly imagine." Police shout "Freeze!" when they want to stop a suspect and protect themselves. And *you* can freeze out harmful thinking by capturing every thought and making it "obedient to Christ." Paul says: "This is not a wrestling match against a human opponent. We are wrestling with...spiritual forces" (Eph 6:12 GWT). Your thoughts have power. To win over them, you must submit to Christ and control what you allow your mind to dwell on.

WORRIED ABOUT MONEY?

Do not worry.

MATTHEW 6:31 NIV

The Psalmist said, "I was young and now I am old, yet I have never seen the righteous forsaken or their children begging bread" (Ps 37:25 NIV). Has God ever failed you? No, and He won't now: "You will have plenty to eat, until you are full, and you will praise the name of the Lord your God, who has worked wonders for you" (Joel 2:26 NIV). Stop trying to figure everything out. Instead, lean on God. "Trust in the Lord, and do good; so shalt thou dwell in the land, and verily thou shalt be fed. Delight thyself also in the Lord; and he shall give thee the desires of thine heart. Commit thy way unto the Lord; trust also in him; and he shall bring it to pass" (Ps 37:3-5). Just keep doing what God has told you to do. "Obey all the law my servant Moses gave you; do not turn from it to the right or to the left, that you may be successful wherever you go. Do not let this Book of the Law depart from your mouth; meditate on it day and night, so that you may be careful to do everything written in it. Then you will be prosperous and successful... do not be discouraged, for the Lord your God will be with you wherever you go" (Jos 1:7-9 NIV). Don't be anxious; God won't fail you. "Do not worry, saying, 'What shall we eat?' or 'What shall we drink?' or 'What shall we wear?'...your heavenly Father knows that you need them. But seek first his kingdom and his righteousness, and all these things will be given to you as well" (Mt 6:31-33 NIV). Relax, He's Jehovah Jireh, "The Lord will provide!"

DON'T LOSE YOUR PASSION FOR GOD!

Love the Lord your God with all your heart.

DEUTERONOMY 6:5 NIV

There's an interesting sequence of events leading up to Peter's denial of Christ. First, Jesus warned Peter that he was a target: "Satan hath desired to have you, that he may sift you as wheat: But I have prayed for thee, that thy faith fail not: and when thou art converted, strengthen thy brethren" (Lk 22:31-32). Next we read that when the authorities came to arrest Christ, Peter "followed afar off" (Lk 22:54). Notice, Peter had grown distant from Christ. Then the man who swore he'd die for Jesus denied knowing Him. At that point the rooster crowed, Peter remembered his promise to Jesus, and "went out, and wept bitterly" (Lk 22:55-62).

Observe how it works: (a) You're unprepared for Satan's attack when it comes. (b) You allow work and family pressures to cause you to forget that your first commitment must always be to God. (c) You end up spiritually defeated. You say, "That will never happen to me." That's what Peter said! The reason "Satan hath desired to have you," is because he knows that when you become passionate about God's purposes, you're unstoppable. Indeed, the very desire that's burning within you right now is the fuel that enables you to withstand his attacks.

There's a reason the crucifixion has been referred to as "The Passion." The Bible says of Christ: "Who for the joy that was set before Him endured the cross, despising the shame, and has sat down at the right hand of the throne of God" (Heb 12:2 NKJV). Even as He was dying, Jesus was ministering to others. *That's* passion! So the Word for you today is, "Don't lose your passion for God."

ARE YOU NEGLECTING YOUR LOVED ONES?

Live a life of love.

EPHESIANS 5:2 NIV

The great Scottish essayist and historian Thomas Carlyle married his secretary, Jane Welsh. She continued to work for him but when she got ill, Carlyle, who was deeply devoted to his work, didn't seem to notice, so he allowed her to keep working. But she had cancer and eventually she was confined to bed. Although Carlyle truly loved her, he found that he didn't have much time to stay with her or much attention to give to her. Then she died. After the funeral Carlyle went up to Jane's room, noticed her diary lying on the table, picked it up and began to read. On one entire page she'd written a single line: "Yesterday he spent an hour with me and it was like heaven: I love him so much." A reality he had somehow been too blind to see now revealed itself with crushing clarity. He'd been too busy to notice how much he meant to Jane. He thought of all the times he'd been preoccupied with his work and simply failed to notice her. He hadn't seen her suffering. He hadn't seen her love. Turning to the next page, he read words he'd never forget: "I've listened all day to hear his steps in the hall, but now it's late and I guess he won't come today." He put her diary back on the table and ran out of the house. Friends found him at the side of her grave, covered with mud. His eyes were red from weeping; tears were rolling down his face. "If only I'd known, if only I'd known," he cried. After Jane's death, Carlyle made little attempt to write again. *Are you neglecting your loved ones?*

PRACTICE COURTESY

Be courteous...that you may inherit a blessing.

1 PETER 3:9 NKJV

Common courtesy is becoming less common every day. And that's not good, because the Bible says, "Be courteous... that you may inherit a blessing." Sometimes we're not sure how to go about pleasing God. Preachers have made it complicated: a series of long-drawn-out, deeply painful acts designed to appease a God who delights in making us squirm. The prophet Micah simplifies it: "What does the Lord require of you...to love kindness" (Mic 6:8 NAS). Could language be clearer? Here are ten "not-so-common" courtesies you should work on every day, and teach your children. After all, if they don't learn common courtesy from you, where are they going to learn it? (1) Go out of your way to speak to people. "Pleasant words are ...healing" (Pr 16:24 NIV). (2) Try to remember their names— it shows you value them. (3) Smile; it increases your "face value." (4) Be friendly and helpful. If you do, people will return it (See Pr 18:24). (5) Show genuine interest. You can find something good in almost anybody, if you try (Php 4:8). (6) Be generous with your praise and cautious with your criticism. (7) Be slow to judge. There are three sides to every story—your side, their side, and the right side. (8) Instead of "using" others, serve them: "By love serve one another" (Gal 5:13). (9) Start trusting people—it builds lasting relationships. (10) Be humble. Oswald Chambers said, "When a saint becomes conscious of being a saint, something has gone wrong."

Courtesy does two things: (a) It speaks well of your parents. Jesus said, "Live so that [people] will...praise your Father" (Mt 5:16 NCV). (b) It determines your level of blessing. "Be courteous...that you may inherit a blessing."

GIVING UP "CENTER STAGE"

Let each of you look out...for the interests of others.

PHILIPPIANS 2:4 NKJV

The Bible says, "Let each of you look out not only for his own interests, but also for the interests of others." In other words, give up "center stage." Now that's easier said than done because we tend to be preoccupied with one person—me!

You ask someone, "How's it going?" Thinking you really want to hear, they start sharing a recent success. That's your signal. You jump in mid-sentence, blow their light out and say, "Think that's something? Let me tell you about..." You're off and running, right over the deflated ego of your friend who's wishing they'd kept walking when they first saw you. They'd hoped to hear something like, "That's wonderful, tell me more." Instead they get treated to a litany of your opinions and achievements. Whatever happened to "Rejoice with those who rejoice" (Ro 12:15 NIV). That command cuts across our preoccupation with self and says, "Get over yourself! Vacate center stage. Learn to focus on others." Practice saying, "Enough about me. I want to hear about you. How's your business... wife...health...church?" Stifle the urge to interrupt; just listen! Listen with your ears, your eyes, your mind and your spirit. Try to understand the feelings behind their words. If they're celebrating, "Rejoice with them." If they're hurting, "Mourn with those who sorrow." The acid test of Christian character is our ability to celebrate another's success, or share their burden as though it were our own. There's no better way to serve and encourage others.

THE "WATER TEST"

Bring them down to the water, and I will test them.

JUDGES 7:4 NKJV

If somebody keeps refusing to support you, let them go—or you'll wish you had. This is especially hard to accept if you're a nurturer by nature, somebody who's invested in making relationships work, come what may. You can't convert the fearful into the faithful. That's God's job, and His "water test" showed Gideon who he could count on and who he couldn't. God told Gideon: "You have too large an army…they'll take…credit… Make [an]…announcement: 'Anyone…who has any qualms… may leave'…Twenty-two companies headed…home. Ten… were left. God said…'There are still too many. Take them down to the stream and I'll make a final cut'" (vv. 2-4 TM).

When the opposition is arrayed against you like "sand on the seashore" (v. 12 TM) is often the time when you lose the most support. Don't worry, God is at work. During the first cut, when Joshua lost 22,000 men, what looked like a set-back was actually a *set-up* from God to determine who was dependable. "Gideon took the troops down to the stream…Three hundred lapped…from their cupped hands…the rest knelt to drink. God said…'I'll use the three hundred… to…give Midian into your hands'" (vv. 5-7 TM). We learn two lessons from this story: *(1) You need to be able to see your enemy approaching.* Those who knelt to drink, sacrificed their vision to satisfy their immediate need. *(2) When God reduces your support, it's to give you a miraculous victory.* It's to show how somebody without formal credentials can run a company, or somebody who's lost everything can make a comeback. So when the people around you can't pass God's "water test," let them go and trust God. He has something better in mind.

CELEBRATING VICTORY, YET DYING OF THIRST

I die of thirst.

JUDGES 15:18 NKJV

The Bible says: "The Spirit of the Lord came mightily upon him; and…his bonds broke loose…He found a fresh jawbone…took it, and killed a thousand men…Then he…cried out to the Lord and said, 'You have given this great deliverance… now shall I die of thirst?'" (vv. 14-18 NKJV). Notice three things in this story:

(1) Samson allowed the enemy to bind him. What has you tied up today? What's holding you back? Counselors, programs and self-help manuals are good, but it took God's Spirit to set Samson free. And that's what it's going to take to set you free too. Come on, you've talked your problems to death; even your friends don't want to hear about them any more. The time for advice is over—it's time to cry out to God, to allow His Spirit that can break every habit to set you free (See Isa 10:27). *(2) Samson needed to see what had already been given him.* Just the jawbone of a donkey, but with God's help it was enough to win the day. Ask God to show you what you've got, put it to work and He'll give you success. Stop looking in faraway places; the answer's right under your nose. Recognize what God's given you and use it. *(3) Samson was celebrating victory, yet dying of thirst.* It happens, particularly to those who work for God but don't spend enough time with Him. Paul warns: "Lest Satan should take advantage of us" (2Co 2:11 NKJV). When you give out but don't take in, Satan gets the advantage and you end up in Delilah's lap. So spend more time with God. The One who gives you victory, can also quench your thirst.

WILL YOU BE ONE OF THEM?

If My people.

2 CHRONICLES 7:14 NKJV

Not so long ago we were all celebrating a great economy. Wow, can't times change? Skyrocketing fuel prices have us carpooling, parking our gas-guzzlers and riding the bus. We'd never heard of a "sub-prime mortgage crisis;" now the equity in some of our homes is evaporating like steam, or they're being auctioned off on the courthouse steps. The headlines say a tsunami hits Burma and 100,000 people die. Earthquakes hit China and thousands of children perish in the rubble of their school. Twisters, fires and floods hit the U.S. heartland leaving untold heartache and ruin. It seems our security blanket has been stripped away and our comfort zone shaken to its core.

But there's a groundswell. If you listen you'll hear it: "It's time to seek God, to repent, to change the way we're living." It's an old message for a new generation. "If My people who are called by My name will humble themselves, and pray and seek My face, and turn from their wicked ways, then I will hear from heaven, and will forgive their sin and heal their land." You say, "The people around me aren't saying that." Then examine the company you're keeping! Jesus said that when the blind lead the blind they both end up in a ditch.

We don't need a majority to turn things around. God told Abraham that just fifty people with a heart for righteousness could save Sodom. Even in a pampered church that majors in "what God will do for you, and how to get Him to do it" there's a remnant who know what revival means, and how to seek God until it comes. The question is, will *you* be one of them?

DEALING WITH DISAPPOINTMENT (1)

Samuel grew, and the Lord was with him.

1 SAMUEL 3:19

Welcome to life; disappointment guaranteed! Webster defines disappointment as, "When expectations fail to be met, producing anger, frustration, sadness and discouragement." Here are some examples to help you when:
(1) You're disappointed with those you look up to. Think of Samuel and Eli (1Sa 1-4). Samuel's mother entrusted her child to Eli the High Priest, confident he'd mentor and prepare him for God's service. But Eli had a serious character flaw. He was a weak, passive parent who stood by while his sons abused their priestly privilege, bringing shame and disrepute to the ministry. Who'd have blamed young Samuel for taking a nose dive when the man he looked up to failed so badly? But no, he fielded his disappointment and kept his eyes on God: "Samuel grew, and the Lord was with him." As a result God turned him into one of Israel's greatest prophets. So keep your eyes on the Lord. *(2) You're disappointed in those you live with.* If anyone wouldn't let you down, surely it would be your family. Right? Wrong! Ask young Joseph. When God promised him a big promotion he thought his brothers would celebrate. Instead they responded with jealousy, ridicule and resentment, selling him into slavery. Far from friends and home he languished in prison for a crime he didn't commit. What an invitation to bitterness, to rehearsing the wrongs done him while plotting his revenge. But if he'd done that he'd have died an unknown convict in a foreign jail. Instead he allowed God to vindicate him, using his circumstances to position, prepare and promote him to being Egypt's Prime Minister—and that's how you deal with disappointment.

DEALING WITH DISAPPOINTMENT (2)

Now go, lead the people.

EXODUS 32:34 NIV

Here are two more types of disappointment you'll deal with in life:

(1) Disappointment in those you work with and depend on. To succeed, you need people; you can't make it without them. And when those people fail you it's painful. Imagine Moses' disappointment. He leaves his brother Aaron in charge while he attends a summit conference with God and receives the Ten Commandments. Returning, he finds Israel in anarchy, idolatry and unspeakable perversion. Where's Aaron? Leading the rebellion! When Moses needs him most, Aaron fails him miserably. But watch Moses; true leadership shines in deep disappointment. He confronts Aaron, takes the mess to God for resolution, and prays forgiveness for Israel. God listens, then reminds Moses of his assignment. "[It's disappointing, Moses, but] 'go, lead the people...my angel will go before you'" (v. 34). Disappointment doesn't cancel your assignment—or God's presence. Do what He sent you to do. *(2) Disappointment in those you've poured your life into.* Let's check in again with Moses, Founding Pastor of the First Church of the Critical and the Ungrateful, a congregation of former slaves, delivered, abundantly blessed, en route to the Promised Land, but without a shred of loyalty or gratitude for the man who put everything on the line to make it possible. Fresh out of Egypt they turn on Moses, accusing, blaming and berating him (See Ex 14). Was Moses disappointed and hurt? Yes. But each time he wanted to quit he'd discuss it with God, pray for his complaining flock, receive fresh orders from headquarters and return to work. It's what God-called men and women do when they're disappointed and feel like giving up.

DEALING WITH DISAPPOINTMENT (3)

But we have this treasure in earthen vessels.

2 CORINTHIANS 4:7

Finally there's: *Disappointment in ourselves*. It's potentially the most debilitating kind of disappointment because it can throw you into a downward spiral that's hard to stop or recover from. Peter had sworn undying love and fidelity to Jesus. "Lord, everybody else may abandon you, but not me! I'm yours till death" (See Mt 26:33-75). And he meant every word of it. But under the pressures surrounding the crucifixion he yields, and three times denies knowing Jesus. Later, remembering Jesus' words, "Before the rooster crows, you'll deny me three times," Peter, heartbroken by his own dismal failure, "went outside and wept bitterly" (Lk 22:62 NIV). Ever asked, "God, how can you possibly use someone as messed up as me?" Peter failed to meet his own expectations and went on a downer. But Jesus wasn't shocked. He was well aware of Peter's flaws when he called him into the ministry. He also knew that his blustering, outspoken disciple had a tender heart, so He extended grace to him rather than remove him from office. When Christ gave post-resurrection orders to "tell His disciples and Peter" (Mk 16:7 NIV) to meet Him in Galilee, He reaffirmed His choice of the failed disciple. The rest of Peter's story is New Testament history.

When (not if!) you confront failure: (1) Don't add insult to injury by letting disappointment mire you in hopelessness and despair. (2) Humble yourself and repent. Confess your sin; don't excuse, rationalize or blame circumstances and people. (3) Receive God's grace and forgiveness by faith, not by feelings. Don't let Satan convince you your case is beyond grace. (4) Get whatever help you need to get back on track—sooner, not later.

THE PRIVILEGES AND RESPONSIBILITIES
OF MEMBERSHIP

You are...fellow citizens...
members of God's household... a holy temple.
EPHESIANS 2:19-21 NIV

If your children stood outside your house pleading to get in, what would you think? Wouldn't you say, "Come in, you're my flesh and blood, I love you, you don't need to beg?" Well, we can come into God's presence at any time. We are "No longer strangers...but fellow citizens...of the household of God ...a holy temple" (NKJV). What privileges:

(a) As "fellow citizens" we represent God's kingdom on the earth. We are His ambassadors (2Co 5:20). "What does an ambassador do?" you ask. He stays in communication with his king, understands his will and makes sure it's carried out. He also knows he doesn't belong there permanently, so he lives, ready for recall at a moment's notice. Getting the idea? (b) Because we belong to the "household of God" we can come confidently before God at any time, with any need, and know that we'll be received with love. God is the father you always hoped for and you are the child He always wanted. If you have any doubts, look at the cross; *that's* how much God values you. But remember, every family member is supposed to contribute, be loyal, and make sure the family's good name is protected. (c) We are "a holy temple." In the Old Testament God had a temple for His people, but now God has a people for His temple. The Bible says, "Do you not know that your body is a temple of the Holy Spirit, who is in you, whom you have received from God? You are not your own; you were bought at a price. Therefore honor God" (1Co 6:19-20 NIV).

FROM SURVIVING—TO THRIVING!

Increase...and possess the land.

DEUTERONOMY 8:1 NIV

After four hundred years of slavery God handed the Israelites the deed to a lush, plentiful land they could finally call home. Up until now everything they owned had been provided for them by their Egyptian captors. But slavery had crushed their will and destroyed their initiative: consequently, God had to break them of their reliance on people rather than on Him. (People-dependency can make you vulnerable and stunt your growth.) So when God led the Israelites into the wilderness and the leeks and onions they enjoyed in Egypt were gone, they were forced to develop an appetite for manna—something only God can provide! Understand this: When God takes away an old source or system and gives you a new one, it doesn't mean the old one was no good. It just means He's chosen a *new* way of guiding and providing.

When God makes you a promise He always keeps it, but you have to be willing to remove the training wheels of your reliance on people. In the wilderness the Israelites griped and bellyached for the comfort of the familiar, even though it meant going back to an old season that was over. But they couldn't, and you can't either! When God said, "Increase...and possess the land," His plan for them went beyond surviving—to thriving. It meant being weaned off the breast milk of people-dependence and on to the meat of God-dependence. Paul writes: "Not that we are sufficient of ourselves...but our sufficiency is from God" (2Co 3:5 NKJV). When God pushes you out of your comfort zone en route to your destiny, expect to go through some unfamiliar, anxiety-producing territory. It's the only way to go from surviving—to thriving.

LOOK FOR THE HONEY!

There was...honey...And he took thereof.

JUDGES 14:8-9

In their book, *The Laws of Lifetime Growth*, authors Dan Sullivan and Catherine Nomura explain: "Continual learning is essential for lifetime growth. You can have a great deal of experience and be no smarter for all the things you've done, seen, and heard. Experience alone is no guarantee of lifetime growth. But if you regularly transform your experiences into new lessons, you'll make each day of your life a source of growth. The smartest people are those who can transform even the smallest events or situations into breakthroughs in thinking and action. Look at all of life as a school and every experience as a lesson, and your learning will always be greater than your experience."

In an old *Peanuts* cartoon, Charles Schulz shows Charlie Brown at the beach building a magnificent sandcastle. It's a work of art. As he stands back to admire it, suddenly it's destroyed by a big wave. In the last frame he says, "There must be a lesson here, but for the life of me I don't know what it is." That's how many of us feel after a potentially valuable experience. We go through it but don't grow. We attend meetings designed to help us learn, then do nothing with what we've heard after closing our notebooks. Don't get excited about a learning event, get excited about learning! And you haven't really learned it until you've *applied* it.

A few days after slaying a lion, Samson returned to the scene of victory and discovered two things in the carcass: (a) Bees, that sting. (b) Honey, that tastes sweet. "And he took thereof." In life, move beyond the pain and look for the honey!

USE WHAT GOD GAVE YOU!

With the ability...God supplies.

1 PETER 4:11 NKJV

Peter says, "If anyone ministers...do it...with the ability... God supplies." When God gives you an assignment He gives you *all* that's needed to fulfill it. In fact, by studying your core competencies you can actually discern your calling. Winston Churchill said: "To each there comes in his or her lifetime a special moment when they are tapped on the shoulder and offered the chance to do a very special thing, unique to them and fitted to their talent. What a tragedy if that moment finds them unprepared or unqualified for that which could have been their finest hour."

You can't always be what *you* want to be, but you can be everything *God* wants you to be. That's because He assigns and directs us "each according to [one's] own ability" (Mt 25:15 NKJV). What do you love doing and do consistently well? Is music your forte? Crunching numbers? Working with kids? Paul says, "The Spirit has given each of us a special way of serving" (1Co 12:7 CEV). That means some of the things other people find boring, will actually energize and enrich you.

The Bible says that God is building a "spiritual house" (1Pe 2:5). And there's a place for each of us in it. Knowing this dispels the misconception that you're not valuable because you don't have the same talents others do. It also defines your actual responsibility by doing away with the myth that you're supposed to do *everything*. No, your goal should be to stay within the boundaries of God's plan for you. So instead of apologizing for the skills you don't have, discover the gifts God has given you and put them to work for His kingdom.

LESSONS FROM LYSTRA

And in Lystra.

ACTS 14:8 NKJV

The Bible says: "In Lystra a…man…who had never walked …heard Paul speaking…Paul…observing…that he had faith to be healed, said…'Stand up straight on your feet!' And he leaped and walked" (vv. 8-10 NKJV). That's extraordinary. Without months of therapy to get his brain's neurological system functioning and his atrophied muscles activated, this man who couldn't stand up suddenly started walking. That's like winning American Idol or the Eurovision Song Contest without a single voice lesson. Or getting your paintings displayed at the Louvre without having an art class. God reverses the damage of your past and blesses you with success. You "walk into it" by His power and grace. Sometimes that's how God works.

Next we read: "When the people saw what Paul had done, they raised their voices, saying…'The gods have come down to us'…When the apostles…heard this, they tore their clothes… crying out…'why are you doing these things? We also are men'" (Ac 14:11-15 NKJV). Here we go again! We keep wanting to make gods out of people. Someone that nobody's ever heard of hits the high note, gets a record deal and becomes an overnight star—and we set them up as a role model. Lord, help us! It even happens to preachers; you struggle, God blesses you and enables you to build a great ministry, now people can't even talk to you without an appointment (unless they happen to be big donors). Paul and Barnabas didn't go out and buy a wardrobe commensurate with their new image, or hire a publicity agent. No, they "tore their clothes" and cried, "We also are men." Wise up! The crowd that worshipped Paul yesterday, stoned him today. *Bottom line: be humble, love people, but trust only in God.*

PITFALLS FOR LEADERS

Work hard and become a leader.

PROVERBS 12:24 NLT

If you are a leader, try to avoid these pitfalls: *(1) Micromanaging vs. leading.* Managing people requires an eye for detail, whereas leading involves vision-sharing, goal-setting and motivating. And you must know the difference. When you micromanage rather than lead, morale plummets because people need clear objectives and the freedom to figure out how to reach them. Don't micromanage; it diminishes the sense of "ownership" those under and around you need for good team dynamics and problem-solving. President Eisenhower once said: "Pull the string and it'll follow you wherever you wish. Push it, and it'll go nowhere."

(2) Confusing individual loyalty with team building. It's good to work closely with key individuals, but it's also important for people to stay "connected to each other" (Ro 12:5 GWT). Make sure everybody gets to be on the team, feels valued and learns how to interact with one another.

(3) Being afraid to try things. Stretching people into new areas means they'll make mistakes. While locking them into the same routine may keep them (and you) safe, it takes the motivational wind out of their sails. Being a leader means risking other people's failures and biting your lip as you let them "toddle" out into the unknown. Like a parent who prays harder when their teen takes the family car out for their first drive, you must accept that some challenges which frighten you are liberating to others. Solomon said, "Work hard and become a leader." That raises a question. If you are leading others, who is leading you? The best way to lead, is to follow God and obey His Word!

WHEN YOUR MIRACLE COMES LATE

I am...old...and my wife is [too].

LUKE 1:18 NKJV

When an angel told Mary she'd conceive, although it wasn't something she'd been praying for, she said, "Let it be... according to your word" (Lk 1:38 NKJV). However, when an angel appeared to Zechariah, "he...was gripped with fear." When the angel told him, "Your prayer has been heard... Elizabeth will bear you a son...Zechariah asked...'How can I be sure...I am...old...and my wife is well along in years'" (Lk 1:12-18 NIV). What do you do when God answers your prayer and you don't know if you can still handle it? When He sends you a son whose name has already been chosen, who doesn't necessarily resemble you, and whose destiny is already decided? Or when He gives you the job you always wanted, the relationship you never thought you'd have, or the ministry opportunity you didn't think would come again? You can either say, "I can't," or "I'm willing. Bring it on, Lord!"

"When the right time came, God sent his Son" (Gal 4:4 NLT). Notice, God doesn't consult us to make sure His plans line up with our timetable and meet with our approval. He simply directs our steps (See Ps 37:23). He calls the shots, even when it means we have to run to keep up!

But sometimes God will shake your foundation in order to develop your "core muscles." If you work out, you know that lifting weights is much easier when you're on solid ground. When you're on a balance ball, for example, you have to work hard to insure the weights don't come back down and crush you. When your miracle arrives late, God is strengthening your faith and teaching you to stay balanced under pressure.

HE'S ALWAYS ON TIME

The time came for the baby to be born.

LUKE 2:6 NIV

Jon Walker writes: "We manage, waste, spend and save time. We wish it would come…we wish it would pass…we see it fly and we feel it drag. We watch clocks and carry calendars, creating the illusion that somehow we control it. God controls time….Do you think He was surprised that 'while they were there, the time came for the baby to be born'? We're surprised by unexpected developments…God's never surprised, even by the most disastrous turn of events.

"How would your faith be, if you knew God wasn't surprised by your circumstances and is working towards a holy and healthy conclusion? George Mueller once waited on the dock for a special chair to be delivered because he had a bad back and needed it for his ocean voyage. When departure time came and it still hadn't arrived his friends offered to buy him one, but Mueller said, 'Either God will provide…or…give me grace to do without.' Then, just like a Hollywood ending…the chair arrived…right on time! How would *you* act, think, and live differently if you were absolutely certain God was at the end of your deadline…even if there were only seconds left? The Bible says, 'Jesus Christ is the same yesterday, today, and forever' (Heb 13:8 NLT). Time doesn't diminish His love, or His power to work within your life. He was there in the past; He's here now, and He will be there in your future. A thousand years are like a few hours to Him. He's interested in bringing you into eternity, not just getting you through until the weekend." When you see it like *that*, it changes the big picture, doesn't it?

YOU'RE IN THE RIGHT FAMILY!

Joseph...went...to...Bethlehem...
because he was of the house...of David.

LUKE 2:4 AMP

Face it, there are times in life when we wish we'd been born into a different family. George Burns quipped, "Happiness is having a large, caring, close-knit family—in another city!" All joking aside, the family you're in is no accident. God told Jeremiah, "Before I formed you in the womb, I knew you... before you were born I [set you apart for a special purpose]" (Jer 1:5 NKJV).

We tend to think of Jesus' family only in terms of His heavenly Father. But He had a human family too; one that didn't always understand Him. God used His family to mold Him and move Him towards His destiny, right down to where He would be born. "Joseph...went...to...Bethlehem...because he was from the family of David...While they were in Bethlehem, the time came for Mary to have the baby" (vv. 4-6 NCV). Notice the words "the time came." There's no coincidence or confusion on God's calendar. He plans our lives right down to the minutest detail. He says, "What I have planned, that will I do" (Isa 46:11 NIV). Jesus likely became a carpenter because that was Joseph's trade. And because of His obligations as the oldest son, He probably waited till he was thirty to begin public ministry. "What does all this mean to me?" you ask. Simply put: God will use your family to prepare you for the assignment He's given you in life. He placed you there to shape you and make you more like Him—hopefully through godly role models and loving relationships. But even when you're born into a dysfunctional, emotionally-distant family, He can still turn a curse into a blessing (See Dt 23:5). So, trust Him!

NIGHT VISION (1)

Who is among you who...fears the Lord...
yet...walks in darkness?

ISAIAH 50:10 AMP

God promises us peace, but not smooth sailing or immunity from life's problems. The Bible says you can "fear the Lord ...yet...walk in darkness and...trouble." Check your Bible: (a) *Job* lived an exemplary life yet he lost everything. Troubled and perplexed, he cried, "God has blocked my way [and]...plunged my path into darkness" (Job 19:8 NLT). (b) *Jeremiah,* after preaching to a rebellious people who beat and imprisoned him, said, "Oh, that...my eyes [were] a fountain ...I would weep day and night for...my people" (Jer 9:1 NIV). (c) *John the Baptist* was puzzled about why his cousin Jesus, who could raise the dead, had left him to languish in prison. So he sent him a message asking, "Are you the one who was to come, or should we expect someone else?" (Lk 7:19 NIV). (d) *Paul* suffered so much he "despaired even of life" (2Co 1:8).

Faith is like film; it's developed in the dark. Dark days make us lean on God in ways we normally wouldn't. The truth is, if our faith was never tested we wouldn't be motivated to pursue God and draw closer to Him. The hymn writer wrote: "When darkness seems to hide His face, I rest on His unchanging grace. When all around my soul gives way, He then is all my hope and stay. On Christ the solid rock I stand, all other ground is sinking sand." It's easy to praise God when your health is good and your bills are paid. It's when light suddenly turns to darkness that we discover what our faith is made of and where our trust truly lies. It's in those seasons, that we develop night vision!

NIGHT VISION (2)

I will give you treasures hidden in the darkness.
ISAIAH 45:3 NLT

Sometimes God doesn't tell us *why* because He wants us to know *who*. In Psalm 23, David goes from talking *about* God, "The Lord is my Shepherd," to talking *with* Him, "Thou art with me." What happened in between? David learned that no matter how dark the way is, the Lord is there to guide us. He discovered that it's better to walk through the valley with God than stand on the mountaintop alone. God doesn't always light the path in advance, but He promises, "When thou passest through the waters, I will be with thee; and through the rivers, they shall not overflow thee" (Isa 43:2). When you feel like you're out of your depth or in over your head, claim the promise! Job had many unanswered questions, but when he began to understand the difference between *reason* and *relationship*, he told God, "I...heard about you before, but now I have seen you" (Job 42:5 TLB). When you can't find the reason, trust the relationship. God won't fail you.

Contrary to what you may think, darkness isn't always the work of the enemy. Sometimes it's one of God's best teaching tools. "About the fourth watch of the night He came to them, walking on the sea...And when they saw Him...they were greatly amazed...beyond measure, and marveled" (Mk 6:48-51 NKJV). You get to know the Lord by going through storms with Him. The Psalmist said, "To you the night shines as bright as day. Darkness and light are the same to you" (Ps 139:12 NLT). So instead of running from your problems, ask God to develop your night vision, to show you "the treasures of darkness...hidden in secret places" (NRS).

NIGHT VISION (3)

You who live in your own light...
will soon fall down in great torment.

ISAIAH 50:11 NLT

When the darkness you're experiencing is God-ordained, don't try to create your own light: "You who live in your own light...will soon fall down in great torment." Abraham decided to kindle his own fire when God's promise of an heir didn't materialize quickly enough. Tired of waiting, he decided to go it alone by fathering Ishmael, and ended up creating problems that would last for generations. God had already promised to liberate Israel, but Moses took it upon himself to do things his way. As a result he killed an Egyptian slave master and spent the next forty years in the wilderness (See Ex 2:11-15). Peter promised to follow Jesus to prison and to death (See Lk 22:33), but because he didn't wait for instructions he ended up lopping off an innocent man's ear.

When you're in darkness by divine design you don't have to be afraid, God will bring you through. Why are we so sure? Because the Bible gives us great promises like: "Light arises in... darkness for the upright" (Ps 112:4 AMP), and "Weeping may endure for a night, but joy cometh in the morning" (Ps 30:5). The forty days Moses spent alone on the mountain, Elijah's stay on Mount Horeb, and Paul's years in the Arabian Desert weren't wasted experiences; they were part of God's plan. Jesus said, "What I tell you in the dark, speak in the daylight" (Mt 10:27 NIV). Notice two things in this Scripture: (1) It's in your worst moments that God gives you some of your best insights. (2) People will listen to you because you've "earned the right to speak." So sit tight and let God teach you things which can only be learned in the dark.

KNOWING WHAT SEASON YOU'RE IN

Be ready in season and out of season.

2 TIMOTHY 4:2 NKJV

We live our lives in seasons, and seasons have *beginnings* and *endings*. So, diversity is the key to longevity. If you don't understand that you can lose your sense of purpose, because when one season is over you've nothing left to carry with you into the next. That's why successful farmers keep rotating their crops. They plant corn in one field, then when it goes out of season they plow that field and let it rest. At the same time they're busy elsewhere harvesting alfalfa to make hay, after which *that* field goes through the same process. In spring they change the order of things so the field where corn once grew now produces alfalfa, and so forth.

When Paul told Timothy, "Be ready in season and out of season," he was encouraging him to broaden his spiritual horizons. In Timothy's case he needed to understand there's a time to correct people, and a time to comfort them (See 2Ti 4:25 NKJV). Timing is so important. The Psalmist compared the blessed man to "a tree...which yields...fruit in *season*" (Ps 1:3 NIV). To succeed, you must recognize what season you are in!

And you must also understand that God is more concerned with the depth of your roots than the height of your branches; more interested in quality than quantity. With God "the quality goes in, before the name goes on." That's why He takes your struggles and uses them to cultivate the kind of soil (and soul) necessary to produce good fruit. And one more thing: From time to time He will permit storms to blow away those *people* and *things* that hinder what He's working to produce in you.

S.M.A.R.T. START THE NEW YEAR!

The righteous keep moving forward.

JOB 17:9 NLT

Whoever said, "Procrastination is the thief of time," was right. We keep postponing, promising ourselves we'll do better. Be honest, how many of last year's resolutions did you keep? This year do things differently. Make your goals S.M.A.R.T. In other words, make them:

Specific: Get up earlier in order to read your Bible and pray before going to work. Make time for your family. Exercise. Eat right. Take care of your body; it's God's temple (See 1Co 6:19-20).

Moderate: Tackling more than one project at a time dilutes your focus and makes it harder to stick with. When you start too much you finish too little. Start small and build on your successes by mastering and maintaining one thing at a time (See Php 3:13).

Achievable: Don't try to swallow the whole elephant in one bite. Baby steps are the name of the game. Talk in terms of what you *will* do instead of what you *won't*. For example, instead of saying, "I'm not going to be so critical," say, "Today I'm going to look for something good in everybody I meet" (See Php 4:8).

Recordable: You can't manage what you can't measure. Documenting your progress (or lack of it!) makes you accountable, shows how far you've come and what you need to work on.

Time-specific: Review your goals weekly (or daily if you're struggling). That way you can trouble-shoot early, and change direction when necessary. The Bible says, "Throw yourself into your tasks so...everyone will see your progress" (1Ti 4:15 NLT). Come on, make up your mind, get up off the couch and go for it!

An Inspirational Collection of Wit, Wisdom, Humor and Fascinating Facts. (Colorado Springs, Colo.: Honor Books, 2005). Pgs. 18-19, 39-40.

Aurandt, Paul. *More of Paul Harvey's the Rest of the Story.* (New York: Bantam Books, 1981). Pgs. 15-16; 18-23; 30-31; 49-50; 190-192.

Blackaby, Henry. *Experiencing God.* (Nashville, Tenn.: Broadman & Holman, 1998). Pgs. 170; 188-189.

Carlson, Richard Ph.D. *Don't Sweat the Small Stuff with Your Family.* (New York: Hyperion, 1988). Pgs. 184-185.

Campolo, Tony. *Who Switched the Price Tag?* (Nashville, Tenn.: Word Publishing, 1986). Pgs. 58-61; 65-68; 72-73.

Campolo, Tony. *Let Me Tell You a Story.* (Nashville, Tenn.: Word Publishing, 2007).

Chambers, Oswald. *My Utmost for His Highest: Updated Edition.* (Grand Rapids, Mich.: Discovery House, 1992).

Clements, Jonathon. "Nine Tips for Investing in Happiness." *The Wall Street Journal,* October 8, 2006.

Cowman, L.B. *Streams in the Desert: Updated Edition.* (Grand Rapids, Mich.: Zondervan, 1997). Pgs. 373-374; 376-377.

Evans, Tony. *Free At Last.* (Chicago: Moody, 2001).

Foster, Gary, Ph.D. *Mindset Makeover.* (Nutrition Newsletter).

Hendricks, Howard G. and Wm. W. Hendricks. *Living By The Book.* (Chicago: Moody, 1993).

Hodgin, Michael E. *1001 Humorous Illustrations.* (Grand Rapids, Mich.: Zondervan, 1992). Pgs. 255-256.

Kennedy, D. James with Jerry Newcombe. *New Every Morning.* (Portland, Ore.: Multnomah, 1996).

Leonard, Dennis. *Happiness Matters: 21 Thoughts That Could Change Your Life.* (Denver, Colo.: Legacy Publishers International, 2006). Pgs. 133-138.

Lucado, Max. *Cure for the Common Life: Living in Your Sweet Spot.* (Nashville, Tenn.: W. Publishing, 2005). Pgs. 1-4.

Lucado, Max. *Every Day Deserves a Chance.* (Nashville, Tenn.: Thomas Nelson Publishing, 2007). Pgs. 105-109, 110-113.

Lucado, Max. *Just for You: Readings from He Chose the Nails.* (Nashville, Tenn.: W. Publishing Group, 2001).

Lucado, Max. *Facing Your Giants*. (Nashville, Tenn.: W Publishing Group, 2006).

Mason, John. *The Impossible Is Possible: Doing What Others Say Can't Be Done*. (Minneapolis, Minn.: Bethany House, 2003). Pg. 181.

Maxwell, John. *Talent Is Never Enough*. (Grand Rapids, Mich.: Zondervan, 2007).

Ortberg, John. *God Is Closer Than You Think*. (Grand Rapids, Mich.: Zondervan, 2005). Pgs. 16-18.

Ortberg, John. *When the Game Is Over It All Goes Back in the Box*. (Grand Rapids, Mich.: Zondervan, 2007).

Rogers, Adrian. *Standing for Light and Truth*. (Wheaton, Ill.: Crossway Books, 2003). Pgs. 67-77.

Sala, Harold. *Profiles in Faith*. (Uhrichsville, Ohio: Barbour Publishing, 2003). Pgs. 131-134, 226-230.

Sala, Harold. *Guidelines for Finding Your Way*. (Uhrichsville, Ohio: Barbour Publishing, 2003). Pgs. 152-160; 224-226; 273; 377-379.

Sheets, Dutch. *Intercessory Prayer*. (Ventura, Calif.: Regal Books, 1996). Pg. 57.

Sutton, Mark A. & Bruce Hennigan, M.D. *Conquering Depression*. (Nashville, Tenn.: Broadman & Holman, 2001).

Swindoll, Charles. *A Life Well Lived*. (Nashville, Tenn.: Thomas Nelson Publishing, 2007). Pgs. 31-32.

Swindoll, Charles R. *Growing Wise in Family Life*. (Portland, Ore.: Multnomah Press, 1988).

Swindoll, Charles R. *Perfect Trust*. (Nashville, Tenn.: J. Countryman, 2000).

Verdell, David. *Riches Stored in Secret Places*. (Nashville, Tenn.: Word Publishing, 1994). Pgs 7-11.

Walker, Jon. "A Descendant of Joseph." Posted Dec. 14, 18, 2007. The Purpose Driven Life Daily Devotional Online. *www.purposedrivenlife.com*

Walker, Jon. "Heroes." Posted Oct. 4, 2007. The Purpose Driven Life Daily Devotional Online. *www.purposedrivenlife.com*

Walker, Jon. "Bursting at the Seams." Posted April 28, 2008. Grace Creates. *www.gracecreates.com*

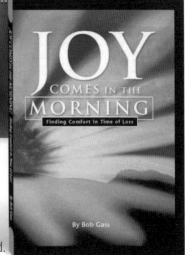

You Can Be Healed
God Still Heals Today

Bob addresses your concerns:
- Is it God's will to heal?
- Why are some not healed?
- How to maintain your healing.
- The importance of knowing God's Word.

Paperback

Be Not Afraid
How to Conquer Your Fears

In this book, Bob Gass shows you how to conquer your financial fears, family fears, fear of sickness, and even fear of death. This book will change your life! *Hardback*

Joy Comes in the Morning
Finding Comfort in Time of Loss

At some time we all lose what we love …This insightful book will show you how to deal with loss and turn your grief into a healing force.
Hardback